The system of liability of articles III and IV of the Hague (Visby) Rules

The system of liability of articles III and IV of the Hague (Visby) Rules

Academisch Proefschrift

ter verkrijging van de graad van doctor
aan de Universiteit van Amsterdam
op gezag van de Rector Magnificus

prof. dr. D.C. van den Boom

ten overstaan van een door het college
voor promoties ingestelde commissie

in het openbaar te verdedigen in de Agnietenkapel
op donderdag 15 mei 2008, te 14:00 uur

door

Nicholas John Margetson

geboren te Colchester, Verenigd Koninkrijk

Promotor: prof. dr. C.E. du Perron
Copromotor: dr. M.L. Hendrikse

Overige leden: prof. mr. F.A.W. Bannier
prof. dr. M.A. Clarke
prof. dr. M.A. Huybrechts (em.)
prof. dr. M.B.M. Loos
prof. mr. G.J. van der Ziel (em.)

Faculteit der Rechtsgeleerdheid

© 2008 N.J. Margetson

Behoudens de in of krachtens de Auteurswet 1912 gestelde uitzonderingen mag niets uit deze uitgave worden verveelvoudigd, opgeslagen in een geautomatiseerd gegevensbestand, of openbaar gemaakt, in enige vorm of op enige wijze, hetzij elektronisch, mechanisch, door fotokopieën, opnamen of enige andere manier, zonder voorafgaande toestemming van de uitgever.

Voorzover het maken van kopieën uit deze uitgave is toegestaan op grond van art. 16h Auteurswet 1912 dient men de daarvoor wettelijk verschuldigde vergoedingen te voldoen aan de Stichting Reprorecht (Postbus 3060, 2130 KB Hoofddorp, <www.reprorecht.nl>). Voor het overnemen van (een) gedeelte(n) uit deze uitgave in een bloemlezing, readers en andere compilatiewerken (art. 16 Auteurswet 1912) kan men zich wenden tot de Stichting Pro (Stichting Publicatie- en Reproductierechten Organisatie, Postbus 3060, 2130 KB Hoofddorp, <www.cedar.nl/pro>).

Hoewel aan de totstandkoming van deze uitgave de uiterste zorg is besteed, aanvaarden de auteur(s), redacteur(en) en uitgever geen aansprakelijkheid voor eventuele fouten en onvolkomenheden, noch voor gevolgen hiervan.

All rights reserved. No part of this publication may be reproduced, stored in a retrieval system, or transmitted in any form or by any means, mechanical, photocopying, recording or otherwise, without prior written permission of the publisher.

A trade edition of this book is published by Uitgeverij Paris, Zutphen, The Netherlands, ISBN 97890-77320-59-4.

Table of contents

List of abbreviations / 13

Preface / 15

1 Introduction / 17
1.1 When do the H(V)R apply? / 17
1.2 Construction of the Rules / 18
1.3 Research question / 18
1.4 Method used to answer the research question / 18
1.5 Researched legal systems / 19
1.6 Topics of research / 19
1.7 The UNCITRAL draft convention / 21

2 Construction of the Hague (Visby) Rules / 23
2.1 Introduction / 23
2.2 Terminology / 23
Treaty, convention, instrument / 23
Protocol / 24
Construction and interpretation / 24
Rules of construction / 24
Uniform construction / 25
Autonomous / 25
Uniformity / 26
Application / 26
2.3 Aids to the construction of the H(V)R / 26
2.3.1 Stag Line / 27
a) Plain meaning of the words / 27
b) Broad principles of general acceptance / 27
2.3.2 Pyrene Co. Ltd. v. Scindia Navigation Co. Ltd. / 28
c) The French text / 28
2.3.3 The Bunga Seroja / 28
d) History of the Rules: compromise character and English roots / 28
e) Reading the Hague Rules as a whole / 29
2.3.4 The Jordan II / 29
f) Purposive construction / 29
g) Travaux Préparatoires / 29
h) The views of the textbook writers / 29
i) The decisions in foreign jurisdictions / 30
Third party bill of lading holders? / 30

Strict construction of the exceptions? / 30
2.4 Problems regarding uniform construction of the H(V)R / 31
2.4.1 Politics / 31
2.4.2 Older law dealing with the same issue / 32
2.4.3 Manner of implementation / 32
2.4.4 National legal concepts / 33
2.5 Ways to improve uniform construction of the H(V)R / 34
2.6 Conclusion / 35
Textual (or objective) / 36
Subjective / 36
Teleological / 36

3 Duties of the carrier / 37
3.1 Introduction / 37
3.2 What is meant by 'voyage'? / 37
3.3 What is meant by 'before and at the beginning of the voyage'? / 39
3.3.1 Before the voyage / 39
3.3.2 The beginning of the voyage / 41
3.4 Why is the requirement restricted to the period 'before and at the beginning of the voyage'? / 42
3.5 What is meant by 'due diligence'? / 43
3.5.1 Common law: absolute warranty of seaworthiness / 43
3.5.2 Hague (Visby) Rules: Due diligence / 45
3.5.3 Dutch cases / 48
3.5.4 Conclusion / 48
3.6 Is the duty to exercise due diligence to make the ship seaworthy delegable? / 49
3.7 What is the meaning of seaworthiness? / 52
3.8 What is meant by 'properly and carefully'? / 55
3.9 Is the duty contained in art. III(2) delegable? / 58
3.9.1 English law: general remarks / 58
The Jordan II / 59
The views of the textbook writers, decisions in foreign jurisdictions and third party bill of lading holders / 60
Decisions in foreign jurisdictions / 60
3.9.2 U.S. Law / 62
3.9.3 Dutch law / 62
3.9.4 UNCITRAL / 63
3.9.5 The intended construction of art. III(2) / 64

4 The relationship between the duties of the carrier and the exceptions / 67
4.1 Introduction / 67
4.2 Causes of damage / 67
4.3 The expression 'overriding obligation' / 69
4.3.1 Common law / 69
Summary / 70
4.3.2 The H(V)R / 70
Summary / 72
4.4 The requirement of causal connection / 72

TABLE OF CONTENTS

4.4.1   American law / 72
4.4.2   English law / 72
4.4.3   Dutch law / 73
4.5   Doctrines concerning the relationship between art. III and art. IV / 74
4.5.1   England / 74
        The requirement of due diligence to make the ship seaworthy / 74
        The requirement of care for the cargo / 74
4.5.2   The United States / 75
4.5.3   The Netherlands / 75
        The requirement of due diligence to make the ship seaworthy / 75
        The requirement of care for the cargo / 76
4.6   Concurrence of culpable and non-culpable causes of damage / 76
4.6.1   Common law: The Lilburn / 76
        Common law: Summary / 78
4.6.2   H(V)R / 78
4.6.2.1 American law: Vallescura Rule / 79
4.6.2.2 English law / 80
4.7   Why is art. III(2) not also considered an overriding obligation under English law? / 82
4.8   The intended construction of the relationship between the duties and the exceptions / 83

5   Art. IV(1) and some of the exceptions of art. IV(2) H(V)R / 85
5.1   Art. IV(1): loss or damage due to unseaworthiness / 85
5.1.1   Introduction / 85
5.1.2   Is art. IV(1) an exception from liability or merely a division of the burden of proof? / 86
5.1.2.1 English law / 86
5.1.2.2 Dutch law / 88
5.1.2.3 U.S. law / 88
5.1.2.4 The intended construction of rule IV(1) / 89
5.2   The 'nautical fault' exception / 90
5.2.1   Introduction / 90
5.2.2   What is meant by 'navigation of the ship'? / 90
5.2.3   What is meant by 'management of the ship'? / 93
        Conclusion / 98
5.2.3.1 The primary purpose test / 98
5.2.3.2 The author's opinion / 99
5.2.3.3 An alternative for the primary purpose test? / 101
5.2.4   The intended construction of art. IV(2)a / 102
5.3   The fire exception / 102
5.3.1   Introduction / 102
5.3.2   The Fire Statutes and the fire exception / 103
5.3.2.1 Introduction / 103
5.3.2.2 The historical background of the Fire Statutes / 104
5.3.2.3 The English Fire Statute / 106
5.3.2.4 The American Fire Statute / 107
5.3.3   American decisions / 107

5.3.3.1 Application of the Fire Statute on its own: breach of non delegable duty by others than owner is not to be considered 'design or neglect of the owner' / 108
Earle & Stoddart v. Ellerman's Wilson Line / 108
A/s J. Mowinckels Rederi v. Accinanto (The Ocean Liberty) / 108
5.3.3.2 When both the Fire Statute and COGSA apply: the 9th Circuit contrary to the other circuits? / 109
Asbestos Corp v. Compagnie de Navigation Fraissinet et Cyprien Fabre (2nd Cir. 1972) / 109
Liberty Shipping (9th Cir. 1975) / 110
Sunkist (9th Cir. 1979) / 111
Ta Chi Navigation (2nd Cir. 1982) / 113
Damodar Bulk Carriers, Ltd. v. People's Insurance Company of China (9th Cir. 1990) / 114
Hyundai Explorer (9th Cir., 1996) / 116
Conclusion: 9th Circuit contra 2nd, 5th and 11th Circuits? / 117
5.3.3.3 What if COGSA applies alone and not besides the Fire Statute? / 118
5.3.3.4 Conclusion / 118
5.3.4 The proviso 'unless caused by the actual fault or privity of the carrier' in the fire exception / 119
5.3.5 What is meant by 'fire' in the fire exception? / 122
Dutch law: Fire / 122
English law: Fire / 123
American law: 'Fire' / 124
5.3.6 What is meant by 'actual fault or privity'? / 124
Dutch law: 'Actual fault or privity' / 124
English and American law: 'Actual fault or privity' / 125
Conclusion / 126
5.3.7 Which persons are meant by 'the carrier'? / 126
Dutch law: 'the carrier' / 127
English law: 'the carrier' / 127
American law: 'the carrier' / 128
5.3.8 The relationship between the duties of the carrier and the fire exception / 130
American law / 130
Dutch law / 130
English law / 131
Conclusion / 133
5.3.9 The burden of proof / 133
Dutch law: the burden of proof / 133
English law: the burden of proof / 134
American law: the burden of proof / 134
5.3.10 The intended construction of the fire exception / 135
5.3.11 Conclusion / 136
5.4 Perils of the sea / 137
5.4.1 Introduction / 137
5.4.2 Elements that may constitute a peril of the sea / 138
5.4.3 The construction of the exception under various legal systems / 139
5.4.3.1 English law / 139
The requirement that the event was unforeseeable / 139
Extraordinary nature of the damage causing event / 142

5.4.3.2 American law / 143
The requirement that the event was unforeseeable / 143
Extraordinary nature of the event / 145
5.4.3.3 Canadian law / 146
The requirement that the event was unforeseeable / 146
Extraordinary nature of the event / 148
5.4.3.4 Australian law / 149
The requirement that the event was unforeseeable / 150
Extraordinary nature of the event / 151
Bunga Seroja: comments / 152
5.4.3.5 Dutch law / 153
The requirement that the event was unforeseeable / 153
Quo Vadis / 154
Extraordinary nature of the event / 155
5.4.3.6 The intended construction of the perils of the sea exception / 156
5.5 The catch all exception / 157
5.5.1 Introduction / 157
5.5.2 Which events are covered by the words 'any other cause'? / 158
5.5.3 How do the words 'actual fault or privity' relate to the words 'fault or neglect'? / 160
5.5.4 Which persons are meant with 'agents or servants of the carrier'? / 160
Agents / 160
The Chyebassa / 161
5.5.5 How is the burden of proof divided? / 161
5.5.6 What is the meaning of the word 'or' in the exception? / 164
5.5.7 Dutch law / 164
Royer's system / 164
5.5.8 The intended construction / 167
5.5.9 Conclusion / 167

6 Division of the burden of proof under the H(V)R / 169
6.1 Introduction / 169
6.2 In general / 169
The Popi M / 169
The burden of proof under the H(V)R in general / 172
6.3 Common law / 172
6.3.1 In general / 172
6.3.2 The Glendarroch / 173
6.3.3 The Canadian Highlander / 173
6.3.4 The Maltasian. Obiter dictum grounds / 175
Court of Session (Inner House) / 175
House of Lords / 175
6.3.5 The views of some authors / 175
6.3.6 Common Law: conclusion / 176
6.4 Dutch Law / 177
6.4.1 Authors / 177
6.4.2 Dutch decisions / 177
6.4.3 Dutch law: conclusion / 178

6.5	Some other continental authors / 178
6.6	The author's opinion: the division of the burden of proof depends on the invoked exception / 178
6.7	The intended division of the burden of proof / 181
6.8	Conclusion / 182

7 Conclusions / 183
7.1	The intended construction of the H(V)R / 183
7.2	Duties of the carrier / 183
7.3	Overriding obligation / 183
7.4	Art. IV(1): loss or damage due to unseaworthiness / 184
7.5	The 'nautical fault' exception / 184
7.6	The fire exception / 184
7.7	Perils of the sea / 185
7.8	The catch all exception / 185
7.9	Division of the burden of proof / 185

Summary / 187
1	Introduction / 187
2	Construction of the Hague (Visby) Rules / 187
3	Duties of the carrier / 187
4	The relationship between the obligations of the carrier and the exceptions / 188
5	Some of the exceptions provided by art. IV H(V)R / 188
5.1	Art IV(1): loss or damage due to unseaworthiness / 188
5.2	The 'nautical fault' exception / 189
5.3	The fire exception / 189
5.4	Perils of the sea / 189
5.5	The catch all exception / 190
6	Division of the burden of proof under the Hague (Visby) Rules / 190

Samenvatting / 191
1	Inleiding / 191
2	Uitleg van de Hague (Visby) Rules / 191
3	Verplichtingen van de vervoerder / 191
4	De verhouding tussen de verplichtingen van de vervoerder en de ontheffingsgronden / 192
5	Enige excepties uit artikel IV H(V)R / 193
5.1	Artikel IV (1): schade of verlies door onzeewaardigheid / 193
5.2	De nautische fout exceptie / 193
5.3	De brandexceptie / 193
5.4	Perils of the sea / 194
5.5	De q-exceptie / 194
6	Bewijslastverdeling onder de H(V)R / 195

Appendix I Hague Visby Rules / 197

Appendix II Harter Act / 205

TABLE OF CONTENTS

Appendix III Carriage of Goods by Sea Act 1936 / 207

Appendix IV Carriage of Goods by Sea Act 1971 / 217

Bibliography / 225

Case List / 233

Index / 237

Curriculum vitae / 239

List of abbreviations

A.C.	Law Reports Appeal Cases
A.M.C.	American Maritime Cases
App.	Appendix
App. Cas.	Law Reports Appeal Cases
art.	article
C.L.R.	Commonwealth Law Reports
CA	Court of Appeal
Cir.	Circuit
COGSA	Carriage of Goods by Sea Act
E.D.N.Y.	Eastern District of New York
ETL	European Transport Law
F	Federal Reporter (West's)
F.2d	Federal Reporter (West's)
F.3d	Federal Reporter (West's)
F.C.	Canada Federal Court Reports
F.Supp.	Federal Supplement (West's)
F.T.R.	Federal Trial Reports (Canada)
H(V)R	Hague (Visby) Rules
HL	House of Lords
J.B.L.	Journal of Business Law
K.B.	Law Reports King's Bench Decisions
Ll.L.L.Rep.	Lloyd's List Law Reports
Lloyd's Rep.	Lloyd's Law Reports
N.Z.L.R.	New Zealand Law Reports
NJ	Nederlandse Jurisprudentie
NJB	Nederlands Juristen Blad
P	Law Reports Probate
p.	Page
PC	Privy Council
PDAD	Probate Divorce and Admiralty Division
Rechtspr. Ant.	Rechtspraak van de haven van Antwerpen
S&S	Schip en Schade
S	Staatsblad
s.	Section
S.C.R.	Supreme Court Reports (Canada)
S.D.N.Y.	Southern District of New York
SCN	Supreme Court of The Netherlands
T.B.H.	Tijdschrift voor Belgisch Handelsrecht

LIST OF ABBREVIATIONS

U.S.	United States Supreme Court Reports
U.S.C.	United States Code
UNCITRAL	United Nations Commission on International Trade Law

Preface

This book was written in the course of four years of research. In those years a number of publications of which the author of this book and dr. M.L. Hendrikse of the University of Amsterdam (Universiteit van Amsterdam) are the authors. A significant pre-study for this book was 'Capita Zeerecht', Kluwer: Deventer 2004, chapters 3, 4, 5, 6 and 7. Chapter 6 of this book was published as Hendrikse & Margetson 2006. Chapter 6 is largely based on that publication, written by the author of this book and dr. M.L. Hendrikse on an equal basis. § 5.2 is based on Hendrikse & Margetson 2005b which was also written by those authors on an equal basis. Although these pre-studies formed the basis for this book this book is not merely a compilation of the pre-studies. It has been completely re-written and constantly adapted for different insights which emerged in the course of my continuing research. Obviously this book as the finished product contains significantly different insights than previous publications. This is a new book on the system of liability of art. III(1)/(2) and art. IV(1)/2 H(V)R.

At this point I shall take the opportunity to thank prof. C.E. du Perron for acting as my supervisor and dr. M.L. Hendrikse for acting as co-supervisor. I am also grateful to the members of the dissertation committee, prof. F.A.W. Bannier, prof. M.A. Clarke, prof. M. Huybrechts, prof. M.B.M. Loos and prof. G.J. van der Ziel who all read the manuscript and provided me with valuable advice and comments. I thank my father and mother for their constant support, my brother N.H. Margetson, LL.M for reading the manuscript and providing practical comments based on his years of experience as a practising maritime lawyer, my fiancée R. Simi, LL.M for her support and for reading the manuscript and my friend and colleague R.C.A. van 't Zelfde, LL.M for reading the manuscript. I should also like to express my gratitude to my friend and colleague dr. H.P.A.J. Martius who wrote his recent dissertation in the same period as I did and with whom I could share the burdens which accompany the writing of a dissertation. Finally I thank all my friends and family and my colleagues for their advice and support.

The text was completed at the beginning of January 2008. However, on 1 February 2008 the Supreme Court of the Netherlands rendered an important judgement holding that the duty to exercise due diligence to make the ship seaworthy extends to containers provided to the shipper by the carrier (SCN 1 February 2008, C06/082HR, The NDS Provider). It was however still possible to add a paragraph to § 3.5.3 wherein I briefly discussed the case.

Nick Margetson
Rotterdam, January 2008

Chapter 1
Introduction

1. The International Convention for the Unification of Certain Rules of Law Relating to Bills of Lading of 25 August 1924 is generally known as the 'Hague Rules' and those Rules as amended by the Protocols of 23 February 1968 and 21 December 1979 as the 'Hague Visby Rules'. The abbreviation 'H(V)R' refers to either the Hague Rules or the Hague Visby Rules. These are instruments of uniform international private law concerning the carriage of goods under a bill of lading. The H(V)R regulate many of the carrier's duties under a bill of lading and also provide the carrier with clauses excluding liability for loss of or damage to the cargo.

In this book the construction of art. III(1) and III(2) of the H(V)R and the construction and application of some of the exclusions to liability contained in art. IV of the H(V)R is researched to establish the system of the carrier's liability for loss or damage under the H(V)R. Because those articles are the same for the Hague Rules as well as for the Hague Visby Rules the abbreviation 'H(V)R' is used. For the same reason the expression 'the Rules' is also used indicating either the Hague Rules or the Hague Visby Rules.

1.1 When do the H(V)R apply?

2. The application of the H(V)R is not discussed in this book. I shall suffice with a few remarks on the applicability of the H(V)R in this introduction. The Protocol of Signature to the Hague Rules provides that 'The High Contracting Parties may give effect to this Convention either by giving it the force of law or by including in their national legislation in a form appropriate to that Legislation the rules adopted under this Convention.'

In the United Kingdom treaties and conventions have no direct effect and require to be enacted by the legislator. The enacting legislation for the Hague Visby Rules is the Carriage of Goods by Sea Act (COGSA)[1] 1971.[2] COGSA 1971 repealed COGSA 1924 which had provided that the Hague Rules were to 'have effect' in relation to the types of carriage that were identified. In COGSA 1971 the terminology was changed. Art. 1(2) COGSA 1971 provides that 'The provisions of the [Hague Visby, NJM] Rules (...) shall have the force of law'. This suggests that the primary rules for the application of the Hague Visby Rules in the UK are to be found in art. X of the Hague Visby Rules.[3]

---

1. This abbreviation is used in many English speaking countries for the national enactment of the H(V)R. Thus different COGSA's exist around the world.
2. See Carver 2005, p. 530.
3. Aikens et al 2006, p. 217. COGSA 1971 provides additional rules for the application which I shall not go into. See for the application of the Rules in the UK see inter alia Carver 2005, p. 530 etc and Aikens et al 2006, p. 216.

In the United States the Hague Rules were incorporated into the domestic law with the enactment of the Carriage of Goods by Sea Act 1936 (COGSA 1936).[4] The U.S.A. are not party to the Hague Visby Rules.

In 1956 the Hague Rules were initially incorporated into the Dutch Commercial Code.[5] In 1991 the system was changed and the Hague Visby Rules were given direct effect by art. 8:371 Dutch Civil Code.

1.2 Construction of the Rules

3. In chapter 2 of this thesis the necessity of uniform construction of the H(V)R is emphasised. If the Rules are applied differently under different legal systems the object of establishing an international regime governing the carriage of goods by sea under a bill of lading would be defeated.

As the formal title of the Hague Rules shows, the intention of the convention was unification of certain rules of law relating to bills of lading. This intention of the Rules has however not been achieved. Over eighty years of case law has created diversity instead of uniformity. This is the failure of the Hague Rules.

1.3 Research question

4. The task of any tribunal which is asked to apply or construe a treaty can be described as the duty of giving effect to the expressed intention of the parties, that is, their intention as expressed in the words used by them in the light of the surrounding circumstances.[6]

However, if a Rule is applied the same in all legal systems it means there is uniformity of law and the question of what the expressed intention was will not arise. The expressed intention of the parties to a treaty will only become relevant if there is no established uniform construction. Then a tribunal will have to answer the question of how the Rule should construed. Therefore the research question is:

If uniform construction of a Rule does not exist, how should the Rule be construed?

1.4 Method used to answer the research question

5. In chapters 3, 4 and 5 the existing differences in the construction and application of articles III(1), III(2), IV(1) and IV(2) are identified through international law comparison. Per topic of research questions are formulated. These questions are answered under the different legal systems. After having established the existing differences I establish the intended construction. To discover the intended construction of the Rules I have established rules of, and aids to the construction of the H(V)R.[7]

---

4. 46 U.S.C. App. § 1300-1315. E.g. § 1303 is also referred to as 'section 3 COGSA'.
5. Art. 468-471 Dutch Commercial Code.
6. McNair 1961, p. 365.
7. See infra chapter 2.

1.5 Researched legal systems

6. The legal systems considered are primarily: U.S. law, English law and Dutch law.[8] Incidentally Canadian and Australian law are considered and even more incidentally Belgian law. Because of the history of the Rules, English and U.S. law are the most important legal systems for the construction of the Rules. It is widely accepted that the Harter Act[9] is the ancestor of the Hague Rules and that the Hague Rules were greatly influenced by American and English law.[10] In the *Bunga Seroja* case of the Australia High Court this was pointed out by judges Gaudron, Gummow and Hayne:

> '..., the fact is that the "immediate impetus for the Hague Rules came from the British Empire". Furthermore, British lawyers and representatives of British carrier and cargo interests dominated the Committees responsible for the drafting of the rules which eventually became the Hague Rules. That being so, it seems likely that the English common law rules provided the conceptual framework for the Hague Rules – certainly the key terms of arts. III and IV are the subject of much common law doctrine. The rules should be interpreted with that framework in mind. That conclusion is strengthened by the fact that there appears to have been very little discussion at the Convention of arts. III, r. 2 and IV, r. 2(c).'[11]

7. The historical background of the Rules and the fact that I am qualified under Dutch law led to the choice to mainly compare Dutch law to Anglo/American law because the latter are two of the most relevant legal systems of maritime law. Of course there are other legal systems which I could have researched. However, a research has to be restricted and I chose the mentioned legal systems for the reasons given above.

1.6 Topics of research

8. After a discussion of how to construe the Rules and establishing rules of, and aids to the construction of the Rules the following topics are discussed:

Chapter 3: the duties of the carrier contained in art. III(1) and III(2);

Chapter 4: the relationship between art. III(1) and (2) and art. IV(1) and (2);

Chapter 5: the application of art. IV(1) and the exceptions provided by art. IV(2), a, b, c and q; These specific elements of art. IV were chosen for different points of interest specific to those elements and because they are amongst the most important of the carrier's exceptions.

---

8. It is important for civil lawyers to note that at common law and the systems derived from the common law a policy of stare decisis exists. That is the doctrine that, when court has once laid down a principle of law as applicable to a certain state of facts, it will adhere to that principle, and apply it to all future cases, where facts are substantially the same. Common lawyers on the other hand should note that in civil law systems various different court decisions can exist at the same time. There is no policy of stare decisis.
9. 46 U.S.C. App. § 190-196.
10. See inter alia Carver 2005, p. 525, Carver 1982, p. 294-301, Royer 1959, p. 18, Blussé 1929, p. 54-56.
11. Great China Metal Industries Co. Ltd. v. Malaysian International Shipping Corporation Berhad (*Bunga Seroja*), [1999] 1 Lloyd's Rep. 512, sub point 73.

Art. IV(1) is either treated as an exemption from liability or as a division of the burden of proof. The nautical fault exception provided by art. IV(2)a is special because, contrary to most exceptions, it is a far reaching exception which can even exculpate the carrier for damage caused by his fault. This and the vagueness of the expression 'management of the ship' make the nautical fault exception interesting to research. Also the fire exception is of special interest because of the proviso it contains; the carrier is not responsible for loss or damage caused by fire *unless caused by his actual fault or privity*. Because of the proviso the fire exception is an almost unbreakable exemption. It is interesting to see how this exception is applied under different legal systems and how the relationship between the duties of the carrier and the fire exception is influenced by the proviso. The 'perils of the sea' exception lends itself for discussion because of its wide application and the overwhelming amount of case law that it has given rise to. Finally the 'catch all' q-exception is of interest because of its general wording and the fact that it contains its own division of the burden of proof. The research has led me to the conclusions that the division of the burden of proof (discussed in the last chapter) depends on the specific exception invoked, as does the way the relationship between the duties (or the non fulfilment thereof) and the exceptions is influenced.

9. Of course there are more aspects of liability of the carrier under the Rules. E.g. the question of when the rules actually apply, the 'said to contain clause' and limitation of liability are only some of the topics which are also governed by the Rules and play a role in cargo claims. However, I have restricted my research to the duties of the carrier contained in art. III(1) and III(2), the relationship between those duties, some of the exceptions in art. IV and the division of the burden of proof.

10. In Chapter 6 the division of the burden of proof is established.

11. Chapter 7 contains my conclusions. One general conclusion is that, although the Rules contain uniform international private law which was meant to lead to uniformity, that uniformity does not exist. This becomes especially clear for art. IV(1), which is either treated as a division of the burden of proof or as a defence against responsibility for cargo damage.[12] Another example is the application of the fire exception. In the U.S.A. the application of the fire exception differs from the application in the other legal systems researched. Under American law the fire exception can even apply if the fire was caused by the carrier's failure to exercise due diligence to make the ship seaworthy. There is also a subtle difference between the way the 9th Circuit construes the fire exception and the way the other circuits construe the exception. However, this difference in construction does not seem to lead to a difference in application and effect of the fire exception.[13] As a final example I shall mention the perils of the sea exception. Under U.S. law the perils of the sea defence provided by art. IV(2)c H(V)R is more or less rendered useless as a defence for the carrier. Under English, Australian and Dutch law the construction is more realistic, providing the carrier with an important defence.[14]

In chapter 2 some suggestions are given to improve uniform construction and application of the Rules.

---

12. See infra § 5.1.
13. See infra § 5.3.
14. See infra § 5.4.

1.7 The UNCITRAL draft convention

12. In 1996 UNCITRAL considered a proposal to include in its work program a review of current practices and laws in the area of the international carriage of goods by sea, with a view to establishing greater uniformity.[15] Another issue was the need for a legal basis for the use of electronic bills of lading.[16] The result is the UNCITRAL Draft Convention on carriage of goods [wholly or partly] [by sea]. The most recent draft in January 2008 (the date of completion of this book) is dated 14 January 2008.[17] It is thought that the convention will be ready for ratification at the end of 2008.[18] It has not been decided how many states will be required to ratify before the convention comes into force. The UNCITRAL draft is an important development in the law concerning the carriage of goods by sea. However, it is likely that it will take years before the instrument will have significant effect in practice.[19] Until then the H(V)R will still be the regime most often encountered. The H(V)R are a very mature regime with 83 years of world wide case law to study. For that reason I have only briefly touched upon the draft proposal and (as the title of this book shows) have focused on the system of liability under the H(V)R.

13. I hope that this book will help to lead to a more uniform construction and application of the H(V)R in the different national legal systems.

---

15. Karan 2004, p. 38.
16. Van der Ziel 2004-I, p. 276.
17. Document WP.101 of UNCITRAL Working Group III. See <www.uncitral.org>.
18. Van der Ziel 2006, p. 203.
19. Compare the Hamburg Rules which were adopted in March 1978 and only came into force on November 1, 1992.

Chapter 2
Construction of the Hague (Visby) Rules

2.1 Introduction

14. Uniform interpretation and construction of maritime law is of the essence. This has been recognised by courts worldwide for years. In the *Lottowanna* case (1874) the U.S. Supreme Court held:

> 'The maritime law is part of the law of nations, one of the great beauties of which is its universality. Uniformity has been declared to be its essence. The worst maritime code would be one which should be dictated by the separate interest and influenced by the peculiar manner of only one people.'[20]

The reference to the 'maritime code' was in fact to the maritime codes of various nations, both ancient and contemporary:

> 'Such was the declaration of the civil law, which in the Roman ports furnished the role as well for the Roman ship as for the ship of the barbarian. Such was the declaration of the maritime codes (...) And when those great systems of law are referred to, the reference is in no proper sense to local law, but to the general law as known throughout the civilized world, including for a long period, England.'[21]

15. This chapter will deal with the question of how uniform construction and interpretation of the H(V)R should be achieved. Before discussing that question however, I shall clarify some of the terminology used (§ 2.2).

2.2 Terminology

Treaty, convention, instrument

16. The word 'treaty' is usually, but far from consistently, reserved for the more solemn agreements such as treaties of peace, alliance, neutrality, arbitration.[22] There is a tendency to describe certain multilateral law-making treaties such as e.g. treaties concluded under auspices of the League of Nations or under the auspices of the United Nations

---

20. The Lottowanna, 88 U.S. 558, 565-566.
21. The Lottowanna, 88 U.S. 558, 565. This case was recently discussed in the Tulane Maritime Law Journal: Marva Jo Wyatt, 'Cogsa comes ashore ... and more: The Supreme Court makes inroads promoting uniformity and maritime commerce in Norfolk Southern Railway v. Kirby', Tulane Maritime Law Journal 2006, p. 101-136.
22. McNair 1961, p. 22.

as a 'convention'. But the term 'convention' is by no means confined to multipartite treaties.[23] Kiantou-Pampouki notes that the terms 'treaty' and 'convention' are used interchangeably, without discrimination.[24] The word 'instrument' is used in a broad sense to indicate any international agreement containing uniform law.

Protocol

17. This usually denotes a treaty amending or supplemental to another treaty.[25] E.g. the Visby Protocol of 1968.

Construction and interpretation

18. The words 'construction' and 'interpretation' are often used synonymously. Black's Law Dictionary says that this is incorrect: 'In strictness, interpretation, is limited to exploring the written text, while construction goes beyond and may call in the aid of extrinsic considerations, ...'[26]

The following makes the difference even clearer: 'Construction' is a term of a wider scope than 'interpretation'. While the latter is concerned only with ascertaining the sense and meaning of the subject-matter, the former may also be directed to explaining the legal effects and consequences of the instrument in question. Hence interpretation precedes construction, but stops at the written text.[27] On the other hand another dictionary treats the words as synonyms.[28] Below I shall use the words construction and interpretation in the meaning given in Black's Law Dictionary.
This chapter will therefore deal with the problem of uniform construction and interpretation of the H(V)R.

Rules of construction

19. Successive generations of writers, arbitrators and judges have elaborated rules for the interpretation and construction of treaties, borrowing mainly from the private law of contract.[29] According to Jacobs modern approaches to interpretation can be classified in three broad groups: the subjective, the textual and the teleological.[30] The subjective approach looks primarily to the actual intentions of parties. The principal question in this approach is concerned with the 'real will' of the parties. It attempts to elucidate the text of the treaty, which on this view is merely an expression of the will of the parties, by reference to the whole course of negotiations leading to the conclusion of the treaty, and seeks to investigate the actual intentions of the parties at the time of the adoption of the final text. The textual approach places the principal emphasis on

---

23. McNair 1961, p. 23.
24. Kiantou-Pampouki 1991, p. 9.
25. McNair 1961, p. 23.
26. Black's Law Dictionary 1968, p. 386.
27. Black's Law Dictionary 1968, p. 954.
28. Wharton's Law Lexicon, 14th edition.
29. McNair 1961, p. 364-365.
30. Francis G. Jacobs 2004, p. 297. This description of the rules of construction is from Francis G. Jacobs 2004, p. 298.

the actual words of the treaty. This approach is also known as the objective approach.[31] While the subjective approach deals with the question 'what did the parties really mean?' the textual approach deals with the question 'what did the parties say?' The teleological approach seeks to construe the treaty in the light of its objects and purposes. To a certain extent this approach is a combination of the subjective and textual approach.

Uniform construction

20. The necessity of uniform construction is often pointed out in case law. Regarding the principle of uniform construction and interpretation of the Hague Rules Lord Macmillan said in the *Stag Line* case:

> 'It is important to remember that the Act of 1924 was the outcome of an international conference and that the rules in the schedule have an international currency. As these rules must come under the consideration of foreign Courts, it is desirable in the interests of uniformity that their interpretation should not be rigidly controlled by domestic precedents of antecedent date, but rather that the language of the rules should be construed on broad principles of general acceptance.'[32]

21. The necessity of uniform construction should be born in mind by anyone dealing with the Rules. Uniform construction is not an aid to construction or a rule of construction. It is a point of view which should always be taken into account regardless of the rule of construction applied.

Autonomous

22. In *Morris v. KLM Royal Dutch Airlines* Lord Steyn explained what is meant by autonomous construction and interpretation of an instrument. That case concerned the meaning of the words 'bodily injury' under the Warsaw convention. Lord Steyn said:

> 'It follows from the scheme of the Convention, and indeed from its very nature as an international trade law convention, that the basic concepts it employs to achieve its purpose are autonomous concepts. It is irrelevant what bodily injury means in other contexts in national legal systems. The correct inquiry is to determine the autonomous or independent meaning of "bodily injury" in the Convention: R. v. Secretary of State for the Home Department, ex p. Adan [2001] 2 A.C. 477. And the premise is that something that does not qualify as a "bodily injury" in the Convention sense does not meet the relevant threshold for recovery under it.'[33]

23. In other words the instrument (here the Warsaw Convention) is to be seen as a separate source of law which exists besides the national law. That instrument should be

---

31. Kiantou-Pampuki 1991, 23.
32. Foscolo, Mango & Co., Ltd., and H.C. Vivian & Co., Ltd. v. Stag Line, 41 Ll.L.L.Rep. 165, 174. See also The Muncaster Castle case, [1961] 1 Lloyd's Rep. 57, 88 and Bunga Seroja, [1999] 1 Lloyd's Rep. 512.
33. Morris v. KLM Royal Dutch Airlines, [2002] UKHL 7, [2002] 2 A.C. 628, 636.

construed in its own light regardless of existing national law.[34] This means that the case law and doctrine of other states should be compared to discover the prevailing construction of an instrument.[35] If all parties to an instrument construe the instrument autonomously it may lead to a uniform construction of that instrument. That is however not always the case. It is possible that different autonomous constructions of a uniform instrument lead to various different solutions. Uniform construction can only be reached if the same solution is chosen in all the involved jurisdictions.

Uniformity

24. Uniform law creates legal certainty between those who are party to international contracts. An international instrument which applies instead of the domestic law of one state can greatly improve the required legal certainty.[36] If all parties to the H(V)R construe the Rules as an autonomous instrument uniformity *could* be achieved. Autonomous construction does not however mean that all parties will reach the same construction. Indeed, different points of view on what the correct autonomous construction of a certain rule is can co-exist. Only if all parties apply the same (autonomous) construction of a rule it will lead to uniformity of law.

Application

25. Uniformity of law does not necessarily lead to uniform application of that law, i.e. the way the uniform law is applied in the various legal systems of the states who are parties to the convention. Uniform application will be impeded if certain aspects are not regulated by the convention. E.g. the division of the burden of proof is not regulated by the H(V)R. This means domestic law will apply. National concepts of law, such as e.g. the English doctrine of bailment will then impede the uniform application of the Rules.

2.3 Aids to the construction of the H(V)R

26. As was said in chapter 1, the task of any tribunal which is asked to apply or construe a treaty can be described as the duty of giving effect to the expressed intention of the parties, that is, their intention as expressed in the words used by them in the light of the surrounding circumstances.[37]
Rules of construction are points of view which can be used to ascertain what the parties meant by the words which they used. There are some who are sceptical 'as to the value of these so-called rules and are sympathetic to the process of their gradual devaluation' because these rules would create the danger of diverting a tribunal from its true task of ascertaining what the parties meant by the words which they used, into a wilderness of conflicting decisions of tribunals and opinions of writers.[38] The example is given that one party invokes a rule of liberal construction and the other counters

---

34. See also Nieuwenhuis 1994, p. 205.
35. See Haak 2007, p. 163.
36. It has been said that legal certainty through unification is the main goal in international transport (Haak 2007, p. 156).
37. McNair 1961, p. 365.
38. McNair 1961, p. 366.

with a rule that an obligation created by a treaty should be construed restrictively that is, so as to impose the least restriction upon the freedom or sovereignty of the State undertaking this obligation.[39] This warning should be heeded when applying rules of construction. Below I shall create a list of aids to construction which can help when applying one of the rules of construction mentioned above. The aids to construction have been derived from case law.

2.3.1 Stag Line

a) Plain meaning of the words

27. Lord Atkin said in the *Stag Line* case:

> 'In approaching the construction of these rules it appears to me important to bear in mind that one has to give the words as used their plain meaning, and not to colour one's interpretation by considering whether a meaning otherwise plain should be avoided if it alters the previous law.'[40]

b) Broad principles of general acceptation[41]

28. And Lord Macmillan said:

> 'It is important to remember that the Act of 1924 was the outcome of an international conference and that the rules in the schedule have an international currency. As these rules must come under the consideration of foreign Courts, it is desirable in the interests of uniformity that their interpretation should not be rigidly controlled by domestic precedents of antecedent date, but rather that the language of the rules should be construed on broad principles of general acceptation.'[42]

29. It has been said that the broad principles of general acceptation are rules based on a general theory of law.[43] Van Delden created a list of 24 of such principles for his inaugural lecture in 1986. Examples are the principal that nobody may wilfully cause damage to another person without having to pay for the damage,[44] the principle that a contract is only binding between parties to the contract and that third parties can not derive rights from that contract nor be harmed by that contract[45] and the principle that a promise should be kept.[46]

---

39. McNair 1961, 365-366.
40. Foscolo, Mango & Co., Ltd., and H.C. Vivian & Co., Ltd. v. Stag Line, 41 Ll.L.L.Rep. 165.
41. See also The Rafaela S, [2005] 1 Lloyd's Rep. 247, 359 and Nieuwenhuis 1994.
42. Foscolo, Mango & Co., Ltd., and H.C. Vivian & Co., Ltd. v. Stag Line, 41 Ll.L.L.Rep. 165, 174.
43. Van Delden 1986, p. 16.
44. 'Damni culpa dati reparatio'. See Van Delden 1986, p. 14 (example 20). See also Nieuwenhuis 1994, p. 208.
45. Van Delden 1986, p. 11 (example 7).
46. 'Promissorum implendorum obligatio'. See Nieuwenhuis 1994, p. 208.

30. If the meaning of the words is clear but lead to an absurd result then the objective construction has failed. Broad principles of general acceptance can be used to test if a result is absurd.[47]

2.3.2 Pyrene Co. Ltd. v. Scindia Navigation Co. Ltd.

c) The French text

31. French is the only authentic language of the Hague Rules. Though the preliminary work was done in the English language the official text is French, and the English version merely a translation of that. However, under the United Kingdom Act of 1924 the English wording has statutory force.[48] It was held permissible to look at the French text by Devlin J in *Pyrene Co. Ltd. v. Scindia Navigation Co. Ltd.* Devlin J. said:

> 'If there is any doubt, the French text (set out in Carver, 9th ed., p. 1065) makes it quite clear. Having regard to the preamble to the [Carriage of Goods by Sea Act, 1924] and the fact that the French text is the only authoritative version of the Convention, I think, notwithstanding [Counsel's] objection, that it is permissible to look at it.'[49]

2.3.3 The Bunga Seroja

d) History of the Rules: compromise character and English roots

32. 'The aim of the rules was to harmonize the diverse laws of trading nations and to strike a new arrangement for the allocation of risk between cargo and carrier interests. However, the Hague Rules were a compromise rather than a codification of any accepted and uniform practice of shippers. Consequently, one needs to be cautious about using the pre-existing law of any country in interpreting the rules. But that said, the fact is that the "immediate impetus for the Hague Rules came from the British Empire". Furthermore, British lawyers and representatives of British carrier and cargo interests dominated the Committees responsible for the drafting of the rules which eventually became the Hague Rules. That being so, it seems likely that English law provided the conceptual framework for the Hague Rules – certainly the key terms of arts. III and IV are the subject of much common law doctrine. The rules should be interpreted with that framework in mind.'[50]

33. The history of the rules leads to two aids to construction: the Anglo-American[51]/common law[52] background and the compromise between shippers and carriers.

---

47. I have applied this method in § 3.9.5.
48. Carver 2005, p. 527.
49. Pyrene Company, Ltd. v. Scindia Steam Navigation Company, Ltd. [1954] 1 Lloyd's Rep. 321.
50. Bunga Seroja, [1999] 1 Lloyd's Rep. 512, par. 73.
51. See also Nieuwenhuis 1994, p. 204.
52. See also Van der Ziel 2006, p. 205.

e) Reading the Hague Rules as a whole

34. 'It is rudimentary to an understanding of the rules that they must be read as a whole so as to achieve the comprehensive objectives suggested by their language, history and purposes. Clearly, they are intended to strike a commercially practical and reasonable balance between the competing claims of cargo-owners, which have suffered loss, and carrier interests bound to standards of proper and careful conduct, but no more.'[53]

35. E.g. in the *Bunga Seroja* case the construction of the perils of the sea exceptions was discussed in the light of the responsibilities of the carrier:

> 'The "perils of the sea" exception cannot be properly understood if it is divorced from its context. It is an immunity created in favour of the carrier and the ship and it is necessary, then, to consider what are the responsibilities of the carrier.'[54]

2.3.4 The Jordan II[55]

f) Purposive construction

36. The plain text of the convention may be construed literally or purposively. In Jordan II a purposive construction of the Rules was preferred above a literal construction.[56]

g) Travaux Préparatoires

37. Regarding the Travaux Préparatoires Lord Steyn said:

> 'It is, of course, a well established supplementary means of interpretation (...) It is, however, equally well settled that the Travaux can only assist if (...) they (...) clearly and indisputably point to a definite legislative intention, ...'[57]

38. The Travaux Préparatoires may be used as an aid to construction. They may be useful to find out what the framers meant or intended with the words they used.

h) The views of the textbook writers

39. In *Jordan II* as well as in other cases the views of writers are taken into account. These views can help to find the intended construction.

---

53. Bunga Seroja, [1999] 1 Lloyd's Rep. 512, par. 142.
54. Ibid., par. 24.
55. Jordan II, [2005] 1 Lloyd's Rep. 57.
56. See infra § 3.9.1.
57. See also Fothergill v. Monarch Airlines, [1980] 2 Lloyd's Rep. 295 and Berlingieri 2004, p. 154-155.

i) The decisions in foreign jurisdictions

40. Foreign decisions were discussed in the *Jordan II* case to establish the international dominant point of view. Foreign decisions are an essential aid to achieve uniform construction.

Third party bill of lading holders?

41. In *Jordan II* the interests of third party bill of lading holders were considered. Lord Steyn said:

> 'It is true, as Counsel for cargo interests emphasized, that third party bill of lading holders will in practice often not have seen the charter-party or had advance notice of relevant charter-party clauses. This is a point of some substance. It is, however, an inevitable risk of international trade and cannot affect the correct interpretation of art. III, r. 2.'

Strict construction of the exceptions?

42. Tetley is of the opinion that exceptions should be construed strictly.[58] The main plank in Tetley's argument is the *Gosse Millerd Ltd. v. Canadian Government Merchant Marine Ltd.* In that decision Greer L.J. said:

> 'I think it is incumbent on the Court not to attribute to Art. IV (2) (a) a meaning that will largely nullify the effect of Art. III (2), unless they are compelled to do so clear words. The words "act, neglect, or default ... in the navigation or in the management of the ship", if they are interpreted in their widest sense, would cover any act done on board the ship which relates to the care of the cargo, and in practice such an interpretation, if it did not completely nullify the provisions of Art. III (2), would certainly take the heart out of those provisions, and in practice reduce to very small dimensions the obligation carefully to handle, carry, keep, and care for the cargo, which is imposed on shipowners by the last-mentioned rule. In my judgement, a reasonable construction of the rules requires that a narrower interpretation should be put on the excepting provisions of Art. IV (2) (a).'[59]

43. I am of the opinion that the rule of strict construction of art. IV(2)a applies specifically for that exception and that it is not a general rule for all the exceptions. Art. IV(2)a must be strictly construed otherwise it would also cover incidents which cannot be qualified as either 'management of the ship' or 'management of the cargo'. If, in those instances, the exception were to be applied in favour of the carrier the duty contained in art. III(2) would be undermined.[60] This is also Greer's argument for strict construction of art. IV(2)a. However, it does not mean that the rule of strict construction is a general rule which applies for all exceptions.

---

58. Tetley 2004, § VII.6.
59. *Gosse Millerd Ltd. v. Canadian Government Merchant Marine Ltd.*, (1927) 29 Ll.L.L.Rep. 190, 197.
60. See infra § 5.2.

44. A surprising rule of construction was formulated by professor Huybrechts in his valedictory address at Antwerp University on 2 March 2007. Huybrechts formulated the rule of construction that there is a presumption that the carrier is not liable for cargo damage. This presumption is based on the fact that the carrier can often rely on one of the exceptions of art. IV H(V)R.[61] The rule is surprising because it is contrary to the French rule that there is a presumption of liability of the carrier in cases of cargo damage.[62] The presumption of liability says that the carrier is liable for cargo damage unless he can successfully invoke an exception. The rule of Huybrechts however, says that the carrier is not liable as long as he can successfully invoke an exception. Both rules illustrate the system of the H(V)R. The rule of Huybrechts seems to emphasise that the carrier will be able to rely on an exception more often than not. However, both rules boil down to the same result; if the cargo interests prove cargo damage the carrier is liable unless he can successfully invoke an exception.

45. Before concluding how the rules of, and aids to construction are to be applied I shall discuss some problems regarding the uniform construction of the H(V)R and suggest some ways to expedite uniformity.

2.4 Problems regarding uniform construction of the H(V)R

2.4.1 Politics

46. In studying the liability of the carrier under the Hague Rules I encountered a number of recurring problems regarding uniform construction of the Hague Rules.[63] The first major influence I encountered could be called 'politics'. The clearest example of political views which intend to influence objective construction is the difference in application of the perils of the sea exception. The American construction of some of the exceptions seems to be based on political grounds which intend to protect cargo interests. This can be explained by the fact that in the past United States cargo interests relied on British ships that carried their goods under British bills of lading.[64] The narrower view, more favourable to cargo interests, would favour nations of cargo-owners (such as the United States of America, Australia and many developing nations).[65] The expansive notion of 'perils of the sea' for the purposes of the immunity provided by the Hague Rules, art IV(2) c might have developed in England reflecting the interest of great fleet-owning nations.[66]

47. Although the American construction of the perils of the sea exception is so strict that the carrier usually cannot rely on it to escape liability the American construction of the fire exception is more in favour of the carrier. This can however be explained by the history of the fire exception which is based on the English Fire Statute. The English Fire Statute leads to the result that the carrier will rarely be responsible for damage by fire. In the 19th century this allowed English carriers to keep their freight rates down.

---

61. Huybrechts 2007, p. 37.
62. See e.g. Lamy Transport 2007, p. 378 and Rodière 1997, p. 341.
63. See also Berlingieri 2004.
64. See e.g. Bunga Seroja, sub point 11.
65. See also Bunga Seroja, sub 121.
66. Bunga Seroja, sub point 12.

History shows that the American legislator was determined to give American shipowners the same benefit in order to be able to compete with the English shipowners.[67]

2.4.2 Older law dealing with the same issue

48. A second problem regarding uniform construction is the applicability of older (statutory) law dealing with the same issue. This problem becomes very clear when studying the different points of views regarding the application of the fire exception.[68] The English and American Fire Statutes and the fire exception provided by art. IV(2)b H(V)R both deal with the exemption from liability of the carrier for damage caused by fire. The English and American Fire Statutes existed before the Hague Rules. The applicability of two different regulations to the same legal problem (is the carrier exempted from liability for damage caused by fire or not?) has led to controversy under US law. The controversy concerns the question if the carrier who wants to rely on the fire exemption is obliged to prove that he used due diligence to provide a seaworthy vessel or not. The answer to this question will influence the division of the burden of proof. The question is answered differently by the 9th Circuit on the one hand and the various circuit courts in the US.[69] This is an example of an obstacle to uniformity caused by the existence and applicability of an older regulation for a problem which is also dealt with by the Hague Rules.

2.4.3 Manner of implementation

49. Another possible obstacle to uniformity could be the manner of implementation of the Hague Rules.[70] As mentioned above the protocol of signature of the Hague Rules provides two options to contracting parties to give effect to the Rules. Either by giving the convention the force of law or by including the Rules in their national legislation in a form appropriate to that legislation. Art. 8:371 of the Dutch Civil Code is an example of the former option. That article defines the conditions under which the Hague Rules will be applicable to a Bill of Lading under Dutch law. Initially however the Netherlands had chosen for the latter option of codification of the Rules in their Commercial Code. This led to a problem. According to the legislative history and the Dutch Supreme Court this possibility to choose how the Rules should be implemented, meant that the Rules had no direct effect.[71] The result was that the Rules were not directly effective in the Netherlands. Later the problem was solved when the Netherlands became party to the Visby Protocol. The Dutch legislator added article 8:371 par 3 to the Dutch Civil Code. That article regulates when article 1 to 9 of the Hague Visby Rules shall apply to a Bill of Lading.

---

67. See infra § 5.3.2.
68. See infra § 5.3.
69. See infra chapter 5.
70. See also Berlingieri 2004, p. 154.
71. SCN 8 November 1968, S&S 1969, 10 (Portalon). See for a discussion of this decision: Swart 1971. See also Boonk 1993, p. 37 and Haak 2007, p. 160.

2.4.4 National legal concepts

50. The existence of different legal concepts such as e.g. causality can also be an obstacle to uniformity. Also the existence of, or the use of, specific concepts of national law which are unknown in other jurisdictions. E.g. the contact of carriage of goods by sea is a contract of bailment under English law. The division of the burden of proof under a contract of bailment differs from the traditional division of the burden of proof under a contract of carriage of goods by sea under a Bill of Lading.[72] There have been judgements rendered which apply the bailment division the burden of proof to a contract of carriage under a Bill of Lading.[73] This has led to lack of uniformity with regard to the correct division of the burden of proof under the Rules.[74]

51. In *Bunga Seroja* Kirby identified this problem and pointed out that:

> 'In construing a text such as the Hague Rules, this Court, to the greatest extent possible, should prefer the construction which is most consistent with that which has attracted general international support rather than one which represents only a local or minority opinion. That is a reason why it would be a mistake to interpret the Hague Rules as a mere supplement to the operation of Australian law governing contracts of bailment. That law, derived from the common law of England, may not be reflected in, or identical to, the equivalent law governing carriers' liability in civil law and other jurisdictions. The Hague Rules must operate in all jurisdictions, whatever their legal tradition.'[75]

52. For the same reason uniform law should not be drafted in the idiom of any one legal system or family of legal systems.[76]

53. Another problem arising from the incorporation of the Rules into the various legal systems is that different versions of the text exist which can lead to differences in the way they are construed.[77] An example are the words 'subject to the provisions of article 4' in art. III(2) of the Rules. Under English law this led to the doctrine that the duty contained in art. III(1) is an overriding obligation and art. III(2) is not.[78] Because the words 'subject to the provisions of article 4' were left out of the U.S. COGSA this distinction is not made in American law.[79]

54. According to Mankabady the incorporation of the Rules into national legal systems caused states to treat that legislation as domestic law instead of as an international instrument. In his opinion the Rules should have been 'adopted' instead of 'incorporated' into the legal systems of each contracting state. Then the way would have been open for uniformity because the Rules would be considered international rules by

---

72. See chapter 6 on the division of the burden of proof.
73. Ibid.
74. See also Mankabady 1974, p. 132.
75. Bunga Seroja, sub point 138.
76. Clarke 2000, p. 127.
77. See also Yiannopoulos 1965, p. 387-388.
78. See infra § 4.3.1.
79. See infra § 4.3.2.

each contracting state.[80] However, Mankabady wrote this in 1974 and since then the concept of autonomous construction has become widely accepted.[81]

55. A last obstacle to uniformity which I shall mention is the problem that certain issues are not dealt with by the Rules.[82] Issues such as the division of the burden of proof and the question if the duties of the carrier contained in art. III(1) and (2) are delegable or not. The first issue is dealt with in the draft UNCITRAL instrument for the carriage of goods by sea. Unfortunately the second question is not dealt with in the draft instrument.

2.5 Ways to improve uniform construction of the H(V)R

56. An easily accessible database containing cases and arbitral decisions in cases concerning the H(V)R is one way to improve uniform construction.[83]

57. An important existing source for the H(V)R is Westlaw. Westlaw does however have a number of drawbacks. It only contains English, US and Canadian cases and materials. Because of the history of the Hague Rules these are of course important jurisdictions for the H(V)R. However it would be good to have a database which also contains Australian and continental cases. A good example of such a database is the CISG database of Pace Law School containing case law from numerous jurisdictions, translated to English and summarised.[84] The database also contains legislative history and scholarly writings. A similar CISG database is the UNILEX database which is maintained by the Centre for Comparative and Foreign Law Studies in Rome. It would be ideal if such a database existed for the H(V)R.

58. Secondly it would be an improvement if unclear terminology were defined on a greater scale than the present definitions of art. I H(V)R. Art. 1 of the UNCITRAL draft convention on the carriage (wholly or partly) by sea is an improvement on art. 1 H(V)R.[85] In that instrument the unclear exception concerning damage due to an error in the management of the ship has been deleted. However the ambiguous 'perils of the sea' has been kept without defining it.

59. It has been said that the use of regulations for the construction of an instrument could be incorporated in the instrument to improve uniformity.[86] This would give judges a clear indication of the principles to adhere to when construing the instrument. An existing example is art. 7(1) CISG which reads:

> 'In the interpretation of this convention, regard is to be had to its international character and to the need to promote uniformity in its application and the observance of good faith in international trade.'

---

80. Mankabady 1974, p. 131-132.
81. See the cases discussed below. See also Haak 2007, p. 163.
82. See also Mankabady 1974, p. 132.
83. See Kruisinga 2004, p. 16-17 on the development of such databases for cases concerning the CISG.
84. <www.cisg.law.pace.edu/cisg/text/cisg-toc.html>.
85. See <www.uncitral.org> under Working Group III.
86. See in general Magnus 2001, p. 578 and Trompenaars 1989, p. 135-162.

CONCLUSION 2.6

The framers of the UNCITRAL draft instrument for the carriage of goods by sea incorporated the wording of art. 7(1) CISG into the UNCITRAL instrument.[87] The Hamburg Rules contain a similar article. The article will remind courts and other tribunals that the international character and need to promote uniformity above national law. As is seen in numerous cases discussed in this book, this is already a generally accepted principal and I do not believe that the article will make a lot of difference.

60. Another method to counter divergence in the construction of an international instrument and to ensure that any tendencies towards divergence shall be corrected, would be the establishment of an international tribunal with ultimate jurisdiction to decide on questions arising out of the interpretation and construction of the international instrument. National courts could be required to suspend their decisions until after the judgement of this tribunal and then decide in accordance with that judgement. A similar procedure already exists within the framework of the European Community.[88] It is probably unrealistic to suggest that such an international tribunal should be restricted to dealing with cases concerning the carriage of goods by sea. How would such a specialised commercial tribunal be financed? It is therefore suggested that an international commercial court is established, e.g. within UNCITRAL, which deals with questions with regard to all trade and transport treaties.

2.6 Conclusion

61. Although uniformity was intended there is diversity in the interpretation and construction of the Hague Rules. This diversity has a number of reasons, some of which were discussed in this chapter such as politics, different legal traditions, manner of implementation and art. VIII H(V)R. In my opinion the best solution to achieve real uniformity is the establishment of a supra national court such as the Court of Justice of the European Communities. The decisions of such a court would have to be binding otherwise the problems discussed above will continue to diversify the way an instrument is applied.
A second best solution would be the establishment of a database such as discussed above.

62. The object of the Rules is uniformity.[89] This should always be the main rule regardless of which of the rules of construction are applied. The necessity of uniform construction means that foreign decisions and doctrine should also be consulted.
In case of absence of uniformity it is necessary to give effect to the expressed intention of the parties, that is, their intention as expressed in the words used by them in the light of the surrounding circumstances. Rules of, and aids to construction are used to achieve this intended construction.

---

87. See page 12 of document A/CN.9/WG.III/WP.56 at <www.uncitral.org under> 'Working Group III'.
88. See also J. Felemegas, 'The United Nations Convention on Contracts for the International Sale of Goods: Article 7 and Uniform Interpretation', Review of The United Nations Convention on Contracts for the International Sale of Goods (CISG), 2000-2001, p. 115-379. The publication is also available in the Pace Law database.
89. This is made clear by the formal name: 'The International Convention for the Unification of Certain Rules of Law Relating to Bills of Lading of 25 August 1924'.

2.6 CONCLUSION

63. The three main rules of construction are the textual (or objective), the subjective and the teleological rule. The aids to construction which I derived from the cases discussed above are grouped under each main rule of construction.

Textual (or objective)

64. The plain text of the convention should prevail if it is clear. The Rules should be read as a whole. The French text should prevail if another language is unclear. If the objective construction leads to an absurd result a different rule of construction should be applied. Broad principles of general acceptance can be used to test if a result is absurd.

Subjective

65. If possible the Travaux Préparatoires can be used to find out what the framers meant by the words they used if the words are not clear. The common law background should be taken into account when necessary.

Teleological

66. The text of the convention can be construed so as to meet the object of the Rules. The compromise character of the Rules should be borne in mind.

67. These are the rules of and aids to construction which I shall apply in this thesis to discover the expressed intention of the parties to the Hague Rules, that is, their intention as expressed in the words used by them in the light of the surrounding circumstances.

Chapter 3
Duties of the carrier

3.1 Introduction

68. The duties of the carrier are contained in art. III (1 and 2) H(V)R:[90]
1. The carrier shall be bound *before and at the beginning of the voyage* to exercise due diligence to:
(a) Make the ship seaworthy;
(b) Properly man, equip and supply the ship;
(c) Make the holds, refrigerating and cool chambers, and all other parts of the ship in which goods are carried, fit and safe for their reception, carriage and preservation.[91]
2. *Subject to the provisions of Article IV*, the carrier shall *properly and carefully* load, handle, stow, carry, keep, care for, and discharge the goods carried. (emphasis added, NJM)

69. Art. III par. 1 and 2 raise the following questions which will be discussed below:

What is meant by *voyage*? (3.2)
What is meant by *before and at the beginning of the voyage*? (3.3)
Why is the requirement restricted to the period before and at the beginning of the voyage? (3.4)
What is meant by *due diligence*? (3.5)
Is the duty to exercise due diligence to provide a seaworthy ship delegable? (3.6)
What is the meaning of *seaworthy*? (3.7)
What is meant by *properly and carefully*? (3.8)
Is the duty to properly and carefully load, handle, stow, carry, keep, care for, and discharge the goods carried delegable? (3.9)

3.2 What is meant by 'voyage'?

70. A voyage can be subdivided into several stages. During a voyage a ship may call at various intermediate ports for loading and discharging of goods. At common law the carrier is under an absolute obligation to provide a seaworthy ship at the beginning of each stage of the voyage.[92] That this is no longer the case is clear from the wording of Art III(1) H(V)R. Under the Rules the voyage is the contractual voyage and not the stages within it.[93] In consequence, the carrier need only exercise due diligence to make the

---

90. In the Dutch Civil Code the obligations are contained in art 8:381(1 and 2) DCC.
91. The three aspects of seaworthiness are the physical condition of the ship, the quality of the crew and the cargoworthiness of the ship (art. III(1) a, b and c H(V)R).
92. See e.g. Carver 2005, p. 503-504 and Cooke et al. 2007, p. 971.
93. The Makedonia, [1962] 1 Lloyd's Rep. 316, 329-330.

vessel seaworthy at the port where the cargo is loaded.[94] Royer[95], Boonk[96], Cooke et al.[97] and Cleveringa[98] hold the same view. Royer in particular, but implicitly also the other aforementioned authors, believe that a contract of carriage only refers to two ports: the port of loading and the port of discharge. What lies before and after these ports is irrelevant to the contract of carriage. This view was held by Hewson J. in *The Makedonia*:

> 'I see no obligation to read into the word "voyage" a doctrine of stages, but a necessity to define the word itself. (...) "Voyage" in this context means what it has always meant: the contractual voyage from the port of loading to the port of discharge as declared in the appropriate bill of lading. The rule says "voyage" without any qualification such as "any declared stage thereof".'[99]

71. Carver notes that the wording 'before and at the beginning of the voyage' appears to leave no room for the doctrine of stages.[100]

72. The term 'voyage' can be construed as covering the entire voyage covered by the bill of lading, irrespective of calls at intermediate posts. The doctrine of stages does not apply under the Rules.[101] The voyage for a cargo is the contractual voyage as stated on the Bill of Lading for that cargo.
Schoenbaum, however, cites US cases in which it was held that the doctrine of stages can be revived under certain conditions. Schoenbaum writes:

> '..., the doctrine of "seaworthiness by stages" holds that where the ship is *en route* and calls at a port, a substantial and actual intervention by the owner or his agents will revive the duty to exercise due diligence to make the ship seaworthy, so that the ship must be seaworthy at each particular stage of the voyage.'[102]

73. To support this statement Schoenbaum cites cases which were not governed by the Hague Rules. One of them is *The Glymont*. In that case the 2nd Circuit said:

> 'Here is a case where master and crew have surrendered their management and have made appeal to the owner to resume control himself. Response to that appeal destroys the continuity of the voyage, as if it were broken into stages. (...) An owner intervening in such circumstances must be diligent in inspection or forfeit his immunity. Negligence at such a time is not the fault of servants employed to take the owner's place for the period of a voyage. It is the

---

94. Tetley 4th edition, chapter 15, p. 16.
95. Royer 1959, p. 367.
96. Boonk 1993, p. 121-122.
97. Cooke et al. 2007, p. 971. Cooke et al. observe that the period 'before and at the beginning of the voyage' embraces at least the period from the beginning of loading till the moment the ship leaves on her voyage.
98. Cleveringa 1961, p. 467.
99. The Makedonia, [1962] 1 Lloyd's Rep. 316, 329.
100. Carver 2005, p. 567.
101. This also becomes clear from Leesh River Tea Co. v. British India steam Nav. Co. [1966] 2 Lloyd's Rep. 193.
102. Schoenbaum 2004, p. 684: The Glymont, 66 F.2d 617, The Steel Navigator, F.2d 590 and The Isis, 290 U.S. 333, 354.

fault of the owner personally, exercising his own judgement to determine whether the voyage shall go on.'[103]

74. However, as was said above, none of the cases mentioned by Schoenbaum in this respect were governed by the Hague (Visby) Rules or a Carriage of Goods by Sea Act based on those rules. These cases are therefore irrelevant for cases governed by the H(V)R.

3.3 What is meant by 'before and at the beginning of the voyage'?

75. One can wonder which time span is entailed by the expression 'before and at the beginning of the voyage'; how long *before* the voyage begins, does the obligation apply and when has the voyage begun? These questions are discussed below.

3.3.1 Before the voyage

76. In *Maxine Footwear* the Privy Council said:

> 'In their Lordships' opinion "before and at the beginning of the voyage" means the period from at least the beginning of the loading until the vessel starts on her voyage. The word "before" cannot in their opinion be read as meaning "at the commencement of the loading". If this had been intended it would have been said. The question when precisely the period begins does not arise in this case hence the insertion above the words "at least".'[104]

77. According to this decision the period *before the voyage* extends at least to the time of actual commencement of the loading. The question remains when the period begins. Carver notes that the phrase 'Before (...) the voyage' is vague and that there will often be cases where the breach of duty treated as eventually giving rise to the loss or damage, occurred very considerably before loading.[105]
The extent of the period 'before the voyage' will depend on the facts of the situation. In my view common sense says that the period will include the time which an ordinary careful and prudent owner would require to achieve the degree of fitness of the vessel required to encounter the voyage and the suitability of the ship for carrying the cargo contemplated, on the voyage contemplated.[106]

78. E.g. in the Kriti Rex case[107] the ship's engine failed due to contaminated lubricating oil causing failure to deliver cargo. It was apparent from the ship's rough engine room logs that for some months prior to the casualty those on board had been keeping a detailed record of main engine filter flushings. These reports showed that the filters were flushed between 5 and 10 times a day which is more often than acceptable.[108] Flushing was required to clear the filters of debris filtered out of the lubricating oil. As

---

103. The Glymont, 66 F.2d 617.
104. Maxine Footwear, [1959] 2 Lloyd's Rep 105, 113.
105. Carver 2005, p. 567.
106. The degree of fitness required: Carver 2005, p. 501-502.
107. The Kriti Rex, [1996] 2 Lloyd's Rep. 171, 185 (QBD).
108. According to J.K. Langendoen who sailed as an engineer on Dutch vessels in the 1990's and who I interviewed on this point, 2 to 4 times a day would be the acceptable limit for an old engine.

to the question whether the owners exercised due diligence to make the vessel seaworthy Judge Moore-Bick said:

> 'The question whether the owners exercised due diligence to make the vessel seaworthy does not loom large in this case because they accepted that having failed to have regular analyses of the lubricating oil carried out it would be difficult for them to argue successfully that they had done all that they could reasonably have done to ensure that the oil was fit for service. In my judgement they were right to make that concession since regular independent analysis of the lubricating oil is a standard precaution against contamination by water and other foreign matter.
> Regular independent analysis of the lubricating oil is a standard precaution against contamination by water and other foreign matter and would probably have shown that there was excessive particulate matter in the oil. However, I do not think that criticism of the owners can be confined to their failure to have such analyses regularly carried out. The unusually high frequency of filter flushings which had been a continuous feature of this engine's operation prior to the voyage was sufficient to indicate that there was a large amount of sludge in the sump tank which ought to have been cleaned. I accept that the sump tank was not easy to enter because of its size and construction, but I am not satisfied, as I have said, that it was completely inaccessible, much less that it was impossible to remove sludge from it by one means or another. In these circumstances I am satisfied that the owners did fail to exercise due diligence in the respect I have mentioned and that their failure to do so caused or contributed to the casualty.' [109]

79. This case shows that knowledge concerning the condition of the vessel over a series of voyages can lead to the conclusion that the carrier failed to exercise due diligence to make the ship seaworthy before a specific voyage.

80. Royer correctly points out that the ship should be ready to receive the cargo, i.e. the ship should be cargoworthy, at the moment that loading commences. This follows from art. III(1) H(V)R.[110]

81. If there is no contract of carriage the owners will be under no obligation to exercise due diligence. That duty only begins when a contract of carriage comes into existence. The contract of carriage will also determine when the voyage is to commence. In conclusion it can be said that the contract of carriage will determine when the voyage will commence and the duty to exercise due diligence begins when the owner entered into the contract of carriage.

---

109. As opposed to the following consideration by Channell J. in the common law decision McFeddon v. Blue Star Line, [1905] 1 K.B. 697: 'There is, of course, no warranty at the time the goods are put on board that the ship is then ready to start on her voyage; for while she is still loading there may be many things requiring to be done before she is ready to sail. The ordinary warranty of seaworthiness, then, does not take effect before the ship is ready to sail, nor does it continue to take effect after she has sailed: it takes effect at the time of sailing, and at the time of sailing alone.'
110. Royer 1959, p. 370-371.

3.3.2 The beginning of the voyage

82. The moment of departure is the beginning of the voyage. The voyage commences, when the ship breaks ground for the purpose of departure.[111] Thereafter, under the Hague Rules the obligation to use due diligence for seaworthiness ends. The carrier may avoid liability for damage caused by unseaworthiness occurring after the voyage commenced by relying on art. IV(1) or art. IV(2)p H(V)R unless the unseaworthiness was discoverable by the use of due diligence before and at the beginning of the voyage. Carver refers to decisions in which the courts inferred unseaworthiness from a breakdown occurring soon after the ship sailed.[112] The question whether or not the voyage had already started, was the subject under discussion in the American case of *Mississippi Shipping Co. v. Zander & Co. (S.S. Del Sud)*.[113] The court held:

> 'In a very real sense the voyage had begun. The ship had no further purpose at the dock. She was made ready for sea. She was being turned around for the purpose of leaving. The lines to the dock were fast not to keep her there, or to continue her stay at the wharf. They were there solely as an essential step in her navigational manoeuvring. They were no less vital than the hawser to the straining tug off the starboard quarter. The ship's engines were actively manoeuvring to accomplish the swing and officers and men were stationed for simultaneous undocking and departure. The ship was literally and figuratively in the sole command of the master on the bridge (...) What we decide is consistent with the ancient observation of Judge Story that "..., the voyage commences, when the ship breaks ground for the purpose of departure, ..." (...) Once it is determined that the hole in the ship's side occurred after the voyage had begun within the meaning of Cogsa Section 3, the failure of the master to inspect and repair damage at Santos was likewise an error in navigation and management and also excused under Section 4.'

83. Furthermore, the court held that

> 'the use of "before and at" does not make the commencement of the voyage – whenever it is – any less a beginning. When the voyage begins, it is the voyage, and not the beginning of it, which continues. The dual reference is to make doubly sure that with respect to cargo then being loaded the vessel must be seaworthy at the time of the receipt of cargo and must continue in that state until the ship sails. That the duty reaches backward from the commencement does not make it reach forward, as the Act prescribes that the latest point of performance is at the beginning. The voyage must have some place (and time) of beginning. After that, it is not the beginning, but the voyage itself which transpires.'[114]

---

111. The Brutus (1815), 4 Fed.Cas., p. 490, 495. See also Von Ziegler 2002, p. 131.
112. Carver 2005, p. 572. E.g. The Assunzione, [1956] 2 Lloyd's Rep. 468.
113. Mississippi Shipping Co. v. Zander & Co. (S.S. Del Sud), 270 F.2d 345.
114. S.S. Del Sud, 270 F.2d 345, Von Ziegler 2002, p. 132. Tetley finds the judgement in the Del Sud case controversial but notes that it is the prevailing doctrine (Tetley 4th ed., Chapter 15, p. 16).

3.4 WHY REQUIREMENT RESTRICTED TO 'BEFORE AND AT BEGINNING OF THE VOYAGE'?

84. In the light of these principles a majority of the Court therefore concluded that the voyage had commenced at the time the damage to the ship's side was sustained.

85. According to this case the test is not 'can the ship actually manoeuvre freely' (the physical theory) but that the ship is not being controlled from land but entirely from the ship (the command theory). The deciding factor in this last theory is that the ship is totally ready to leave port and commence the voyage.[115]

86. The following consideration of the Amsterdam Court of Appeal is incorrect:

> 'The "beginning of the voyage" is the time of loading. When cargo is loaded in three ports, the beginning of the voyage is the moment the ship leaves the first port.'[116]

Both sentences are not in accordance with the aforementioned English and American doctrine and case law. The court of appeal's consideration may be due to its unfamiliarity with the Hague Rules in 1952.[117]

3.4 Why is the requirement restricted to the period 'before and at the beginning of the voyage'?

87. The *ratio legis* of the limitation of the period in which the carrier is required to exercise due diligence for a seaworthy ship is that the carrier has no more influence on the state of the ship after she sails.[118]
At the ILA 1921 Hague Conference[119], Sir Norman Hill gave the following explanation, whereupon the present text of the opening sentence of Article III was adopted:

> '... , As I understood it, and I think that is as the cargo interests generally understood it, the obligation in regard to seaworthiness is up to the time of starting on the voyage. To begin with, a ship worthy to take that cargo, and when she leaves on the voyage she must still be seaworthy. *If you go further than that, and you say that there is an absolute obligation on the part of the shipowner to keep the ship seaworthy throughout the voyage, then, of course, you render quite valueless most of your exceptions.* For instance, if, through the negligent navigation of the pilot, the ship is run on the rocks and holed, she ceases to be seaworthy. There cannot be an overriding obligation on the shipowner to keep the ship seaworthy throughout the voyage: he is excused, and we will agree, as I understand, that he should be excused, because the damage has been done through the negligence in the navigation. When this was drafted, I think all of the interests clearly agreed that the obligation, and the only obligation, they wanted to put on the shipowner was that the ship shall be seaworthy when she starts loading, that she shall be seaworthy when she starts on her voyage. If he has done that, he

---

115. The Willowpool, 12 F. Supp. 96 (S.D.N.Y. 1935) and 86 F.2d 1002 (2d Cir.). Von Ziegler 2002, p. 131.
116. Amsterdam Court of Appeal 12 November 1952, NJ 1954, 370 (The Deido).
117. The Hague Rules were enacted for the Netherlands on 18 February 1957 (Trb. 1957, no. 24).
118. Von Ziegler 2002, p. 130.
119. A conference of the International Law Association in preparation of the Hague Rules in 1921.

has done his duty, and then the voyage is made under the conditions set out in No. 2, and with the exemptions set out in Article 4.'[120] (emphasis added, NJM)

88. I do not follow Sir Norman Hill's reasoning. If the cause of damage is unseaworthiness which was caused by an excepted peril, then the dominant cause of the damage will be the excepted peril. If an excepted peril can be proven it means the carrier was not negligent, otherwise the peril could not be proven.[121] As the carrier is not liable for damage caused by unseaworthiness which was not a lack of his due diligence (art. IV(1) H(V)R) Sir Norman Hill's remark is not entirely correct.
It should be noted that Sir Norman Hill refers to a ship that *is* seaworthy before loading. This is not completely correct. The Hague Rules replaced the common-law requirement of absolute seaworthiness (seaworthiness as a condition of the ship) with the obligation to exercise *due diligence* to make the ship seaworthy.[122]
I agree with Von Ziegler that a temporal limitation of the period in which due diligence for the seaworthiness has to be exercised is no longer justified.[123] In these days of modern aids to communication and safe/reliable ships with systematic maintenance plans it no longer makes sense to limit the period in which due diligence to make the ship seaworthy ought to be exercised to a period before and at the beginning of the voyage. In that sense the new UNCITRAL draft instrument is an improvement, because article 15 of this draft provides that the carrier is obliged to exercise due diligence before, at the beginning of and during the voyage to make and keep the ship seaworthy.[124] This means that under the future UNCITRAL convention the carrier will no longer be able to escape liability for cargo damage caused by unseaworthiness which was not a result of lack of due diligence before and at the beginning of the voyage.

3.5 What is meant by 'due diligence'?

3.5.1 Common law: absolute warranty of seaworthiness[125]

89. At common law the duty of the carrier to provide a seaworthy ship is an absolute duty of the carrier.[126] That means that even if the cause of unseaworthiness was not discoverable by due diligence the carrier will still be liable. The duty is also referred to as an absolute warranty. At common law the carrier also, however, has complete freedom of contract. He can escape liability by negotiating his own terms. Even the implied duty to furnish a seaworthy ship can be reduced or excluded.[127] Abuse of the carriers' stronger bargaining position resulted in the curtailment of this freedom by the Hague Rules. The forerunner of the Hague Rules is the (U.S.) Harter Act.[128] The object of the Hague Rules and the Harter Act was to protect cargo interests from widespread ex-

---

120. Travaux Préparatoires, p. 145-146.
121. See chapter 6.
122. See § 3.5.
123. Von Ziegler 2002, p. 133 and 140.
124. Document WP.101 of UNCITRAL Working Group III. See <www.uncitral.org>. G.J. van der Ziel discusses this issue in TVR 2004, p. 44.
125. See also Rhidian Thomas 2006.
126. The Muncaster Castle, [1961] 1 Lloyd's Rep. 57. Also Schoenbaum 2004, p. 607 and Gaskell 2000, p. 272.
127. Cargo ex The Laertes (1877) 12 P.D.; Varnish & Co. Ltd v. Kheti (Owners) 82 Ll.L.L.Rep. 525. See also Carver 2005, p. 505.
128. 46 U.S.C. 191 et cetera. See Carver 2005, p. 525 for the historical development of the Harter Act.

clusion of liability by carriers. Art. III (8) of the Hague Rules ensures that the carrier is bound by the Hague Rules.[129] On the other hand the Hague Rules and the Harter Act reduced the absolute warranty of seaworthiness to a duty to exercise due diligence to provide a seaworthy ship. The intent of the U.S. Congress was to relieve the shipowner from liability without fault.[130]

90. Under a contract of marine insurance this means that seaworthiness is a condition precedent and if not complied with the insurance never attaches.[131] In carriage of goods by sea however, unseaworthiness does not affect the carrier's liability unless it causes the loss.[132] In *McFadden v. Blue Star Line* Channell J. said the following regarding the absolute warranty of seaworthiness:

> 'Now I think it is clear that, apart from the Harter Act, that warranty is an absolute warranty; that is to say, if the ship is in fact unfit at the time when the warranty begins, it does not matter that its unfitness is due to some latent defect which the shipowner does not know of, and it is no excuse for the existence of such a defect that he used his best endeavours to make the ship as good as it could be made. And there is also another matter which seems to me to be equally clear -- that the warranty of seaworthiness in the ordinary sense of that term, the warranty, that is, that the ship is fit to encounter the ordinary perils of the voyage, is a warranty only as to the condition of the vessel at a particular time, namely, the time of sailing; it is not a continuing warranty, in the sense of a warranty that she shall continue fit during the voyage.'[133]

91. This consideration makes clear that though the standard of the duty is absolute, there is no requirement that the ship be perfect. The duty is to use a ship that is fit to encounter the ordinary perils of the voyage.
The absolute warranty of seaworthiness can result in a type of liability without fault in cases concerning damage caused by concurrent causes of which one is unseaworthiness. In *Smith, Hogg & Co. v Black Sea & Baltic General Insurance Company, Ltd.* Lord Wright said:

> '..., the contract may be expressed to be that the ship owner will be liable for any loss in which those other causes covered by exceptions co-operate, if unseaworthiness is a cause, or if it is preferred, a real, or effective, or actual cause.'[134]

92. The standard set by the law is measured by reference to the standards that an ordinary careful owner would demand in respect of his own ship. If a ship goes to sea with

---

129. He can, however, take on a more extensive liability than the minimum prescribed by the Hague Rules.
130. The Irrawaddy, 171 U.S. 187, 192-193 and The Southwark, 191 U.S. 1, 24. See also Schoenbaum 2004, p. 681.
131. The Europa, [1908] P.84, Smith, Hogg & Co., Ltd. v. Black Sea & Baltic Insurance Company, Ltd., [1940] 67 Ll.L.L.Rep. 253, 258. Under the Harter Act seaworthiness is a condition of exemption even if the unseaworthiness did not cause the loss (The Isis, 290 U.S. 333).
132. The Europa, [1908] P.84, Smith, Hogg & Co., Ltd. v. Black Sea & Baltic Insurance Company, Ltd., [1940] 67 Ll.L.L.Rep. 253, 258. Under the Harter Act seaworthiness is a condition of exemption even if the unseaworthiness did not cause the loss (The Isis, 290 U.S. 333).
133. McFadden v. Blue Star Line, [1905] 1 K.B. 697.
134. Smith, Hogg & Co. v. Black Sea & Baltic General Insurance, 67 Ll.L.L.Rep. 253, 258.

a defect which such an owner would not have tolerated, the ship is unseaworthy.[135] At common law the obligation to provide a seaworthy ship is strict. If a ship is unseaworthy the owner is liable, with no defences or excuses entertained.[136]

3.5.2 Hague (Visby) Rules: Due diligence

93. What is meant by the words 'due diligence' in art. III(1) H(V)R? To answer that question Carver refers to *The Amstelslot*[137], where the court held that lack of due diligence is *negligence*.[138] Lord Reid said:

> 'But where, as here, the defendant meets the *prima facie* case against him by calling two surveyors of unchallenged reputation who are found by the Judge to be impressive and who say what they did and why they did it and why they did not do more, then, unless they can be successfully criticized for their omissions, a Judge is entitled to say that due diligence was exercised (…) It is important to get clear the point to which criticism must be directed. There is here no lack of care and no lack of skilled knowledge. The surveyors were quite familiar with the three methods of examination which it is said that they should have adopted; and they could easily have followed them if they had chosen to do so. What is said against them is that by deciding in effect that these methods were not appropriate to the sort of examination they were conducting, they made an error of judgement which a competent surveyor ought not to have made. Lack of due diligence is negligence; and what is in issue in this case is whether there was an error of judgement that amounted to professional negligence.'

94. In the same case the court held that the mere fact that with hindsight it is possible to see that extra precautions should have been taken does not mean that due diligence was not exercised. Lord Reid said:

> 'It is not enough to say that if those steps had been taken there would have been a better chance of discovering the crack. In a great many accidents it is clear after the event that if the defendant had taken certain extra precautions the accident would or might have been avoided. The question always is whether a reasonable man in the shoes of the defendant, with the skill and knowledge which the defendant had or ought to have had, would have taken those extra precautions.'[139]

95. Regarding the words 'due diligence' in general L.J. Auld said in *The Kapitan Sakharov*:

> 'USC was required under art. III, r. 1, of the Hague Rules to exercise due diligence to make the vessel seaworthy. The Judge correctly took as the test whether it had shown that it, its servants, agents or independent contractors, had exercised all reasonable skill and care to ensure that the vessel was seaworthy at

---

135. Bradley & Sons v. Federal Steam Navigation Co. 24 Ll.L.L.Rep. 446.
136. Rhidian Thomas 2006, p. 87.
137. The Amstelslot, [1963] 2 Lloyd's Rep. 223, 235.
138. [1963] 2 Lloyd's Rep. 223 and Carver 2005, p. 568.
139. [1963] 2 Lloyd's Rep. 223, 230.

the commencement of its voyage, namely, reasonably fit to encounter the ordinary incidents of the voyage. He also correctly stated the test to be objective, namely to be measured by the standards of a reasonable ship-owner, taking into account international standards and the particular circumstances of the problem in hand.'[140]

96. Carver mentions cases in which examples of *due diligence* are to be found regarding the care that should be employed in fumigation,[141] maintaining steering gear,[142] electrical equipment[143] and engines,[144] selecting crew[145] and providing documentation.[146, 147] The presence of dangerous cargo does not necessarily mean that due diligence was not exercised.[148] In *The Kapitan Sakharov* containers of dangerous cargo were stowed below deck and exploded. The dangerous cargo had not been declared by the shipper.
Although the stowage of the containers of dangerous cargo below deck contravened SOLAS[149], IMDG[150] and MOPOG[151] the Court of Appeal held that compliance with the aforementioned instruments was not necessarily determinative of the issue of due diligence. Although the court found the ship was unseaworthy because of the dangerous and undeclared cargo below deck the court held that the carrier's duty of due diligence as to the structure and stowage of its ship did not extend to verification of the declared contents of containers or other packaging in which cargo is shipped unless put on notice to do so. The containers of dangerous cargo were closed with a custom's seal and were not capable of internal examination by the carrier. The court held that the carrier had exercised due diligence with respect to the non detection of the dangerous cargo because he could not with the exercise of reasonable skill and care have detected the presence of the dangerous cargo.[152]
Referring to Canadian, English and American authority, Tetley defines *due diligence* as a serious, competent and reasonable effort on the part of the carrier to fulfil the obligations referred to under Art III(1) H(V)R.[153] It is the effort which a carrier acting with reasonable care would exercise. Tetley has derived the following test from English authority:

---

140. The Kapitan Sakharov, [2000] 2 Lloyd's Rep. 255.
141. The Good Friend, [1984] 2 Lloyd's Rep. 586.
142. The Theodegmon, [1990] 1 lloyd's Rep. 52.
143. The Subro Valour, [1995] 1 Lloyd's Rep. 509.
144. The Antigoni, [1991] 1 Lloyd's Rep. 209 and The Yamatogawa [1990] 2 Lloyd's Rep. 39.
145. The Makedonia [1962] 1 Lloyd's Rep. 316.
146. Ibid.
147. Carver 2005, p. 569.
148. [2000] 2 Lloyd's Rep. 255 and Carver 2005, p. 569.
149. International convention for the Safety of Life at Sea.
150. International Maritime Dangerous Goods code.
151. The Russian Federation's version of the IMDG code.
152. [2000] 2 Lloyd's Rep. 255.
153. Tetley 4th edition, chapter 15, p. 4-5 refers to: F.C. Bradley & Sons v. Federal Steam Navigation Co. (1926) 24 Ll.L. L.Rep. 446 at p. 454 (C.A. per Scrutton L.J.): 'The ship must have that degree of fitness which an ordinary owner would require his vessel to have at the commencement of the voyage having regard to all the probable circumstances of it', cited with approval in The Fjord Wind [2000] 2 Lloyd's Rep. 191 at p. 197 (C.A. per Clarke L.J.); The Lendoudis Evangelos [2001] 2 Lloyd's Rep. 304 at p. 306 (per Cresswell, J.), and The Eurasian Dream [2002] 1 Lloyd's Rep. 719 at p. 736 (per Cresswell, J.) (enumerating the following aspects of seaworthiness: physical condition of the vessel and equipment; competence/efficiency of the master and crew; adequacy of stores and documentation; and cargoworthiness).

'all reasonable skill and care to ensure that the vessel was seaworthy at the commencement of its voyage, namely, reasonably fit to encounter the ordinary incidents of the voyage...'[154]

97. It has been said that in reality the undertaking to use due diligence to make the ship seaworthy is not really less onerous than the old common law undertaking that the ship is in fact seaworthy. This is because the relief to the carrier will occur only in cases where the unseaworthiness is due to some cause which the due diligence of the carrier personally and all his servants and agents could not discover (latent defects not discoverable by due diligence).[155] The English cases *The Muncaster Castle*[156] and *The Happy Ranger*[157] show that a carrier will not be able to escape from liability if the unseaworthiness was due to an error of the carrier's servants, agents or independent contractors. This will even be the case if the servants, agents and or contractors used by the carrier are well-known, experienced and respected so that one should be allowed to trust that the work delegated to such entities would be sound. In *The Happy Ranger* the carrier was found liable for a faulty rams horn hook of a crane on a brand new ship which had only recently come into the carrier's 'orbit'.[158] The carrier was liable because, although the hook had been certified, it had never been proof loaded. In *Muncaster Castle* the carrier was found liable for cargo damage caused by the carelessness of a fitter employed by skilled repairers working for the carriers.[159]

98. Rhidian Thomas remarks that 'the ordinary careful owner test' used by judges does not correspond with the shipping industry's idea of the ordinary careful owner. 'To the mind's eye or the judiciary the ordinary careful owner is a paragon of watchfulness, attentiveness and responsiveness, who keeps abreast of all technical developments, tolerates little that is less than perfect, takes only the best advice, plans ahead with meticulous care, works in harmony with classification societies, employs skilled and experienced superintendents, crew, agents and independent contactors, and uses equally skilled and competent inspectors to supervise everything done on his behalf. Such an owner is no ordinary or reasonable animal in the commercial sense.'[160] Rhidian Thomas correctly remarks that the legal concept and reality are far apart. The standards of the law are therefore very high, demanding and uncompromising. Only in very exceptional circumstances will a defect be overlooked by the law and liability avoided. The one concession relates to want of due diligence by the builder of a ship or a preceding owner from whom the new owner acquires possession, and in respect of which the new owner does not assume responsibility.[161] 'This arises from the language of the Hague Rules which obliges the carrier to use due diligence to make the ship seaworthy. This the carrier can only do if the ship is within his possession and control.

---

154. The Kapitan Sakharov [2000] 2 Lloyd's Rep 255 at p. 266 (C.A.). The Eurasian Dream [2002] 1 Lloyd's Rep 719 at p. 737 and 744: 'The exercise of due diligence is equivalent to the exercise of reasonable care and skill. Lack of due diligence is negligence....'
155. Smith Hogg & Co. Ltd. v. Black Sea & Baltic General Insurance Company Ltd., [1939] 64 Ll.L.L.Rep. 87, 89. See also Seaworthiness-the illusion of the Hague compromise, JIML 12 [2006] 287.
156. The Muncaster Castle, [1961] 1 Lloyd's Rep. 57.
157. The Happy Ranger, [2006] 1 Lloyd's Rep. 649.
158. In The Muncaster Castle, the term 'orbit' is used co-extensively with ownership or service or control.
159. See infra § 3.6.
160. Rhidian Thomas 2006, p. 87.
161. Angliss & Co. (Australia) Pty Ltd v. Peninsular and Oriental Navigation Co., 28 Ll.L.L.Rep. 202.

But even this exception is subject to the neutralising qualification that once the new owner acquires possession he will be liable for failure to detect defects making the ship unseaworthy which he ought to have discovered by the exercise of due diligence.[162]

3.5.3 Dutch cases

99. In *The Deidi* the Amsterdam Court of Appeal held with respect to the concept of due diligence:
'Inspections during the voyage and before loading do not have to be exhaustive, but if no attention was paid to a pipe and socket connection, which could easily have been inspected by tapping it with a hammer, the inspection was inadequate.'[163]
In *The Straat Soenda* the court of appeal held:
'Due diligence' does not include regular and thorough checking of the hundreds of metres of piping.'[164]
In *The Imke* the Amsterdam District Court held:
'In general, the carrier is not responsible for faults in the ship, which were made before he took over the ship, unless he could have reasonably discovered these faults by careful and skilful inspection [after he took the vessel over, NJM]. It would be unreasonable to demand that "due diligence" means that the ship should be inspected for construction errors which are not visible from the outside, especially since Lloyd's has issued a certificate of seaworthiness for the ship'.[165]

In the *NDS Provider* the Supreme Court of the Netherlands held that the duty to exercise due diligence to make the ship seaworthy extends to containers provided by the carrier to the shipper.[166] The Supreme Court of the Netherlands drew an analogy between the holds of the ship and containers and held that the duty contained in art. III(1) H(V)R applied to the containers.
In my opinion it goes too far to extend the scope of art. III(1) to containers. Containers are not a part of the ship and a carrier will have no control over the container when it is ashore to be transported and stuffed. In that period anything could happen to the container outside the carrier's knowledge. The duty imposed on the carrier by the Supreme Court of the Netherlands would mean that the carrier would have to inspect every container coming aboard. Seeing the quantity of containers loaded on modern container ships and the speed of loading this is unrealistic.

3.5.4 Conclusion

100. In my opinion the examples and citations discussed above make clear that a single definition of the expression *due diligence* is not easy to formulate. When assessing if the standards of due diligence were met, the courts will have to rely on common sense, ex-

---

162. Rhidian Thomas 2006, p. 88.
163. Amsterdam Court of Appeal 27 January 1954, S&S 1957, 70 (Deidi).
164. Amsterdam Court of Appeal 5 February 1964, S&S 1964, 44 (Straat Soenda).
165. Amsterdam District Court 2 February 1966, S&S 1966, 37 (Imke).
166. SCN 1 February 2008, C06/082HR. This judgement was rendered after completion of this manuscript but before it was printed, allowing me to briefly discuss it. In a future publication I shall discuss the judgement in depth.

pert information and on domestic and foreign case law.[167] Rhidian Thomas correctly sums it up as follows:

> '[t]he duty to make a ship seaworthy is an exceptionally demanding legal obligation. Rarely will the owner of a defective or deficient vessel avoid liability. The adoption of the Hague Rules of a limited and qualified position, requiring the exercise of due diligence to make the ship seaworthy is not as significant as might first appear. It is more apparent than real, for little has changed from the absolute undertaking of seaworthiness under the common law. The only difference is that under the Hague Rules the carrier is protected from liability in respect to latent defects (*The Amstelslot* [1963] 2 Lloyd's Rep. 223). Even when the fault is outside the orbit of the carrier's assumed or vicarious liability, the consequential protection will often be neutralised by the carrier's direct personal duty to exercise due diligence on the transfer of acquisition of the ship.[168]

However, the Dutch decision *Straat Sunda* of the Amsterdam Court of Appeal seems to be less strict than the English courts.'[169]

3.6 Is the duty to exercise due diligence to make the ship seaworthy delegable?

101. Under English[170] and US[171] law the obligation to exercise due diligence to provide a seaworthy ship is a non-delegable duty. This means that shipowners are responsible for unseaworthiness resulting from lack of diligence by a servant of independent ship repairers, even though they were of high repute and properly appointed by the ship owners.[172] The *leading case* is *The Muncaster Castle*[173], in which the House of Lords found that the words 'due diligence to make the ship seaworthy' had been taken from the Harter Act[174] and similar British Commonwealth statutes. In the interest of uniformity these words should therefore be given the meaning attributed to them prior to the Hague Rules: A carrier was responsible to the cargo-interests unless due diligence in the work had been shown by every person to whom any part of the necessary work had been entrusted, no matter whether he was the carrier's servant, agent, or independent contractor. Therefore in *The Muncaster Castle* the carrier was held liable for the negligent repair work carried out by an independent contractor.

102. In the same case Lord Keith of Avonholm said:

---

167. See also Royer 1959, p. 561.
168. Rhidian Thomas 2006, p. 87.
169. See supra.
170. The Muncaster Castle, [1961] 1 Lloyd's Rep. 57.
171. See e.g. The Colima, 82 Fed. 665 (A decision governed by the Harter Act). See Schoenbaum 2004, p. 684 and the authority cited there: International Navigation Co. v. Farr & Bailey Manufacturing Co., 181 U.S. 218, Cerro Sales Corp. v. Atlantic Marine Enterprises, Inc. 403 F.Supp. 562, The Point Brava, 1 F.Supp. 366, Matter of Complaint of Tecomar S.A., 765 F.Supp. 1150.
172. The Muncaster Castle, [1961] 1 Lloyd's Rep 57.
173. Ibid.
174. 46 USC App. § 190-196.

> 'The Hague Rules abolished the absolute warranty of seaworthiness. They substituted a lower measure of obligation. The old law no doubt worked hardly on shipowners and charterers, in the absence of exception or exclusion. The change in the law, not confined entirely to England, operated to afford relief to shipowners, as well as some protection to shippers. It would, however, be a most sweeping change if it had the result of providing carriers with a simple escape from their new obligation to exercise due diligence to make a ship seaworthy. If this were the plain effect of the statute, *cadit quaestio*. But *in dubio* the Courts should, in a change of the suggested dimensions, lean the other way. The language of the Hague Rules does not, I think, lead to the result contended for by the respondents. The carrier will have some relief which, weighed in the scales, is not inconsiderable when contrasted with his previous common-law position. He will be protected against latent defects, in the strict sense, in work done on his ship, that is to say, defects not due to any negligent workmanship of repairers or others employed by the repairers and, as I see it, against defects making for unseaworthiness in the ship, however caused, before it became his ship, if these could not be discovered by him, or competent experts employed by him, by the exercise of due diligence.'[175]

103. In *The Muncaster Castle* reference was made to *Smith Hogg & Co. Ltd. v. Black Sea & Baltic General Insurance Company Ltd.*,[176] in which the court held:

> 'In appearance the undertaking to use due diligence to make the ship seaworthy is less onerous than the old common law undertaking that the ship is in fact seaworthy. In reality there is no great gain to the shipowner by the substitution. For (...) the relief to the shipowner will occur only in cases where the unseaworthiness is due to some cause which the due diligence of *all his servants and agents* could not discover in the case of latent defects not discoverable by due diligence.'(emphasis added, NJM)

104. Lord Radcliffe said:

> 'It seems to me to be plain on the face of this contract that what was intended was that the owner should, if not with his own eyes, at any rate by the eyes of proper competent agents, ensure that the ship was in a seaworthy condition before she left the port, *and that it is not enough to say that he appointed a proper and competent agent*. It is obvious that the shipowner cannot himself with his own hands make the ship seaworthy; he must act through other persons; *but I do not read the contract as exempting him from liability in the case of the negligence of the agents whom he employs to act for him in this respect...*'[177] (emphasis added, NJM)

105. The *Muncaster Castle* case was brought to the attention of the CMI Sub-Committee on Bills of Lading and discussed during the CMI 1963 Stockholm Conference. The Sub-Committee expressed the opinion that 'the interpretation of the Hague Rules by the courts in the United Kingdom and the United States places a very much heavier bur-

---

175. The Muncaster Castle, [1961] 1 Lloyd's Rep 57.
176. Smith Hogg & Co. Ltd. v. Black Sea & Baltic General Insurance Company Ltd., 64 Ll.L.Rep 87.
177. The Muncaster Castle, [1961] 1 Lloyd's Rep 57.

den on the carrier than is the case in other countries.'[178] According to the Sub-Committee the difference in construction is a result of the difference in wording used in the English and French version of the Hague Rules.[179] In the English version the words 'due diligence' are used whereas the French version uses the expression 'execer une diligence raisonnable' which should have been translated as 'reasonable diligence'. The Sub-Committee reached the conclusion that efforts made to create a uniform rule of construction on this point would come up against a fundamental difference of opinion between notions on the construction of the French version and the attitude of Anglo-Saxon law. Because a solution acceptable to all parties would not be possible the Sub-Committee recommended a status quo, but also recommended an investigation of the actual position in the various countries on this particular point.[180]

106. Some of the reactions to the decision of the Sub-Committee are the following; Britain proposed an amendment of art. III(1) which would lead to protection of the owner who used independent contractors of repute as regards competence. Denmark and Sweden welcomed efforts to try to find a solution to the difficulties caused by the *Muncaster Castle* decision. Also Loeff, the delegate for the Netherlands, was willing to support the amendment proposed by Britain.[181] The U.S.A. however sought international uniformity on this point, preferably on the basis of amendment of the Hague Rules to assure that the jurisprudence of all countries would be brought into accord with the jurisprudence of the U.S. and England.[182]

107. After voting, the Sub-Committee adopted the amendment proposed by Britain at the Stockholm Conference.[183] As is well-known, the proposed amendment was eventually rejected so that the *Muncaster Castle* problem still exists.

108. Monsieur Prodromidés of France however was of the opinion that the *Muncaster Castle* decision had not created a problem. A report on the subject by Monsieur le Doyen van Ryn indeed concluded that the *Muncaster Castle* decision is in line with the law of Sweden, The Netherlands, Italy, France, U.S.A., Denmark, Canada and Belgium.[184] Monsieur Prodromidés asks the question why the members of the CMI Stockholm Conference of 1963 want to try to amend or modify the Convention 'in order to avert the disparities in the various countries, when the quasi unanimity which we desire already exists in most countries.'[185]

109. Today *The Muncaster Castle* view still appears to be generally acceptable in most jurisdictions.[186] A practical reason in support of the *Muncaster Castle* solution was given by Lord Radcliffe in *The Muncaster Castle*:

---

178. Travaux Préparatoires, p. 154.
179. This should not really be a problem as French is the authentic language of the convention.
180. Ibid.
181. Travaux Préparatoires, p. 172.
182. Travaux Préparatoires, p. 150.
183. Travaux Préparatoires, p. 181.
184. See Travaux Préparatoires on p. 150-153. This report was written at the request of the Sub-Committee to investigate the the actual position in the various countries in respect of 'due diligence'.
185. Travaux Préparatoires. p. 174.
186. Tetley 1988, p. 393, Wilson 1993, p. 188, Von Ziegler 2002, p. 119, Boonk 1993, p. 123.

'I should regard it as unsatisfactory, where a cargo owner has found his goods damaged through a defect in the seaworthiness of the vessel that his rights of recovering from the carrier should depend upon particular circumstances in the carrier's situation and arrangements with which the cargo owner has nothing to do; as, for instance, that liability should depend on the measure of control that the carrier had exercised over persons engaged on surveying or repairing the ship, or on such questions as whether the carrier had or could have done whatever was needed by the hands of his own servants or had been sensible or prudent in getting done by other hands. Carriers would find themselves liable or not liable according to circumstances quite extraneous to the sea carriage itself.'[187]

110. Under Dutch law it is unclear for which group of persons the carrier is liable.[188] I disagree with the view taken by some Dutch authors that the problems should be solved by means of the Dutch law of obligations[189], for such a solution is contrary to the need for uniform construction of the convention. I agree with Lord Radcliffe's view quoted above. The carrier is directly liable for cargo damage caused by unseaworthiness as a result of his agents failure to exercise due diligence. If agents of the carrier were responsible for the unseaworthiness then that is no defence against the cargo claim. The carrier, not the cargo interests, is the one who should retrieve the damages from the agent responsible for the unseaworthiness.

111. The framers of the new UNCITRAL instrument have decided not to tackle the problem (if any) in the new instrument. The consensus seems to be that it is not possible to create uniformity on all fronts within the Rules.[190]

3.7 What is the meaning of seaworthiness?

112. The requirements stated in art. III(1)(a), (b) and (c) are features of the warranty of seaworthiness as developed at common law. Existing authority on the common law duty can usually be employed, bearing in mind that common law cases are likely to be based on the absolute or strict obligation of seaworthiness, whereas under Rules the obligation is one of due diligence.[191]

113. The general term 'seaworthiness' entails the fitness of the ship to encounter the voyage and the suitability of the ship for carrying the cargo contemplated, on the voyage contemplated.[192] There is no requirement that the ship be perfect. The duty is to furnish a ship that is fit to encounter the ordinary perils of the voyage. In *Mcfadden v. Blue Star Line* Channell J., citing Carver, said:

---

187. The Muncaster Castle, [1963] 2 Lloyd's Rep. 57, 82. See also Wilson 1993, p. 188-189.
188. Boonk 1993, p. 123-124.
189. Ibid. at p. 125.
190. The author discussed this matter with prof. Van der Ziel who is involved in the framing of the UNCITRAL instrument.
191. Carver 2005, p. 570-571.
192. Carver 2005, p. 501-502.

> 'A vessel must have that degree of fitness which an ordinary careful and prudent owner would require his vessel to have at the commencement of her voyage having regard to all the probable circumstances of it. To that extent the ship-owner, as we have seen, undertakes absolutely that she is fit, and ignorance is no excuse. If the defect existed, the question to be put is, would a prudent owner have required that it should be made good before sending his ship to sea had he known of it? If he would, the ship was not seaworthy within the meaning of the undertaking.'[193]

114. Under art. III(1) a ship can be unseaworthy if it is unfit for the particular voyage anticipated. This can occur when it is improperly crewed, equipped and supplied and where the ship is safe as a navigating entity, but uncargoworthy because it is unfit for the particular cargo to be carried. Von Ziegler derives the following definition from American cases:

> 'Seaworthiness is a *relative term* which looks to such matters as the type of vessel, character of the voyage, reasonably expectable weather, and navigational conditions. [...] The vessel must be *reasonably fit to carry the cargo she has undertaken to transport.*'[194] (emphasis in the original)

115. Von Ziegler also quotes the following English test:

> 'The test in a case of this kind, of course, is not absolute; you do not test it by absolute perfection or by any absolute guarantee of successful carriage. It has to be looked at realistically, and the most common test is: Would a prudent shipowner, if he had known of the defect, have sent the ship to sea in that condition?'[195]

116. Tetley derives the following definition from numerous decisions:

> 'Seaworthiness may be defined as the state of a vessel in such a condition, with such equipment, and manned by such a master and crew, that normally the cargo will be loaded, carried, cared for and discharged properly and safely on the contemplated voyage. Seaworthiness therefore has two aspects: 1) the ship, crew and equipment must be sound and capable of withstanding the ordinary perils of the voyage and 2) the ship must be fit to carry the contract cargo.'

117. In the Australian case *Bunga Seroja* a number of points of view derived from mainly English and US authority were expressed on the issue of seaworthiness.[196]

> '1. [S]eaworthiness is to be assessed according to the voyage under consideration; there is no single standard of fitness which a vessel must meet. Thus, sea-

---

193. McFadden v. Blue Star Line, [1905] 1 K.B. 697, 703 and Carver 2005, p. 500.
194. Von Ziegler 2002, p. 89. Von Ziegler refers to PPG Industries, Inc., v. Ashland Oil Co. – Thomas Petroleum, 592 F.2d 138, 146 (3rd Cir.). In that judgement reference was made to The Isis, 290 U.S. 333, 352.
195. M.D.C., Ltd. v. N.V. Zeevaart Maatschappij (Beursstraat), [1962] 1 Lloyd's Rep. 180, 186 and Von Ziegler 2002, p. 88-89.
196. The Bunga Seroja, [1999] 1 Lloyd's Rep. 512.

worthiness is judged having regard to the conditions the vessel will encounter. The vessel may be seaworthy for a coastal voyage in a season of light weather but not for a voyage in the North Atlantic in mid-winter.[197]

2. Thus, definitions of seaworthiness found in the cases (albeit cases arising in different contexts) all emphasize that the state of fitness required "must depend on the whole nature of the adventure". The vessel must be "fit to encounter the ordinary perils of the voyage"; it must be "in a fit state as to repairs, equipment, and crew, and in all other respects, to encounter the ordinary perils of the voyage insured".[198]

3. Further, if the question of seaworthiness is to be judged at the time that the vessel sails, it will be important to consider how it is loaded and stowed. If the vessel is over laden it may be unseaworthy. If it is loaded or stowed badly so, for example, as to make it unduly stiff or tender it may be unseaworthy.[199]

4. The standard of fitness [is not] unchanging. The standard can and does rise with improved knowledge of shipbuilding and navigation.[200]

5. Fitness for the voyage may also encompass other considerations as, for example, the fitness of the vessel to carry the particular kind of goods or the fitness of crew, equipment and the like. The question of seaworthiness, then, may require consideration of many and varied matters.'[201]

118. Judges Gaudron, Gummow and Hayne went on to consider:

> 'What is important for present purposes is not the detailed content of the obligation to make the ship seaworthy, it is that making the ship seaworthy (or, as the Hague Rules provide, exercising due diligence to do so) requires consideration of the kinds of conditions that the vessel may encounter. If the vessel is fit to meet those conditions, both in the sense that it will arrive safely at its destination and in the sense that it will carry its cargo safely to that destination, it is seaworthy.'[202]

119. Gaudron, Gummow and Hayne summarised:

> 'Thus, the performance of the carrier's responsibilities under art. III, rr. 1 and 2 will vary according to the voyage and the conditions that may be expected.'[203]

> 'In art. III, r. 1, the term "seaworthiness" should be given its common law meaning. Nothing in the rules generally or in the Travaux Préparatoires suggests otherwise. It was a term well-known at common law and, for the reasons I have given, it is probable that that was the meaning that the drafters of the rules intended it to have. What constitutes "seaworthiness" depends on the voyage to be undertaken. The ship must be seaworthy to undertake the voyage

---

197. Ibid. at point 27 per Gaudron, Gummow and Hayne JJ.
198. Ibid. at point 28.
199. Ibid. at point 29.
200. Ibid. at point 30.
201. Ibid. at point 31.
202. Ibid. at point 33.
203. Ibid. at point 35.

planned and to face any expected weather or storms. If, as was the case here, the ship is expected to sail through an area of sea which is renowned for its severe weather, appropriate precautions must be taken to ensure that the ship is fit to undertake that voyage both in respect of the ship itself and the stowage of the cargo. The carrier must exercise due diligence at the start of the voyage to make the ship seaworthy in the light of the anticipated weather conditions.'[204]

120. According to Tetley, a vessel is seaworthy if it is fit to load, discharge and carry the cargo during the intended voyage.[205] Schoenbaum derives the following rule from American case law:

'whether the vessel is reasonably fit to carry the cargo which she has undertaken to transport', and adds to this that such a general rule should be tested on a case by case basis.[206]

121. The open standards and tests of reasonableness make the question whether a ship is sufficiently seaworthy extremely casuistic. However, the Hague Rules furnish a useful test for seaworthiness which makes allowances for various climates and geographical data, and also the technical possibilities. No legal uncertainty has developed despite the flexible standards because carriers and cargo interests are familiar with the particulars of the intended voyage.

3.8 What is meant by 'properly and carefully'?

122. Art III(2) H(V)R provides that the carrier shall *properly and carefully* load, handle, stow, carry, keep, care for, and discharge the goods carried. At the ILA 1921 Hague Conference Sir Norman Hill made the following remark with respect to due care for the cargo:

'And, Sir, you notice that in No. 2 we were very careful in drafting this. No. 1 is "to exercise due diligence"- that is taken from all the existing laws on this subject of all nations. Then in 2 it is positive. It is not a question of the carrier exercising due diligence under 2 it is "The carrier shall be bound to provide for the proper and careful handling, loading, stowage, carriage, custody, care, and unloading of the goods carried". *That is an absolute obligation on the carrier during the voyage, and it is only qualified by the exceptions in Article 4.*'[207] (emphasis added, NJM)

123. Sir Norman Hill's remarks show that from the wording of paragraph art. III(2) with respect to the care for the cargo it follows that the carrier, as a matter of course, guarantees the proper and careful handling of the goods.[208]

124. I agree with the opinion expressed in the Bunga Seroja where Gaudron, Gummow and Hayne said:

---
204. Ibid. per Judge McHugh at point 86.
205. Tetley 4th ed., Chapter 15, p. 4.
206. The Sylvia, 171 U.S. 462, 464 and Schoenbaum 2001, p. 602.
207. CMI Travaux Préparatoires, p. 185.
208. Royer 1959, p. 412.

'Whether the goods are properly and carefully stowed must also depend upon the kinds of conditions which it is anticipated that the vessel will meet. The proper stowage of cargo on a lighter ferrying cargo ashore in a sheltered port will, no doubt, be different from the proper stowage of cargo on a vessel traversing the Great Australian Bight in winter. Thus, the performance of the carrier's responsibilities under art. III rr. 1 and 2 will vary according to the voyage and the conditions that may be expected.'[209]

125. In *The Bunga Seroja* Judge McHugh expressed the following view:

'Notwithstanding the opening words of art. III, r. 2, the terms of art. IV, r. 2 do not in my opinion affect the content of the obligations imposed by art. III, r. 2. The carrier remains under an obligation to "properly and carefully load, handle, stow, carry, keep, care for and discharge the goods carried." But the carrier is not liable if the "loss or damage" to the goods arises or results from one of the matters identified in pars. (a)-(q) of art. IV, r. 2. Where the owner alleges a breach of art. III, r. 2 and the carrier relies on one of the identified matters in pars. (a)-(q) as a defence, the liability of the carrier will turn on whether the loss or damage arose or resulted from the breach or from the identified matters. In that respect, art. III, r. 2 and art. IV, r. 2 effectively track the common law doctrine applicable to bills of lading. The common law position was stated by Mr. Justice Willes in *Grill v. General Iron Screw Collier Co.*:
"In the case of a bill of lading it is different, because there the contract is to carry with reasonable care unless prevented by the excepted perils. If the goods are not carried with reasonable care, and are consequently lost by perils of the sea, it becomes necessary to reconcile the two parts of the instrument, and this is done by holding that if the loss through perils of the sea is caused by the previous default of the shipowner he is liable for this breach of his covenant."'[210]

126. As Boonk remarks, the carrier may not be an expert in the care of certain goods.[211] This implies that the shipper is obliged to inform the carrier of the manner in which he should handle the goods.

127. Regarding the construction of the words 'properly and carefully' Lord Pearson said:

'[t]he word "properly" adds something to "carefully". If "carefully" has a narrow meaning of merely taking care. The element of skill or sound system is required in addition to taking care.'[212]

128. Although the second sentence is not very clear I think Lord Pearson meant that 'properly' goes further than 'carefully'. 'Properly' is 'carefully' plus an element of skill or sound system.

---

209. See also the Bunga Seroja, [1999] 1 Lloyd's Rep. 512 at points 34 and 35.
210. The Bunga Seroja, [1999] 1 Lloyd's Rep. 512 at points 91 and 92.
211. Boonk 1993, p. 130.
212. Albacora S.R.L. v. Westcott & Laurance Line. Ltd., [1966] 2 Lloyd's Rep 53, 64.

129. Regarding the words 'properly and carefully' Lord Reid said:

> '..., I think that "properly" in this context has a meaning slightly different from "carefully". I agree with Viscount Kilmuir, L.C., that here "properly" means in accordance with a sound system[213] (...) and that may mean rather more than carrying the goods carefully. But the question remains by what criteria it is to be judged whether the system was sound.'[214]

130. Lord Reid goes on to formulate a test to judge if operations have been conducted according to a sound system:

> 'In my opinion, the obligation is to adopt a system which is sound in light of all the knowledge which the carrier has *or ought to have* about the nature of the goods.'[215] (emphasis added, NJM)

131. The emphasised phrase immediately raises the question of the extent of the carrier's obligation to inspect. Should he, in case of doubt, ask the Shipper? In some Dutch decisions the norm is the 'reasonably acting carrier'.[216] I.e. what would a competent carrier have done under those circumstances?
Cleveringa uses the following test for the required level of care:

> 'The level of care, which a dedicated carrier, who has the knowledge which might be expected of such a carrier, applies under such circumstances.'[217]

132. I believe this to be a correct construction. It would be unfair if e.g. a carrier, who is specialised in transport of fruit in refrigerated ships from South America to Rotterdam, may defend himself against a cargo claim on the grounds that he was not familiar with the handling of fruit. That would be contrary to the test that was formulated in the *Maltasian* which says that 'the obligation is to adopt a system which is sound *in light of all the knowledge which the carrier has or ought to have* about the nature of the goods.'[218]

133. It is however true that, in the *Maltasian,* Lord Pearce said that 'a sound system does not mean a system suited to all the weaknesses and idiosyncrasies of a particular cargo, but a sound system in relation to the general practice of carriage of goods by sea.'[219] However, I think that this statement should be applied in the correct context. The rule can not be applied to specialist forms of transport such as e.g. refrigerated transport or heavy lift shipping.

---

213. Viscount Kilmuir said this in the case of G.H. Renton & Co., Ltd. v. Palmyra Trading Corp. of Panama, [1956] 1 Lloyd's Rep 379, 388.
214. Albacora S.R.L. v. Westcott & Laurance Line, Ltd., [1966] 2 Lloyd's Rep 53, 58.
215. Ibid.
216. Amsterdam Court of Appeal 14 September 1995, S&S 1998, 80 and Amsterdam District Court 4 April 1990, S&S 1991, 121.
217. Cleveringa 1961, p. 479.
218. Albacora S.R.L. v. Westcott & laurance Line, Ltd (The Maltasian) [1966] 2 Lloyd's Rep 53.
219. Ibid.

134. Carriers should learn from previous cases and new knowledge. *The Flowergate* [220] is a case concerning moisture damage to cocoa. When the cargo was loaded it was apparently in good condition. However, upon arrival the moisture level of the cocoa proved to be too high. The case runs to 47 pages in Lloyd's List Law Reports. Most of the decision is about factual issues concerning the transport of cocoa. The conclusion of the case is that the moisture level of the cocoa was too high at the time of loading. Roskill J. said that the case had yielded a great deal of knowledge of the carriage of cocoa, which had been obscure before. This knowledge, learned during the proceedings, led to the decision that carriers were not responsible for the damage. Reid said:

> 'If in the future and in the light of what is now known, shipowners continue to accept cocoa for shipment merely on the strength of its apparent condition, and heedless of the implications of what its true condition may in fact be by reason of its moisture content, *they may find it said against them hereafter that they have engaged themselves to carry that cocoa safely to destination, whatever that moisture content may ultimately prove to be.*'[221] (emphasis added, NJM)

135. According to Carver *carefully* refers to the absence of negligence. Carver is less clear on the construction of the word *properly*, which, according to Carver, might tend to mean something nearer to strict liability which can only be averted by successfully invoking an exception. However, in *G.H. Renton & Co. Ltd. v. Palmyra Trading Corp*, preference was given to another construction, that is, the meaning of '*in accordance with a sound system.*'[222]

136. *Albacora S.R.L. v. Westcitt & Laurance Line Ltd. (The Maltasian)* is the leading case on the construction of the expression *properly and carefully*. Lord Reid's construction and test quoted above explain the construction of the word *properly*.
I believe Cleveringa's test makes sense: 'the level of care, which a dedicated carrier, who has the knowledge which might be expected of such a carrier, applies under such circumstances.'[223]

3.9 Is the duty contained in art. III(2) delegable?

3.9.1 English law: general remarks

137. Under English law the duty contained in art. III(2) is not delegable for so far as it applies. In that view art. III(2) does not impose duties in respect of loading, handling, stowing and discharge except in so far as the carrier by the contract of carriage undertakes these.[224] Art. III(2) is only directed to the manner in which the obligations under-

---

220. The Flowergate, [1967] 1 Lloyd's Rep 1.
221. The Flowergate, [1967] 1 Lloyd's Rep 1, 46.
222. G.H. Renton & Co., Ltd. v. Palmyra Trading Corporation of Panama, [1956] 2 Lloyd's Rep 379. See also Carver 2005, p. 573.
223. Cleveringa 1961, p. 479.
224. Pyrene Co., Ltd v. Scindia Steam Navigation Co. Ltd., [1954] 1 Lloyd's Rep. 321. G.H. Renton & Co., Ltd. v. Palmyra Trading Corporation of Panama, [1956] 2 Lloyd's Rep. 379. Jindal Iron and Steel Co. Limited v. Islamic Solidarity Shipping Company Jordan Inc. (The Jordan II), [2005] 1 Lloyd's Rep. 57. See also Carver 2005, p. 573-574.

taken are to be carried out. If undertaken the duties are non delegable. In *International Packers London Ltd. v. Ocean Steam Ship Co., Ltd.* McNair J. held:

> 'I can see no difference in principle between the ship owner's obligation under art. III, r. 1, and that under art. III, r. 2. As a matter of law, therefore, I would hold that the defendants would be liable if the surveyor gave negligently wrong advice. A fortiori the ship-owner would be liable if the advice was the result of incorrect or inadequate information given to the surveyor by the ship's officers, or if the action taken (which for this point of law must be assumed to be negligent) was the joint act of the ship's officers and the surveyor.'[225]

138. Under English law the carrier may include a FIOS(T)[226] clause in the agreement. The leading cases are *Pyrene*, *Renton* and *Jordan II*.[227] Citing French decisions Von Ziegler argues that if it can be proven that the FIO or FIOS clause merely refers to the costs and not to the actual handling of the cargo, the carrier will remain liable for exercising due care with respect to the cargo.[228] Von Ziegler believes that when a FIO or FIOS clause has been agreed on by which the shipper is fully responsible for loading and stowing, inadequate performance of those duties will be regarded as a fault on the part of the shipper so that the carrier will be able to rely on art. III(2) (i) H(V)R to escape liability.[229]

The Jordan II [230]

139. In the *Jordan II* the House of Lords was invited by the cargo interests to revise its position regarding the question whether a FIOS clause is allowable under the Hague (Visby) Rules. Lord Steyn came to the conclusion that a purposive construction of the Rules which permits transfer of the responsibility to load and stow the cargo to the cargo interests is to be preferred above a literal construction of the Rules which would lead to an unreasonable result; i.e. a result which would not comply with the existing practice that FIOS(T) clauses are deemed to be acceptable by the involved parties.[231]

140. Carver remarks that in cases such as the *Jordan II* there may be an overriding responsibility on the carrier, exercised by the master, to supervise the loading and stowage. Furthermore in some cases it may be possible to establish that loss is due to faulty supervision or failure to intervene where this was necessary.[232]

---

225. International Packers London Ltd. v. Ocean Steam Ship Co., Ltd., [1955] 2 Lloyd's Rep. 218, 236 per McNair J.
226. The contract of carriage contains a clause providing that the shipper takes care of the loading, unloading and stowing of the cargo. In case of a FIOST clause the shipper also takes care of the trimming of the ship.
227. Pyrene Co., Ltd v. Scindia Steam Navigation Co., Ltd., [1954] 1 Lloyd's Rep 321. G.H. Renton & Co., Ltd v. Palmyra Trading Corporation of Panama, [1956] 2 Lloyd's Rep. 379. Jindal Iron and Steel Co. Limited v. Islamic Solidarity Shipping Company Jordan Inc. (The Jordan II), [2005] 1 Lloyd's Rep. 57.
228. Von Ziegler 2002, p. 152.
229. Von Ziegler 2002, p. 151.
230. [2005] 1 Lloyd's Rep. 57, 62. This case is discussed extensively in chapter 2.
231. In chapter 2 the considerations in the Jordan II case regarding the construction of the Rules are discussed.
232. Canadian Transport Co. v. Court Line [1940] A.C. 934, 937, 943, 951 and Carver 2005, p. 563.

The views of the textbook writers, decisions in foreign jurisdictions and third party bill of lading holders

141. According to Lord Steyn:

> 'Since the decision of the House in *Renton*[233] in 1956 no English textbook writers have challenged its correctness.'

142. I cannot agree. Gaskell points out that that the *Pyrene*[234] case has been criticised because in that case the court held that the carrier was not liable for damage caused by the shipper's poor way of stowing the cargo. Gaskell takes the view that a clause stipulating that the shipper is liable for the loading and stowing of the cargo is in conflict with the provisions contained in art. III(8) H(V)R.[235]
Carver, however, argues that a FIO clause is not in conflict with the H(V)R. His opinion is based on the *Pyrene* decision in which Devlin J. said:

> 'The carrier is practically bound to play some part in the loading and discharging, so that both operations are naturally included in those covered by the contract of carriage. But I see no reason why the Rules should not leave the parties free to determine by their own contract the part which each has to play. On this view the whole contract of carriage is subject to the Rules, but the extent to which loading and discharging are brought within that carrier's obligations is left to the parties themselves to decide.'[236]

Decisions in foreign jurisdictions

143. Lord Steyn also discussed foreign decisions. He said:

> 'Counsel placed great reliance on decisions of the 2nd Circuit Court of Appeal in *Associated Metals and Minerals Corp. v. M/V The Arktis Sky* 978 F.2d 47 (2nd Cir 1992) and the 5th Circuit Court of Appeal in *Tubacex Inc v. M/V Risan*, 45 ƒ 3rd 951 (5th Cir 1995) in which it was held that loading, stowing and discharging under section 3(2) of the United States Carriage of Goods By Sea Act are "non delegable" duties of the carrier. In neither of these decisions is there any reference to the earlier English decisions in *Pyrene* and in *Renton*. Counsel for the cargo owners pointed out that *The Arktis Sky* has been followed at first instance in South Africa: *The Sea Joy* (1998) (1) SA 487 at 504. And with reference to *Tetley, Marine Cargo Claims,* 4th ed in preparation, chapter 25, at p. 21, he said that in France a shipowner may not contract out of responsibility for improper stowage by an F.I.O.S.T. clause.
> On the other hand the *Renton* decision has been followed in Australia: *Shipping Corporation of India v. Gamlen Chemical Co. A/Asia Pty Ltd.* (1980) 147 CLR 142 and *Hunter Grain Pty Ltd. v. Hyundai Merchant Marine Co. Ltd.* (1993) 117 ALR 507; compare, however, doubts expressed in *Nikolay Malakhov Shipping Co. Ltd. v. SEAS Sap-*

---

233. G.H. Renton & Co. Ltd. v. Palmyra Trading Corporation of Panama, [1956] 2 Lloyd's Rep. 379.
234. Pyrene Co., Ltd. v. Scindia Steam Navigation Co., Ltd., [1954] 1 Lloyd's Rep. 321.
235. Gaskell 2000, p. 261.
236. Carver 1982, p. 363-364.

for Ltd. (1998) 44 NS WLR 371, per Handley JA, at 380, Sheller JA at 387-388, and Cole JA, at 418. Similarly, New Zealand courts have applied *Renton*: *International Ore & Fertilizer Corp v. East Coast Fertiliser Co. Ltd.* [1987] 1 NZLR 9. In Pakistan the English rule has been adopted: see e.g. *East and West Steamship Co. v. Hossain Brothers* (1968) 20 PLD SC 15. In India (the country of shipment in the present case) the English rule is followed: see *The New India Assurance Co. Ltd. v. M/S Splosna Plovba* (1986) AIR Ker 176 (Court: Balakrishna, Menon and K Sukumaran JJ).'[237]

144. With respect to foreign decisions Lord Steyn concludes that internationally there is no dominant view. The weight of opinion in foreign jurisdictions is fairly evenly divided. Lord Steyn recognises that third party bill of lading holders will in practice often not have seen the charter-party or had advance notice of relevant charter-party clauses. He says that although this is a point of some substance it is, however, an inevitable risk of international trade and cannot affect the correct construction of art. III(2).

145. After the above analysis Lord Steyn concludes that everything ultimately turns on what is the best contextual construction of art. III(2). He then goes on to consider whether a departure from the *Renton* decision is justified. He points out that an opportunity arose in 1968 to improve the operation of the Hague Rules. But an international conference took the view that only limited changes were necessary.
Lord Steyn went on to say that if in the United Kingdom there had been dissatisfaction with the effect of the *Renton* decision, one would have expected British cargo interests to have raised it when Parliament considered the Bill which was to become the Carriage of Goods by Sea Act 1971. If invited to do so, Parliament could have considered whether Renton should be reversed. The matter was not raised at all. Instead, art. III(2) was re-enacted in unaltered form. Furthermore Lord Steyn repeated his view that no academic writers have argued that the *Renton* decision should be reversed. For these reasons Lord Steyn reached the view that the case against departing from *Renton* is overwhelming. Also ever since the *Renton* decision all sorts of transactions[238] have been entered into on the basis that *Renton* accurately reflected the law. Risks would often have been assessed in reliance on the decision of the House in *Renton* as to how they should be borne. He says that but for the reliance on *Renton* it is likely that different freight rates and insurance premiums would sometimes have been charged.
On top of all the reasons discussed above Lord Steyn cites from an UNCTAD publication[239] in which the *Renton* decision is discussed. Also in that publication it is recognised that according to English law the words of art. III(2) do not define the scope of the contract service but the terms upon which the agreed service is to be performed. The final reason is that the United Nations Commission on International Trade Law (UNCITRAL) is currently undertaking a revision of the rules governing the carriage of goods by sea. This exercise involves a large scale examination of the operation of the Hague (Visby) Rules. Steyn says that it apparently extends to art. III(2). It will take into account representations from all interested groups, including shipowners, charterers, cargo owners and insurers. According to Lord Steyn this factor by itself makes it singularly inappropriate to re-examine the *Renton* decision now [i.e. In the *Jordan II* case, NJM].

---
237. The Jordan II, [2005] 1 Lloyd's Rep. 57, 64-65.
238. Such as bills of lading, voyage charter parties, time charter parties, insurances, etc.
239. Charterparties: a comparative analysis, UNCTAD: Geneva 1990.

3.9.2 U.S. Law

146. The American author Schoenbaum writes that '[l]ike the duty of seaworthiness, the duty of care of the cargo is non delegable'.[240] A study of the American cases and the opinions of other authors prove this to be correct. According to Gaskell[241] it is doubtful whether an FIOS provision could effectively transfer the responsibility for loading and stowing to the cargo owner under U.S. law.[242] Schoenbaum cites cases in which it was ruled that this did not mean the shipper and the carrier could not enter into a valid agreement placing the duty of loading the cargo on the shipper.[243] Tetley is of the opinion that the duty is non delegable ex 46 U.S.C. § 1303(8).[244] The 2nd and 5th Circuits are also of that opinion.[245] The 9th Circuit however, held that FIO shipments are a common and commercially acceptable practice.[246]

In conclusion it can be said that amongst the circuit courts the 2nd and 5th Circuits take the view that the duty is non-delegable. On the other hand the 9th Circuit is of the opinion that a FIO clause is acceptable.

3.9.3 Dutch law

147. In its judgement of 19 January 1968 (*The Favoriet*) the Dutch Supreme court decided that the carrier can leave the stowing of the cargo up to the shipper but that the carrier can not use that fact as a defence against a third party holder of the bill of lading if that third party did not have knowledge of the agreement regarding the stowing.[247] The Dutch authors Boonk[248] and Van Overklift[249] are of the opinion that the same must apply for loading and discharging and I see no reason to disagree. If loading and stowing are delegable why should loading and discharging not be? The circumstances will be the same as those for loading and stowing. In the *Risa Paula* case the Hague Court of Appeal held that parties could agree that the loading of the cargo would be left up to the shipper.[250]

148. Van der Wiel discusses two cases concerning damages due to improper stowing under a charter party containing a FIOS clause. Neither of the two cases were governed by the H(V)R. In the *Atlantic Duke* case steel pipes were carried on deck under a Gencon

---

240. Schoenbaum 2004, p. 687 citing Nichimen Company v. M/V Farland, 462 F.2d 319 (2nd Cir. 1972).
241. Gaskell 2000, p. 262.
242. M/V Arktis Sky, 978 F.2d 47 (see infra) and M/V Farland, 462 F.2d 319 (see supra).
243. Schoenbaum 2004, p. 687 The decisions cited are equivocal. In Sigri Cabon Corp. v. Lykes Bros. S.S. Co., Inc., 655 F. Supp. 1435, 1438 upholding a FIOS clause in the bill of lading and Sumimoto Corp. of America v. M/V Sie Kim, 632 F. Supp. 824, 837 upholding a 'free in/out' provision of a bill of lading. On the other hand there appears to be a split of authority on this issue in the Circuits. On the one hand the 2nd and 5th Circuits will not allow the view that the duty is delegable. The 9th Circuit however, held that FIO shipments are a common and commercially acceptable practice (Atlas Assur. Co. v. Harper Robinson Shipping Co., 508 F.2d 1381, 1389).
244. Tetley 4th ed., chapter 24, p. 8 and 9.
245. Associated Metals and minerals v. The Arktis Sky, 978 F.2d 47 (2nd Cir.) and Tubacex Inc. v M/V Risan, 45 F.3d 951, 956 5th Cir.).
246. Atlas Assur. Co. v. Harper Robinson Shipping Co., 508 F.2d 1381, 1389 (with judge Trask dissenting).
247. SCN 19 January 1968, NJ 1968, 20, De Favoriet.
248. Boonk 1993, p. 131.
249. Van Overklift 2005, p. 37.
250. The Hague Court of Appeal 18 April 1969, S&S 1970, 37 (Risa Paula).

charter party with a FIOS clause.[251] The cargo on two of the hatches was not secured and lashed properly and shifted in rough weather. The vessel had to put into a port to have the cargo re-lashed. The owners demanded payment of the additional costs of the voyage charterer. The court of appeal held that, although the time charterer was responsible for the stowing and lashing of the cargo, the vessels crew had the duty to check if the work had been done properly and that the vessel was seaworthy. This led the court of appeal to hold that the fault of the time charterer was 2/3 and the fault of the owners 1/3. Therefore 2/3 of the owners' claim was awarded. This division was based on construction of the charter party.
A similar case discussed by Van der Wiel in which the court (The Hague Court of Appeal) held that damages were to be divided between charterer and owner is the *Boekanier*.[252]

149. Van der Wiel draws the conclusion from these cases and other Dutch cases that under Dutch law and the H(V)R it is permissible to delegate loading, lashing, stowing and discharging to the cargo interests but that the carrier is responsible to check the work. In case of cargo damage the damages may be divided between the cargo interests and the carrier.[253] Van der Wiel concludes that he finds '..., the Dutch system wherein the damages are divided the best'.[254]
However, after reading the *Atlantic Duke* and the *Boekanier* it becomes clear that the court's decision to divide the damages was based on construction of the charter parties and not on construction of the H(V)R which did not apply in those cases. Therefore I think that Van der Wiel probably meant that *he* is an advocate of the system wherein damages may be divided between the parties. Division of damages in cases of cargo damage under the H(V)R and a FIOS(T) clause is not a general rule that can be derived from the Dutch cases.

150. I agree with the *Favoriet* decision as it recognises existing commercial practice but also protects third party bill of lading holders who do not know of the existence of a delegation of certain duties to the shipper.

3.9.4 UNCITRAL

151. In *Jordan II* Lord Steyn refers to the proposed UNCITRAL treaty. Art. 14 (regarding 'specific obligations' of the carrier') of the proposed instrument reads:[255]

1. The carrier shall during the period of its responsibility as defined in article 12, and subject to article 27, properly and carefully receive, load, handle, stow, carry, keep, care for, unload and deliver the goods.
2. Notwithstanding paragraph 1 of this article, and without prejudice to the other provisions in chapter 4 and to chapters 5 to 7, the parties may agree that the loading, handling, stowing or unloading of the goods is to be performed by the shipper, the docu-

---

251. The Atlantic Duke, The Hague Court of Apeal 27 November 1981, S&S 1982, 24.
252. See Van der Wiel 2001, p. 80 and The Boekanier, The Hague Court of Appeal 7 November 1991, S&S 1993, 47.
253. Van der Wiel 2001, p. 82.
254. Van der Wiel 2001, p. 82.
255. Document A/CN.9/WG.III/WP.8101.

mentary shipper or the consignee. Such an agreement shall be referred to in the contract particulars.

Art. 18 (regarding the basis of liability) contains the following exoneration in paragraph 3 and sub i:

3. The carrier is also relieved of all or part of its liability (...) if, alternatively to proving the absence of fault (...) it proves that one or more of the following events or circumstances caused or contributed to the loss, damage, or delay:

(...)

(i) Loading, handling, stowing, or unloading of the goods performed pursuant to an agreement in accordance with article 14, paragraph 2, unless the carrier or a performing party performs such activity on behalf of the shipper, the documentary shipper or the consignee;

152. Paragraph 2 of art. 14 makes clear that the framers of the proposed UNCITRAL instrument follow the House of Lords decision in the *Renton* case.

153. The exception provided by art. 18(3)i makes it extra clear that the carrier will not be liable for damage caused by loading, handling, stowing or discharging of the goods if the parties had agreed that the loading, handling, stowing or discharging of the goods was to be performed by the shipper. The carrier can avoid liability by either proving the absence of fault or by invoking the i-exception.

154. Art. 18(3)i also provides an exception to that exception. If the loading, handling, stowing or discharging of the goods is performed by the carrier on behalf of the shipper and damage occurs then the carrier will not be able to rely on art. 18(3)i.

155. Art. 18(3)i does not exonerate the carrier for any loss or damage in the period that the cargo is being loaded, handled, stowed or discharged. It only exonerates for the actual activity of loading, stowing, handling or discharging. So if e.g. cargo is stolen during loading (as was agreed between the parties) then the carrier will still be liable for the loss of the stolen cargo.

156. At present there is no international uniformity regarding the allowability of a FIOS(T) clause under the Rules.[256] Uniformity of construction of the Rules is desired. If the proposed UNCITRAL instrument is adopted with the provision mentioned above in the proposed art. 14 par. 2 the desired uniformity will have been reached for this point.

3.9.5 The intended construction of art. III(2)

157. The above shows that there is no agreement on the issue whether the requirement of proper care for the cargo can be delegated. Article III(8) provides that the require-

---

256. See Lord Steyn's speach in Jordan II under point 22.

ment of due care for the cargo cannot be delegated with the result that the carrier is exempted from liability thereof. However, this is not in keeping with existing practise. In *Jordan II* and the earlier English decisions *Pyrene* and *Renton* existing commercial practice was recognised and transfer of the responsibility for loading and stowing was deemed permissible. Under English law however, third party bill of lading holders may be harmed by the existence of a FIO clause between the shipper and the carrier of which they had no knowledge. In my view the Dutch Supreme Court takes a more reasonable view which protects third party bill of lading holders who had no knowledge of a contractual delegation of the duty to load and stow properly and carefully. In the U.S. there is a diversity of authority.

158. Now that the lack of uniformity has been established the question which has to be answered is: what is the intended construction and application of Rule III(2)? A textual, i.e. objective construction of art. III(2) is clear. The carrier has to properly and carefully load and stow. Art. III(8) is also clear: 'Any clause, covenant, or agreement in a contract of carriage relieving the carrier or the ship from liability for loss or damage to, or in connection with, goods arising from negligence, fault, or failure in the duties and obligations provided in this article or lessening such liability otherwise than as provided in these Rules, shall be null and void and of no effect. A benefit of insurance in favour of the carrier or similar clause shall be deemed to be a clause relieving the carrier from liability.'

159. The text seems to be clear. The carrier is responsible for loading, stowing etc and any clause relieving the carrier from those responsibilities is null and void. Although the text is clear the result could be absurd.[257] Was this really what was intended? If a shipper expressly agrees to be responsible for stowing it would be absurd if he could hold the carrier responsible for damage due to bad stowing for which the shipper was responsible himself.
Regarding the duty contained in art. III(2) the following speech of Mr. Louis Franck is included in the Travaux Préparatoires. He said:

> 'Article 3(2) contained an essential clause highlighting that the carrier, except as provided for in article 4, was responsible for seeing that everything required for loading, handling, stowage, carriage, custody, and unloading was provided for the goods to be carried. And the inclusion of every clause permitting the shipowner, without incurring responsibility, to fail in this essential duty of overseeing the preservation of the goods from the point of view of successful stowage, loading, and unloading was null and void. *That was the main element of the convention because it was in this way that, in the past, the use of immunity clauses had given cause for the greatest criticism.* The result had been the creation of different sorts of bills of lading that still bore the form, but whose content was completely destroyed by the force of the immunity clauses.'[258] (emphasis added, NJM)

160. Bearing in mind that the framers of the Rules were practical people it seems unlikely that they would intend to create a duty which does not comply with commercial

---
257. See supra § 2.3.1: If the meaning of the words is clear but lead to an absurd result then the objective construction has failed. Broad principles of general acceptation can be used to test if a result is absurd.
258. Travaux Préparatoires, p. 186.

practise. The emphasised sentence makes clear that the immunity clauses had given cause for criticism. If a carrier were to include a clause exempting him from responsibility for damage due to non fulfilment of art. III(2) such a clause would be null and void. On the other hand a contract between a carrier and a shipper containing a clause saying the shipper should load and stow is not an immunity clause. It is common commercial practise. The House of Lords recognised this and therefore let a teleological construction which expressed the object of the Rules prevail over an objective construction which would lead to absurd[259] results. The object of the Rules was to create a compromise between shippers and carriers. This means the carrier could no longer use immunity clauses. The object was not to change commercial practise whereby shippers and carriers are acting on an equal footing.

---

259. It would be contrary to general principles of law if a shipper who agrees to load an stow would be able to successfully hold the carrier responsible for damage caused by the shipper's failure to fulfil his part of the contract correctly (see Van Delden 1986, p. 10-11).

Chapter 4
The relationship between the duties of the carrier and the exceptions[260]

4.1 Introduction

161. In the H(V)R the duties of the carrier are contained in art III(1) and (2). The duty contained in art III(1) (seaworthiness) is an obligation to use due diligence. The duty contained in art III(2) (regarding the care for the cargo) is an absolute obligation. Art. IV H(V)R contains the exceptions from liability. It has been said that the relationship between the duties and the exceptions is unclear.[261] In this chapter the following topics regarding these articles will be discussed:

Causes of damage: competing and concurring causes (4.2)
The expression 'overriding obligation': common law (4.3.1)
The expression 'overriding obligation': H(V)R (4.3.2)
The requirement of causal connection (4.4)
Doctrines regarding the relationship between art. III(1) and III(2) and art. IV (4.5)
Concurrence of culpable and non-culpable causes of damage: common law (4.6.1)
Concurrence of culpable and non-culpable causes of damage: H(V)R (4.6.2)
Why is art. III(2) not also considered an overriding obligation under English law? (4.7)
The intended relationship between art. III and IV (4.8)

4.2 Causes of damage

162. It is possible that damage was caused by an excepted peril (a non-culpable cause) and by the non-fulfilment of one of the duties of the carrier (a culpable cause). Royer separated the two ways that a culpable and a non-culpable cause can cause damage into two groups. The first group is damage attributable to causes which exist together but whereby there is no causal connection between the causes. The second group contains the events whereby the one cause is the cause of the other cause.[262]
The problem in such cases of cargo damage caused by more than one cause (culpable and non-culpable) is how liability should be apportioned. This problem is discussed in the Report of Working Group III (UNCITRAL) on the work of its 12th session.[263] The reason that this problem was tackled by the UNCITRAL working group, is the proposed abolishment of the nautical fault exception in the proposed UNCITRAL convention which is to replace the H(V)R. Often one of the causes of cargo damage can be qualified as 'management of the ship' so that the carrier will not be liable for that cause. The non-culpable cause will then remain and the carrier will not be liable. However, the

---
260. See for an earlier version of this chapter Hendrikse & Margetson 2005a.
261. Carver 2005, 571.
262. Royer 1959, p. 231.
263. Document A/CN.9/544, p. 42-45.

elimination of the nautical fault exception 'may have the unintended effect of depriving the carrier of every statutory defense in any case in which navigational fault could plausibly be argued'.[264] This could lead to unfair results. E.g. if the carrier is held liable for all the damage when only a small part of the damage is caused by a culpable cause and the larger part of the damage by a non-culpable cause.

A solution of the problem would be that, in cases of more than one cause of damage, a system exists whereby the carrier will only be liable for the damage caused by the culpable cause. The most recent UNCITRAL proposal is that the carrier will be relieved of liability if, alternatively to proving the absence of fault, he proves that one or more of the excepted perils provided by art. 18(3) caused or contributed to the loss, damage or delay.[265]

163. In the Report on the work of the 12th session of Working Group III it was suggested that

> '..., the draft instrument should provide guidance to courts and arbitral tribunals to avoid certain causes of the damage being neglected, for example through excessive reliance on the doctrine of overriding obligations. The discussion focused on paragraph 4 of the third proposed redraft of article 14 [concerning the basis of liability. Art. 14 became art. 17 in the version of 26 March 2007 and it became art. 18 in the version of January 2008, NJM]. It was suggested that, in discussing the issue of apportionment of liability, it might be useful to bear in mind a distinction between concurring causes and competing causes for the damage. In the case of concurring causes, each event caused part of the damage but none of these events alone was sufficient to cause the entire damage (for example, where the damage was attributable to both weak packaging by the shipper and improper storage by the carrier). In the case of competing damages, the court might have to identify an event or the fault of one party as having caused the entire damage, irrespective of the fault of the other party (for example, where the goods were damaged as a result of artillery fire hitting the vessel, a decision might need to be made as to whether the artillery fire was to be regarded as the only cause of the damage, irrespective of the fault the master of the vessel might have committed by bringing the ship into a war zone). It was pointed out that, in this second situation, the doctrine of "overriding obligations" would often apply. It was suggested that draft article 14 dealt only with the situation where concurring faults were at stake and not with the second situation described as "competing faults".'[266]

164. I agree that the distinction should be made between damage caused by competing causes (one cause can cause all the damage) and concurring causes (each cause is the cause of part of the damage). The overriding obligation rule as it exists under common law is unreasonable. It means that a carrier may be responsible for damage which was not caused by non-fulfilment of a duty (see below).

---

264. Document A/CN.9/544, p. 43-44 and A/CN.9/WG.111/WP.34, paragraph 15.
265. Document A/CN.9/544, p. 44 and Document A/CN.9/WG.III/WP.101.
266. Document A/CN.9/544, p. 44.

4.3 The expression 'overriding obligation'

4.3.1 Common law

165. This expression was used by the Privy Council in *Paterson Steamships, Ltd. v. Canadian Co-operative Wheat Producers, Ltd. (The Sarnidoc)*. Lord Wright said:

> 'It will therefore be convenient here, in construing those portions of the Act which are relevant to this appeal, to state in very summary form the simplest principles which determine the obligations attaching to a carrier of goods by sea or water. At common law, he was called an insurer that is he was absolutely responsible for delivering in like order and condition at the destination the goods bailed to him for carriage. He could avoid liability for loss or damage only by showing that the loss was due to the act of God or the King's enemies. But it became the practice for the carrier to stipulate that for loss due to various specified contingencies or perils he should not be liable: the list of these specific excepted perils grew as time went on. That practice, however, brought into view two separate aspects of the sea carrier's duty which it had not been material to consider when his obligation to deliver was treated as absolute. *It was recognised that his overriding obligations might be analysed into a special duty to exercise due care and skill in relation to the carriage of the goods and a special duty to furnish a ship that was fit for the adventure at its inception. These have been described as fundamental undertakings, or implied obligations.* If then goods were lost (say) by perils of the seas, there could still remain the inquiry whether or not the loss was also due to negligence or unseaworthiness. If it was, the bare exception did not avail the carrier (...) [he then quoted Lord Sumner who had said in a different case:]
>
> [T]he exception in the bill of lading (...) only exempts him [the shipowner] from the absolute liability of a common carrier, and not from the consequences of the want of reasonable skill, diligence, and care (...) [I]t was common ground that the ship had to deliver what she received as she received it, unless relieved by excepted perils. Accordingly, in strict law, on proof being given of the actual good condition of the apples on shipment and of their damaged condition on arrival, the burden of proof passed from the consignees to the shipowners to prove some excepted peril which relieved them from liability, and further, as a condition of being allowed the benefit of that exception, to prove seaworthiness (...) the port of shipment, and to negative negligence or misconduct of the master, officers and crew with regard to the apples during the voyage and the discharge in this country.'[267] (emphasis added, NJM)

166. At common law the carrier is absolutely responsible for delivering the goods that were bailed to him in the same order and condition as they were in when he received them. This was the carrier's overriding obligation. The quoted passage above makes clear that later that concept developed into the separate overriding duties to exercise due care in the handling of the goods and the duty to furnish a seaworthy ship. The concept of separate overriding obligations regarding the seaworthiness and the care of

---

267. Paterson SS Ltd v. Canadian Co-operative Wheat Producers Ltd., 49 Ll.L.L.R. 421, 426, 427.

the cargo were a result of the original overriding obligation. At common law the duties 'to exercise care and skill in relation to the carriage of the goods and a special duty to furnish a ship that was fit for the adventure' are overriding obligations.[268]

167. Clarke wrote about the common law phrase 'overriding obligation':

> '..., these obligations were then said to be overriding, in that the parties were presumed not to have intended to except liability for their breach.'[269]

168. Lord Wright explained the phrase as follows:

> 'If then goods were lost, say, by perils of the seas, there could still remain the inquiry whether or not the loss was also due to[270] negligence or unseaworthiness. If it was, the bare exception did not avail the carrier.'[271]

Summary

169. The expression 'overriding obligation' has its origin in common law. Under common law the duty deliver the cargo in good order and condition was an absolute duty and an overriding obligation. If the carrier failed to fulfil that duty and damage occurred due to more than one cause, one being an excepted peril and the other a non-excepted peril *then the non-excepted peril is seen as the only cause*. The carrier will be responsible for the whole of the damage, not merely for such proportion as must have been incurred due to the unseaworthiness.[272] No distinction is made between competing causes and concurring causes.[273]

170. I find this rule unreasonable because it could mean that a carrier will be responsible for all of the damage even though only a small portion of it was caused by a non-excepted peril. This is different under the English law developed under the H(V)R. Under that law the carrier will be allowed to prove for which portion of the damage he is not responsible even if a portion of the damage was caused by the non-fulfilment of art. III(1).[274]

4.3.2 The H(V)R

171. In the *Maxine Footwear* case, concerning the application of the Hague Rules, Lord Somervell of Harrow explained the relationship between art. III(1) and IV of the Hague Rules as follows:

---

268. Paterson SS Ltd v. Canadian Co-operative Wheat Producers Ltd., 49 Ll.L.L.Rep. 421, 426, Clarke 1976, p. 124-125, Carver 2005, p. 499.
269. Clarke 1976, p. 124.
270. In carriage of goods by sea, unseaworthiness does not affect the carrier's liability unless it causes the loss, as was held in the Europe, [1908] P. 84 and in Kish v. Taylor, [1912] A.C. 604.
271. Canadian Co-operative Wheat Producers, Ltd v. Paterson Steamships, Ltd., 49 Ll.L.L.R. 421, 426-427.
272. Smith, Hogg & Co., Ltd v. Black Sea & Baltic General Insurance Company, Ltd. (The Lilburn), (1940) 67 Ll.L.L.Rep., 253.
273. See supra § 4.1.
274. See infra § 4.6.2.

> 'Article III, rule 1 is an *overriding obligation*. If it is not fulfilled and *the non-fulfilment causes the damage, the immunities of Art. IV cannot be relied on*. This is the natural construction apart from the opening words of Art. III, rule 2. The fact that the rule is made subject to the provision of Art. IV and Rule 1 is not so conditioned makes the point clear beyond argument.[275]' (emphasis added, NJM)

172. The words 'and the non-fulfilment causes the damage' do not leave room for the distinction between 'all of the damage' or 'part of the damage', or to use the terminology discussed in the introduction; there is no room for distinction between concurring causes or competing causes. The overriding obligation rule from *Maxine Footwear* assumes that the causes are competing causes, i.e. one of the causes could have caused all of the damage.

173. Regarding the relationship between art. III(2) and art. IV Lord Pearson said in *The Maltasian*:

> 'Art. III, r. 2, is expressly made subject to the provisions of Art. IV. The scheme is, therefore, that there is a *prima facie* obligation under Art. III, r. 2, which may be displaced or modified by some provision of Art. IV. Art. IV contains many and various provisions, which may have different effects on the *prima facie* obligation arising under Art. III, r. 2. The convenient first step is to ascertain what is the *prima facie* obligation under Art. III, r. 2.'[276]

174. So, according to the English construction of the Hague Rules, the expression *overriding obligation* means, that when damage is a consequence of competing causes, i.e. non-fulfilment of art. III(1) and an excepted peril, the exceptions of art IV(2) cannot be successfully invoked.

175. Carver remarks that the full consequences of this overriding nature as applied to the Rules are not clear:

> 'It cannot mean that if the seaworthiness duty is not first proved to have been complied with, the exceptions of Art. IV cannot be invoked at all whether or not the damage occurred in connection with unseaworthiness. (...) Rather, it must mean that if art III(1) is not fulfilled and the non-fulfilment causes the damage the immunities of art. IV cannot be relied on.'[277]

176. Strictly speaking this implies that if art III(2) has been violated and this violation caused the damage, exceptions can still be invoked. This will however depend upon which exception is being invoked. For example, a carrier will not be able to rely on the perils of the sea exception to obtain exoneration from liability if he failed to meet the obligations contained in art III(2).[278] This is because one of the main tests to prove a peril of the sea is that the damage caused by that event was unavoidable. If the carrier

---

275. Maxine Footwear Co. Ltd v. Canadian Government Merchant Marine Ltd (The Maurienne), [1959] 2 Lloyd's Rep. 105, 113.
276. The Maltasian [1966] 2 Lloyd's Rep. 53, 63.
277. Carver 2005, p. 571.
278. See § 5.4 for a detailed discussion of the perils of the sea exception. See in general Carver 2005, p. 609.

could have avoided the damage by e.g. stowing the cargo better the damage was avoidable.

177. This means the carrier will not be able to prove the damage was caused by a peril of the sea.

178. The view also exists that art. IV(1) H(V)R is an indication that art. III(1) contains an overriding obligation.[279] Karan explains this view as follows: '[a]rticle 4(1) of the Hague and Hague-Visby Rules exempts the carrier from liability for loss or damage arising only from unseaworthiness unless caused by want of due diligence. By contrast Article 4(2)(q) of the same Conventions removes liability for loss or damage arising from any occurrence resulting without fault. For that reason, the liability regime under Articles 3(1) and 4(1) is more special, and, thereof, prevails over the one under Articles 3(2) and 4(2).'[280] I do not agree with this view. As is discussed in § 5.1 art. IV(1) was included to change existing American law. The distinction between the overriding obligation of art. III(1) and the non-overriding obligation of art. III(2) is made clear by the words in art. III(2) saying that art. III(2) is subject to the provisions of art. IV. This follows from a simple objective construction of art. III(1) and art. III(2). There is no need for the more complicated aid to construction used by Karan (reading the Rules as a whole).

Summary

179. The expression 'overriding obligation' is used in decisions regarding the H(V)R but in a different meaning than under common law. The meaning under the H(V)R is that if the damage is caused by non-fulfilment of art. III(1) the carrier cannot rely on an exception to escape responsibility for damage caused by non-fulfilment art. III(1).

4.4 The requirement of causal connection

4.4.1 American law

180. Under the Harter Act the carrier has no recourse to exceptions in the case of unseaworthiness prior to the voyage, even if there is no causal connection between the unseaworthiness and the damage.[281] On the other hand it is generally recognised under the H(V)R that causal connection between the non-fulfilment of a duty and the loss or damage is required to disallow the carrier recourse to an exception to escape liability.[282]

4.4.2 English law

181. Also under English law causal connection between a non-excepted peril and the damage is required to prove liability of the carrier. From the *Maxine Footwear* case it follows that there must be causal connection between the non-compliance with art. III(1)

---

279. Clarke 1976, p. 159.
280. Karan 2004, p. 105.
281. The Isis, 290 U.S. 333.
282. Schnell & Co. v. S.S. Vallescura, 293 U.S. 296. See infra § 4.6.2.

and the damage.[283] This also follows from the last words of the text of art. IV(1).[284] This means that the carrier cannot rely on the provisions of art. IV to escape liability for the portion of damage caused by non-compliance with art. III(1). However, if another portion of the damage had a cause other than non-compliance with art. III(1) he does have an escape hatch. In that event the carrier will be allowed to avail himself of the provisions of art. IV.

182. In *Apostolis* (Court of Appeal) it was held that

> 'To show breach of art. III r. 1 AMJ must show that the carriers failed to make the ship seaworthy and that their loss or damage *was caused by* the breach, or in other words was caused by unseaworthiness.'[285] (emphasis added, NJM)

183. This consideration also leads to the conclusion that a violation of art III(1) will only lead to liability of the carrier if a causal connection has been proven between the unseaworthiness and the fire.[286]

184. However, this is not so under Dutch law.

4.4.3 Dutch law

185. The following consideration from the Dutch *Quo Vadis* judgement demonstrates that the Supreme Court of the Netherlands (SCN) applies the overriding obligation rule as it exists in common law, to cases governed by the H(V)R.

> 'If the damage *is due to* two causes, as meant above, the unseaworthiness for which due diligence was not exercised, *ought to be regarded as the only cause*, leaving no possibility to reduce liability by invoking an exception out of the second para of art. 469 [old Commercial Code; currently art. 8:383 (2) Dutch Civil Code].'[287] (emphasis added, NJM)

186. From this consideration it follows that if there is *any* causal connection between a failure to fulfil an obligation and the damage the non-excepted peril is held to be the only relevant cause and the carrier will be liable for all of the damage, not merely for the portion which was caused by the non-excepted peril. This rule blocks the escape hatch of disproving causal connection between the non-excepted peril and a portion of the damage.

187. Another opinion also exists. The Dutch author Schadee gives an example of damage to the cargo occurring on an under manned ship. There is no causal connection between the damage to the cargo and the failure to fulfil the duty to exercise due dili-

---

283. See supra § 4.3.2: Maxine Footwear Co. Ltd v. Canadian Government Merchant Marine Ltd (The Maurienne), [1959] 2 Lloyd's Rep. 105, 113.
284. See § 5.1.
285. A. Meredith Jones v. Vangemar Shipping Co. (The Apostolis), [1997] 2 Lloyd's Rep. 241.
286. As much is also in evidence in The Canadian Highlander, 32 Ll.L.L.Rep. 91 and The Torenia, [1983] 2 Lloyd's Rep. 210, 218.
287. Quo Vadis, SCN 11 June 1993, NJ 1995, 235.

gence to make the ship seaworthy. Even so, Schadee is of the opinion that the carrier has no recourse to an exception.[288] As was said above, this is the view under the Harter Act, but is incorrect under the H(V)R.

4.5 Doctrines concerning the relationship between art. III and art. IV

4.5.1 England

The requirement of due diligence to make the ship seaworthy

188. As was said above, under English law art III(1) H(V)R contains a so called overriding obligation.[289] From the aforementioned decision in *Maxine Footwear* (concerning damage caused by fire) it follows that the fire exception will fail if the fire that caused the damage is a consequence of a failure to exercise due diligence to ensure seaworthiness before and at the beginning of the voyage. The consequence hereof is that the carrier will not be able to rely on any of the exceptions of art IV(2) H(V)R to escape from liability for the damage caused by the non-fulfilment of art. III(1).[290]

The requirement of care for the cargo

189. Art III(2) H(V)R begins with the words '*Subject to the provisions of Article 4*, the carrier shall, ...' (emphasis added, NJM). It has been argued that the emphasised words imply that the obligations contained in art III(2) cannot be deemed to be overriding obligations because of the reference to the exceptions of art IV(2) H(V)R.[291]
This does not however mean that if loss or damage which was caused by a breach of art. III(2) and an event which may qualify as an exception of art. IV(2) the carrier will not be responsible. As was said above, the proof of an excepted peril will often also entail the proof that the duty contained in art. IV(2) was fulfilled.[292] The relevance of the words 'subject to the provisions of art. IV' is that the carrier, in certain instances, will be allowed to rely on a certain exception (e.g. the fire exception) even though the loss or damage was caused by the negligence of his employees or agents in the fulfilment of the duty contained in art. III(2). However, because under English law the duty contained in art. III(1) is an overriding obligation, he will not be allowed to rely on the fire exception if the loss or damage was caused by the failure to fulfil the duty to exercise due diligence to make the ship seaworthy.[293]

---

288. NJB 1954, p. 730.
289. Maxine Footwear Co. Ltd v. Canadian Government Merchant Marine Ltd (The Maurienne), [1959] 2 Lloyd's Rep. 105.
290. Carver 2005, p. 571 where reference is made to the aforementioned Maxine Footwear case.
291. See for example Maxine Footwear v. Canadian Government Merchant Marine, [1959] 2 Lloyd's Rep. 105 and Cooke et al. 2001, p. 925.
292. See supra the example of the 'perils of the sea' exception.
293. See § 5.3 on the fire exception. See also Carver 2005, p. 572-573 and the discussion of English case law. See in the same sense Aikens et al, p. 256-257.

4.5.2 The United States

190. The American COGSA[294] does not contain the proviso 'subject to the provision of article 4' of art III(2) of the H(V)R. However this has not led to an absence of a debate of the 'overriding obligation' of due diligence for a seaworthy ship.[295] The 9th Circuit introduced the concept of an overriding obligation for seaworthiness in America in the *Sunkist* case, regarding the application of the fire defences. This view of he 9th Circuit was based on the *Maxine Footwear* case. In *Maxine Footwear* the words 'subject to the provisions of article 4' in art. III(2) played an important factor in the Privy Council's decision that art. III(1) is an overriding obligation. The 9th Circuit seems to have overlooked that those words were omitted from the U.S. Cogsa.[296] The view of the 9th Circuit does, however, seem to be an exception and, as far as I know, the concept of 'overriding obligation' is not applied to other exceptions and has also not been recognised by the U.S. Supreme Court. According to Schoenbaum the carrier's duty to properly care for the cargo and to exercise due diligence before and at the beginning of the voyage to provide a seaworthy ship are indeed both overriding obligations.[297]

4.5.3 The Netherlands

The requirement of due diligence to make the ship seaworthy

191. In the *Quo Vadis* case, the Supreme Court of The Netherlands (SCN) held that the requirement to exercise due diligence to ensure seaworthiness is an overriding obligation.[298]

192. The carrier had argued that if the damage is a result of concurrent causes[299] (a culpable and a non-culpable cause) fault and liability should be divided. In my view this argument is correct. It is also in line with the *Vallescura* rule.[300] I do not see why the carrier should not be given the opportunity to prove that he is not liable for a part of the damage.

193. At first view the above quoted consideration of the SCN appears to be in accordance with that from *Maxine Footwear* quoted above. The decision of the SCN, however, goes a little further. Whereas in *Maxine Footwear* there is room for a division of damages if some of the damage was caused by a breach of art. III(2) and if the carrier proves that he was not culpable for part of the damage, the Dutch Supreme Court has explicitly ruled this possibility out: if damage in caused by concurrent causes, the culpable cause is considered to be the 'only cause'.
As was said above this was the application of the 'overriding obligation' rule at common law. The decision of the SCN is incorrect as it does not allow room for the carrier

---

294. 46 U.S.C. App. Sec.1303 et cetera.
295. Sunkist Growers Inc v. Adelaide Shipping Lines Ltd., 603 F.2d 1327.
296. See § 5.3.
297. Schoenbaum 2004, p. 605.
298. Supreme Court of The Netherlands 11 June 1993, NJ 1995, 235. See supra § 4.4.3.
299. In Dutch: 'samenwerkende oorzaken', meaning 'causes working together'. Concurrent causes in the terminology used in § 4.1.
300. The Vallescura rule is discussed below in § 4.6.2.1.

to escape from responsibility for the part of the damage not caused by the breach of a duty.

The requirement of care for the cargo

194. Under Dutch law the system of *stare decisis* does not exist, meaning that, especially in the lower courts, conflicting judgements exist.[301] Just for interest I will mention the *Portalon* case because I do not agree with the decision. I do however stress that this is only one of many cases and is not a rule of law under Dutch law.

195. In the *Portalon* case, the Court of Appeal judged that the cargo interest can also deprive the carrier of the fire exception by proving that the carrier did not fulfil the duties contained in art III(1) and (2). The Court of Appeal held that 'the history of the fire exception does not show with certainty that during the framing of the Hague Rules (...) the intention prevailed that, contrary to the other exceptions, the exclusion of liability ought to be allowed under the fire exception, even if the carrier has not fulfilled his *primary obligation* to exercise due diligence to ensure the seaworthiness of the vessel and insufficient care was taken for proper and careful loading, treatment, stowing etc.'[302] (emphasis added, NJM)

196. The Court of Appeal thus held that in relationship to the fire exception the obligation contained in art III(2) of the Hague Rules is an overriding obligation. Considering the intended construction of the fire exception I suggest that this decision is contrary to the correct application of the fire exception.[303]

4.6 Concurrence of culpable and non-culpable causes of damage

4.6.1 Common law: The Lilburn

197. In *The Lilburn* Lord Wright said:

> 'There is always a combination of co-operating causes out of which the law, employing its empirical or common-sense view of causation, will select the one or more which it finds material for its special purpose of deciding the particular case. That this is the test of the significance of an event from the standpoint of causation is clearly illustrated by this very doctrine of seaworthiness and its relation to kindred questions of negligence as applied to the two maritime contracts, marine insurance and sea carriage of goods. In the former, seaworthiness is a condition precedent (at least in voyage policies) and if not complied with the insurance never attaches. In carriage of goods by sea, unseaworthiness does not affect the carrier's liability unless it causes the loss, as was held in the Europa, [1908] P. 84, and in Kish v. Taylor, [1912] A.C. 604. (...) In carriage of goods by sea, the shipowner will in the absence of valid and sufficient exceptions be liable for a loss occasioned by negligence. Apart from express exceptions, the carrier's contract is to deliver the goods safely. But when the practice

---

301. However, the SCN does tend to follow its own decisions.
302. The Portalon, The Hague Court of Appeal, 30 December 1966, S&S 1967, 28.
303. See § 5.3 on the fire exception.

of having express exceptions limiting that obligation became common, it was laid down that there were fundamental obligations, which were not affected by the specific exceptions, unless that was made clear by express words. Thus, an exception of perils of the sea does not qualify the duty to furnish a seaworthy ship or to carry the goods without negligence (see Paterson Steamships, Ltd. v. Canadian Co-operative Wheat Producers, Ltd., *sup.*). *From the nature of the contract, the relevant cause of the loss is held to be the unseaworthiness or the negligence as the case may be, not the peril of the sea, where both the breach of the fundamental obligation and the objective peril are co-operating causes.* The contractual exception of perils of the seas does not affect the fundamental obligation, unless the contract qualifies the latter in express terms.'[304] (emphasis added, NJM)

198. So, to use the terminology introduced in the introduction: when there are competing causes of damage the relevant cause of the loss is held to be the culpable cause. Does this mean the carrier will not be allowed to invoke an exception or disprove the cause of the damage?

199. Regarding this question Lord Wright said:

'The question is (...) would the disaster not have happened if the ship had fulfilled the obligation of seaworthiness, even though the disaster could not have happened if there had not also been the specific peril or action?
There is precise authority for this in the judgement of the Court of Appeal delivered by that great authority on mercantile law, Scrutton, L.J., with the concurrence of Bankes and Atkin, L.JJ., in the Christel Vinnen, [1924] P. 208. Cargo in that case was damaged by leakage through a leaky rivet; the damage might have been checked but for the negligence of the master in not detecting the water in the hold and pumping it out. *It was held (notwithstanding an exception of negligence) that the shipowners were responsible for the whole of the damage, not merely for such proportion as must have been incurred before the inflow of water could have been checked. No distinction was drawn between damage due to perils of the seas alone and that due to perils of the seas and to negligence combined.* Scrutton, L.J., said, at p. 214:
The water which entered and did the damage entered through unseaworthiness; its effects when in the ship might have been partially remedied by due diligence, which the shipowner's servants did not take. But in my view the cause of the resulting damage is still unseaworthiness ... Here the man who has by his original breach of contract caused the opportunity for damage has by the negligence of his servants increased it. *He cannot show any exception to protect him, and cannot show that the dominant cause of the damage was not the unseaworthiness which admitted the water into the ship.*'[305] (emphasis added, NJM)

200. Lord Wright went on to explain that the language used by Carver did not apply to the contract of carriage:

---

304. The Lilburn, (1940) 67 Ll.L.L.Rep. 253, 258.
305. The Lilburn, (1940) 67 Ll.L.L.Rep. 253, 259.

'If I may, however, venture to criticise the language of the learned Lord Justice, I should prefer to avoid the word "dominant", which he takes from the marine insurance cases cited by him, in which it is necessary to find the *causa proxima* or dominant cause. This results by reason of the special character of that contract where the liability to pay depends, broadly speaking, on the casualty being caused directly by the happening which the contract stipulates to be the event on which the indemnity becomes exigible. There may be in marine insurance cases a competition of causes so that it is necessary to determine which event is the dominant cause. Negligence is not material, nor, in time policies, is unseaworthiness material; nor is it material, in one sense, in other classes of marine policies from the point of view of causation, since, if the warranty is not complied with, the risk never attaches.'[306]

201. Lord Wright then explained the law with regard to the carriage of goods by sea:

'In cases, however, of the sea carriage of goods the liability depends, in the words of the Lord Justice, on a "breach of contract", that is, to provide a seaworthy ship. *The sole question, apart from express exception, must then be, "Was that breach of contract 'a' cause of the damage."* It may be preferred to describe it as an effective or real or actual cause, though the adjectives in my opinion in fact add nothing. *If the question is answered in the affirmative the shipowner is liable though there were other co-operating causes, whether they are such causes as perils of the seas, fire and similar matters, or causes due to human action, such as the acts or omissions of the master, whether negligent or not, or a combination of both kinds of cause.*'[307]

Common law: Summary

202. At common law the carrier will be responsible for all of the loss or damage if a cause of the loss or damage or merely some of the loss or damage was the non-fulfilment of a contractual duty. The carrier will not be allowed to invoke an exception or to disprove causal connection between the non-excepted peril and the damage.

4.6.2 H(V)R

203. Under the H(V)R the expression 'overriding obligation' is used in a different meaning than under common law. The meaning which follows from *Maxine Footwear* is that in the case of *competing* causes (i.e. the damage is a result of more than one cause and each of the causes could have caused all of the damage) the culpable cause will be deemed to be the only relevant and the carrier will therefore be liable.

204. In Carver 2005 it is said that the problem of damage caused by concurrent causes under the H(V)R should be solved as follows:

'The technique for solving such problems in English law depends on whether one of the causes is unseaworthiness. If it is, the overriding nature of Article

---
306. The Lilburn, (1940) 67 Ll.L.L.Rep. 253, 259.
307. The Lilburn, (1940) 67 Ll.L.L.Rep. 253, 259-260.

III.1, together with the fact that the excepted perils mostly do not apply where the carrier is negligent, has been held to create the result that the carrier must pay for the whole loss. If however one of the causes is the carrier's other main obligation, of properly and carefully caring for cargo under Art. III.2, this duty is expressly made subject to Art. IV, hence in principle the loss generated by each cause should be determined.'[308] (citations omitted, NJM)

205. The author of the quoted passage refers to *The Fiona* [1994] 2 Lloyd's Rep. 506 and to *The Christel Vinnen* [1924] P. 208, 241 and to *Smith Hogg & Co. Ltd. v. Black Sea & Baltic General Insurance Co. Ltd.* [1940] A.C. 997 as authorities for the statement that when one of the causes for damage is unseaworthiness, the carrier will be responsible for all the damage and will not be allowed to rely on one of the exceptions provided by art. IV. The last two cited cases are cases in which the common law applied and not the H(V)R. In *The Fiona* the question was whether art. IV(6) was the overriding obligation or art. III(1). I do not see how the cited authorities could lead to the statement that when one cause of damage is unseaworthiness the carrier will be liable for all the damages under the H(V)R. Although that is so under common law I do not think it should be so under the H(V)R.

206. If there is a concurrence[309] of negligence in the care for the cargo or the duty to exercise due diligence to make the ship seaworthy and an exception, then the carrier remains liable for the full extent of the damage unless he can prove which part of the damage was caused by an excepted cause. As was said above, the carrier will not be allowed to invoke an exception to escape from liability for the damage *caused by* the non-fulfilment of art. III(1).

4.6.2.1 *American law: Vallescura Rule*

207. This follows from the so-called *Vallescura Rule*.[310] The *Vallescura* judgement is a decision of the U.S. Supreme Court from 1934 under the Harter Act. The rule still applies under U.S. COGSA.[311] In the *Vallescura* it was held that:

> 'Similarly, the carrier must bear the entire loss where it appears that the injury to cargo is due either to sea peril *or negligent stowage*, or both, and he fails to show what damage is attributable to sea peril. (...) upon the evidence, it appears that some of the damage, in an amount not ascertainable, is due to sea peril. That does not remove the burden of showing facts relieving it from liability. If it remains liable for the whole amount of the damage because it is unable to

---

308. Carver 2005, p. 621-622.
309. By a concurrence of causes I mean the situation wherein more than one cause of damage exists and each of the causes caused part of the damage but neither of the causes could have caused all of the damage. In the terminology introduced in § 4.1: 'concurring causes'.
310. Schnell & Co. v. S.S. Vallescura, 293 U.S. 296.
311. See for example 306 F.2d 426 (2nd Cir.) in which it was said that 'Had libelant done this, we would have a parallel to Schnell v. The Vallescura, with one cause proved to be excepted and the other not, and the teaching of that case, which we assume to be applicable to COGSA in this respect, would then place upon respondents the burden of showing how much of the damages came from the excepted as distinguished from the unexcepted cause.'

show that sea peril was a cause of the loss, it must equally remain so if it cannot show what part of the loss is due to that cause.' (emphasis added, NJM)

208. See also the *Irish Spruce* case, in which it was said that:

'The law under the Carriage of Goods by Sea Act is clear that if both an "excepted peril" under s.1304 (2) (...) and unseaworthiness or another element described in (...) s. 1303(1), concur in causing cargo damage, the shipowner is liable for the entire loss unless he can exonerate himself from part of the liability by showing that some portion is attributable solely to the "excepted peril".'[312]

209. In Tetley's view the overriding obligation rule applies when damage is caused by a concurrence of a lack of due diligence for seaworthiness and an excepted cause. In such a case the carrier remains liable for the entire damage. However, if the damage is caused by a violation of art. III(2) and an excepted cause, then the *Vallescura* rule does apply because the concurrence is of two causes of equal weight.[313] I do not agree with this point of view. Under US COGSA no distinction is made between the duties concerning care of the cargo and seaworthiness. Also the doctrine of 'overriding obligations' is not a part of American law.[314]

4.6.2.2 *English law*

210. In the *Canadian Highlander*[315] case damage had been caused by negligence in the care for the cargo and by a nautical fault. Viscount Sumner considered that:

'... unless it be held that negligence merely in discharging cargo is negligence in the management of the ship, [which is clearly not the case; NJM] it is incumbent on the shipowner, on whom the whole burden of proving this defence falls, to show how much damage was done in the subsequent operations, because it is only in respect of them that he can claim protection.'[316]

211. The *Canadian Highlander* case shows that if damage is caused by the non-fulfilment of art. III(2) the carrier will still be allowed to prove that an excepted peril was the cause of a portion of the damage.

212. In *The Torenia* the shell plating of the vessel sprang a leak through some defect in her structure. The carrier pleaded that the loss was caused by one or more latent or other defects in the vessel's port side shell plating (...) not discoverable by due diligence and expressly relied on art. IV(2)(p) as well as art. IV(2)c.
The proof that the defect was a 'latent defect not discoverable by due diligence' was however, not given.

---

312. The Irish Spruce, [1976] 1 Lloyd's Rep. 63, 75-76.
313. Tetley 4th edition, ch. 15, p. 22: 'The rule with respect to due diligence [overriding obligation rule] is stricter because the conflict is not between two equal provisions (an exculpatory exception and care of cargo), but between an exculpatory exception and an overriding obligation (due diligence).'
314. See supra § 4.3.2.
315. Also known as 'Gosse Millerd'.
316. The Canadian Highlander, [1928] 32 Ll.L.Rep. 91 (HL).

213. Mr. Justice Hobhouse said:

> 'The question of the construction of art. IV, r. 2, which I have to consider is whether, where the carrier proves that the loss resulted from a peril of the sea and a defect in the ship, but does not go on to prove that the defect was a "latent defect not discoverable by due diligence", the carrier has proved a defence under r. 2.
> This question seems to me to admit of only one answer. *Where the facts disclose that the loss was caused by the concurrent causative effects of an excepted and a non-excepted peril, the carrier remains liable. He only escapes liability to the extent that he can prove that the loss or damage was caused by the excepted peril alone (e.g., Gosse Millerd Ltd. v. Canadian Government Merchant Marine Ltd., (1928) 32 Ll.L.Rep. 91; [1929] A.C. 223 at p. 98 and 241, per Viscount Sumner). Here the carrier has proved, as concurrent causes, perils of the sea (an excepted peril under par. (c)) and a defect (ex-hypothesis not a latent defect) which is not an excepted peril as it does not satisfy the criteria of par. (p).* I see nothing in the drafting of r. 2 which would justify one in concluding that the carrier is nevertheless relieved of liability.'[317] (emphasis added, NJM)

214. The latent defect which is not an excepted peril must be qualified as unseaworthiness as a result of non-fulfilment of art. III(1). The use of the general words "non-excepted peril" are an indication that the *Gosse Millerd* rule can also apply if a portion of damage was a cause of the non-fulfilment of art. III(1). The fact that the non-excepted peril was in fact non-fulfilment of art. III(1) makes it clear that in *The Torenia* case the rule accepted that a carrier is allowed to prove which part of the damage was not caused by non-fulfilment of the overriding obligation contained in art. III(1). This rule follows indirectly from the *Maxine Footwear* case.[318] As was said above, the carrier will not be allowed to invoke the provisions of art. IV to escape liability for damage *caused by* non-fulfilment of art. III(1). The requirement of causal connection between the non-fulfilment of art. III(1) and the damage indicates that if there is no causal connection the carrier may prove for which portion he is not responsible.

215. English case law shows that the overriding obligation rule and the English version of the *Vallescura Rule* co-exist. The overriding obligation rule follows from the aforementioned *Maxine Footwear*. The English version of the Vallescura Rule follows from *Gosse Millerd*[319] (which judgement was rendered well before Maxine Footwear) and *The Torenia*[320] (rendered some time after Maxine Footwear). Damage as a consequence of a failure to fulfil the duty contained in either art III(1) (*The Torenia*) or art III(2) (*Gosse Millerd*) will be attributed to the carrier. If the carrier can demonstrate which part of the damage was caused by a non-culpable occurrence when a culpable and a non-culpable cause of damage concur, he will not be liable for that part of the damage under English law.[321]

---

317. The Torenia, [1983] 2 Lloyd's Rep. 210, 218-219.
318. See supra § 4.3.2.
319. Gosse Millerd, [1928] 32 Ll.L.Rep. 91.
320. The Torenia, [1983] 2 Lloyd's Rep. 210.
321. This is different under Dutch law. For from *Quo Vadis* (SCN 11 June 1993, NJ 1993, 123) it follows that when there are two possible causes of damage, the culpable cause is considered to be the legally relevant cause. The carrier is not given the opportunity to prove for which part of the damage he is not liable. As was discussed above, this was the rule at common law, but is incorrect under the Hague Rules.

4.7 Why is art. III(2) not also considered an overriding obligation under English law?

216. The question arises why the obligation to use due diligence to make the ship seaworthy is an overriding obligation and the duty to care for the cargo properly and carefully is not. As was seen above in the early days the carrier was strictly liable for the goods as a bailee. Later the view was developed that the carrier had two overriding obligations: care for the cargo and the duty to furnish a seaworthy ship. At common law the duty of the carrier to provide a seaworthy ship is an absolute duty of the carrier. Even if the unseaworthiness was not discoverable by due diligence the carrier would still be liable.[322] Then, under the Hague Rules, the duty regarding seaworthiness was reduced to a duty to exercise due diligence to make the ship seaworthy.[323] The view was developed that the duty to provide a seaworthy ship is overriding and the duty regarding care for the cargo is not. In 1963 an article on seaworthiness was published by Zaphiriou explaining that:

> '[d]uring the last seventy years legislatures, courts and international conferences have tried to strike and maintain a balance between the paramount duty to protect the public (crews, passengers and cargo-owners) and rendering justice to the shipowners. The protection of the public demands ideal standards and an absolute guarantee of safety, while justice to shipowners is based on the realisation of a number of technical and commercial realities that call for relativity. A ship is a complex instrument with potentially hidden defects, some of which are undiscoverable by reasonable human care. The maintenance, repair and inspection of the ship are delegated to experts and qualified registered surveyors and are largely carried out while a ship is in port or in dry-dock. Constantly improving scientific methods of detection minimise the existence of latent defects, though the use of such methods may sometimes involve a commercially unreasonable loss of time or expenditure. All the facets of this problem are reflected in a number of recent English decisions which deal with unseaworthiness.'[324]

217. Von Ziegler cites Zaphiriou and writes that in international trade, involving carriage of goods by sea, the ship is the centre point. All interested parties have to be able to rely on the soundness of the ship. This applies for the parties involved in shipping (owners, the bank, the insurers of the ship and the insurers of the cargo) and for the general public and its interest in an intact environment. Theoretically these interests should lead to an absolute seaworthiness and fitness of the ship which demands that all safety measures shall be taken. A modern ship should be absolutely seaworthy and able to endure the strains of the sea, salt water and the cargo it is carrying.[325]

It seems that the view of Zaphiriou and in particular the view of Von Ziegler is that the duty to exercise due diligence to make the ship seaworthy is also in the public interest and therefore a more important duty than the duty regarding the treatment of the cargo. For that reason the duty regarding seaworthiness is an overriding obligation un-

---

322. See supra § 3.5.1.
323. See supra § 3.5.2.
324. Zaphiriou 1963, p. 221.
325. Von Ziegler 2002, p. 78.

der the English law regarding the Hague Rules and the duty regarding treatment of the cargo is not.

I have not encountered this point of view in case law nor in the Travaux Préparatoires. I also doubt if this was actual reason why the concept of an overriding obligation of seaworthiness was created under the Hague Rules in *Maxine Footwear*.[326] If e.g. the aspect of seaworthiness regarding the cargoworthiness of the vessel is considered it is difficult to see how this could effect the environment or safety of the public. E.g. if certain cargo was loaded into dirty tanks causing contamination of the cargo it would be a fault due to the ship being uncargoworthy and so a breach of the overriding obligation ex art. III(1) H(V)R. How is this different from improper stowing causing cargo damage due to rough weather? The argument heard in practice is that a shipowner is an expert on ships and not an expert on cargo. For that reason the carrier can contract out of loading and stowing the cargo.[327] On the other hand the duty to exercise due diligence to make the ship seaworthy is an overriding obligation and a non-delegable duty. There is indeed something to say for this point of view. On the other hand it can also be said that the essence of the contract of carriage is to transport the cargo and deliver it in the same condition as it was received by the carrier. In my view both duties should be considered overriding. However, it must be concluded that under English law the duty to exercise due diligence to make the ship seaworthy is more important than the duty regarding the cargo (ex art. III(2)) and therefore the duty to exercise due diligence is an overriding obligation. This may be a result of the common law view that the duty to make the ship seaworthy is an absolute duty meaning that the carrier will be liable for damage caused by unseaworthiness even if the unseaworthiness was not discoverable by due diligence.[328]

4.8 The intended construction of the relationship between the duties and the exceptions

218. The framers of the Hague Rules intended art. III(1) to be an overriding obligation and art. III(2) to be subject to the provisions of article IV. This follows from the objective rule of construction that the meaning of the text should prevail if it is clear. This means that if the damage is caused by lack of due diligence to make the ship seaworthy the carrier will be liable for that damage which was caused by the lack of due diligence to make the ship seaworthy. However, if the damage is caused by non-fulfilment of the duties contained in art. III(2), the carrier will be allowed to avail himself of the provisions of art. IV. To understand the intended construction of the Rules the Rules should be read as a whole.[329] Art. IV(1) requires causal connection between the failure to fulfil the duty contained in art. III(1) and the damage. This means that if damage was caused by non-fulfilment of art. II(1) the carrier will not be allowed to invoke the provisions of art. IV.

219. He will however be able to escape liability for a portion of the damage if he can prove which portion of the damage was caused by an excepted peril.

---

326. The reason of public interest is not given in that judgement.
327. See supra § 3.9.
328. See supra § 3.5.1.
329. See supra § 2.6.

4.8 INTENDED CONSTRUCTION OF RELATIONSHIP BETWEEN DUTIES AND EXCEPTIONS

The text of the Rules says nothing about the requirement of causal connection between non-fulfilment of art. III(2) and the damage. However, common sense dictates that causal connection between non-fulfilment or art. III(2) and damage to the goods is required to render the carrier liable.[330] In case of damage caused by non-fulfilment of the duty contained in art. III(2) the carrier can either prove that the damage or part of it was not caused by the non-fulfilment of the duties contained in art. III(1) en (2), or invoke an exception (a provision of article 4).

---

330. In § 5.1 it is made clear that art. IV(1) was included in the Rules to remove the effect of *The Isis* case (rendered under the Harter Act). That decision caused the carrier to be liable if he could not prove that due diligence had been exercised to make the ship seaworthy, even if there was no causal connection between the unseaworthiness and the damage.

Chapter 5
Art. IV(1) and some of the exceptions of art. IV(2) H(V)R

5.1 Art. IV(1): loss or damage due to unseaworthiness

5.1.1 Introduction

220. Art. IV(1) provides that

> '[n]either the carrier nor the ship shall be liable for loss or damage arising or resulting from unseaworthiness unless caused by want of due diligence on the part of the carrier to make the ship seaworthy, and to secure that the ship is properly manned, equipped and supplied, and to make the holds, refrigerating and cool chambers and all other parts of the ship in which goods are carried fit and safe for their reception, carriage and preservation in accordance with the provisions of paragraph 1 of Article III. Whenever loss or damage has resulted from unseaworthiness the burden of proving the exercise of due diligence shall be on the carrier or other person claiming exemption under this article.'

221. Under English law the purpose of art. IV(1) is to divide the burden of proof in case of damage caused by unseaworthiness. The meaning of or reason for art. IV(1) is, however, unclear. Is it meant as merely a division of the burden of proof in cases concerning loss or damage caused by unseaworthiness or is it also meant as an exemption from liability for loss or damage caused by unseaworthiness? This is the primary question which will be discussed below (§ 5.1.2).

222. If the provision is treated as an exemption from liability then only unseaworthiness not due to a lack of due diligence to provide a seaworthy ship will exempt the carrier from liability. The carrier will therefore have to prove that before and at the beginning of the voyage due diligence was exercised to make the ship seaworthy. This becomes clear from the reference to article III(1) in article IV(1). Article III(1) provides that the carrier shall be bound 'before and at the beginning of the voyage' to exercise due diligence to make the ship seaworthy. This makes it clear that the period to exercise due diligence is restricted to the period before and at the beginning of the voyage.[331] The unanimous decision of the CMI sous committee of 21 October 1922 also made this clear. The committee decided that the obligation to use due diligence to make the ship seaworthy is restricted to the period before and at the beginning of the voyage.[332]

---

331. See also Carver 2005, p. 603 where it is noted that this seems to be assumed by the Court of Appeal in Leesh River Tea Co. Ltd v. British India S.N. Co. Ltd [1966] 1 Lloyd's Rep. 450, 457 and Scrutton 1996, p. 441.
332. Travaux Préparatoires, p. 367.

5.1.2 Is art. IV(1) an exception from liability or merely a division of the burden of proof?

5.1.2.1 *English law*

223. Under English law art. IV(1) only protects against latent defects of the ship.[333] At common law the only event which falls under unseaworthiness is unseaworthiness existing before or at the time of sailing. The warranty of seaworthiness is not a continuing warranty, in the sense of a warranty that the vessel shall continue fit during the voyage.[334] If a ship becomes unseaworthy after leaving port art. IV(1) will not be a defence against a claim for cargo damage under English law and the H(V)R. As McNair J. said:

> 'If you get seawater coming into a ship which was initially seaworthy, it does not come in as a result of unseaworthiness, but as a result of perils of the sea.'[335]

224. In *The Leesh River* case due diligence was exercised before the ship departed Calcutta. When the ship was discharging and loading cargo at Port Sudan stevedores stole a storm valve cover plate. After departure from Port Sudan cargo was damaged because seawater could enter through the storm valve. As to the application of art. IV(1) McNair J. said:

> 'The defendants, upon whom the burden lies of bringing themselves within the exceptions contained in Art. IV, first relied upon Art IV, r. 1, set out above, dealing with unseaworthiness. Though it was agreed that the vessel became unseaworthy at Port Sudan when the cover plate was removed and that the ship's officers were not negligent in failing to ascertain that the cover plate had been removed, I have formed the clear opinion, and so hold, that Art. IV, r. 1, only applies to the obligation to exercise due diligence to secure initial seaworthiness "before and at the beginning of the voyage." See the words "in accordance with the provisions of paragraph 1 of Article III" which occur at the end of the first sentence of Art. IV, r. 1. Except that by the rules the absolute obligation to secure seaworthiness at this stage is altered to an obligation to exercise due diligence to secure seaworthiness, the rules do not, so far as is material for present purposes, alter the position as it existed before the Act at common law. In my judgement, this point fails.'[336]

225. On appeal this construction of art. IV(1) was followed.[337]

---

333. See per Lord Wright in Smith, Hogg & Co., Ltd v. Black Sea & Baltic General Insurance Co., Ltd., 67 Ll.L.L.Rep. 253, 257: 'Hence the qualified exception of unseaworthiness does not protect the ship-owner. In effect, such an exception can only excuse against latent defects.'
334. Mcfadden v. Blue Star Line [1905] KB 697.
335. [1966] 1 Lloyd's Rep. 450, 454 (Leesh River Tea Company Ltd., and others v. British India Steam Navigation Company Ltd., The 'Chyebassa').
336. Leesh River Tea Company, Ltd., and others v. British India Steam Navigation Company, Ltd. (The 'Chyebassa'), [1966] 1 Lloyd's Rep. 450, 457 affirmed by the Court of Appeal [1966] 2 Lloyd's Rep. 193.
337. [1966] 2 Lloyd's Rep. 193, 198.

226. This judgement illustrates that under English law the exception provided by art. IV(1) only applies to circumstances that could not be discovered by exercising due diligence before and at the beginning of the voyage. The exception does not apply to unseaworthiness arising after the voyage commenced. It has been said that the reasons for this construction are unclear.[338] Especially the reference to the 'position as it existed before the Act at common law' is hard to place. Did McNair mean by the 'position as it existed at common law' the 'absolute obligation to secure seaworthiness at this stage'? If that was meant then McNair seems to be saying that the absolute obligation (under the Rules mitigated to 'due diligence') still exists under the Rules. This would mean that, in McNair's view, the carrier would be bound to exercise due diligence before every stage of the journey. This, however, would be contrary to the earlier decision of Mr. Justice Hewson in The Makedonia where it was established that the doctrine of stages no longer exists under the Rules.[339] Probably the reason for this construction is that actual unseaworthiness occurring after the beginning of the voyage is not qualified as unseaworthiness under English law because the carrier only needs to exercise due diligence for seaworthiness before and at the beginning of the voyage.

227. Under English law art. IV(1) does play a role in the division of the burden of proof. Carver[340], Scrutton[341] and Cooke[342] refer to the division of the burden of proof in *Minister of Food v. Reardon Smith Line*[343] and consider that division to be applicable to art. IV(1) even though that case concerned the nautical fault exception (art. IV(2)a). The division of the burden of proof was as follows:
1. The cargo interest proves *prima facie* damage.
2. The carrier proves that the damage was caused by an excepted peril.
3. The cargo interest proves that the damage was caused by unseaworthiness.
4. The carrier now has to prove that he exercised due diligence to make the ship seaworthy.

228. Regarding the second sentence of art. IV(1) McNair J. said:

> 'Furthermore, it seems to me that if one treats the matter purely as a matter of contract, the second sentence in Art. IV, Rule 1, strongly supports the submission made on behalf of the ship that no onus as to seaworthiness is cast on the ship-owner, except after proof has been given by the other party that the damage has resulted from unseaworthiness.'[344]

229. It has also been said that under English law art. IV(1) is there to emphasise the overriding obligation of art. III(1).[345]

---

338. See also Clarke 1976, p. 151 and 155.
339. See infra § 3.2.
340. Carver 1982, 377.
341. Scrutton 1996, p. 442.
342. Cooke et al, 2007, p. 1017.
343. *Minister of Food v. Reardon Smith Line*, [1951] 2 Lloyd's Rep., 265.
344. *Minister of Food v. Reardon Smith Line*, [1951] 2 Lloyd's Rep., 265, 272.
345. See chapter 4.

5.1.2.2 *Dutch law*

230. According to Royer and Cleveringa art. IV(1) is an exception that the carrier can invoke to escape liability.[346] On the other hand Boonk does not consider art. IV(1) as a separate exception but as a result of the duties contained in art. III(1). Unseaworthiness can occur even if due diligence was exercised in accordance with art. III(1). Art. IV(1) makes clear that the carrier will not be responsible for such unseaworthiness. Boonk does however remark that if the unseaworthiness occurred during the voyage then art. IV(1) will be a 'real exemption'.[347] Boonk restricts the application of art. IV(1) as an exemption to unseaworthiness that occurred during the voyage.
In a number of recent decisions it has also been recognised that art. IV(1) can be relied upon as an exemption from liability.[348] It is clear that under Dutch law art. IV(1) is considered to be an exemption from liability. The carrier can use unseaworthiness as a defence as long as he can prove that he used due diligence to make the ship seaworthy. Von Ziegler concludes that this is the continental European application of art. IV(1).[349]

231. In the *Singapore Jaya* the District Court of Rotterdam ruled that the ship was unseaworthy at the beginning of the voyage. Referring to Rule IV(1) the court ruled that the carrier had to prove that due diligence had been exercised to make the ship seaworthy.[350] In the *Barentzgracht* the court of appeal ordered cargo interests to prove that the ship was unseaworthy and the carrier was given the burden of proving due diligence.[351] The Hague Court of Appeal ruled that the carrier had to prove that damage was caused by unseaworthiness and that the carrier had exercised due diligence to make the ship seaworthy.[352]
In the *Hea* the ships engine failed, forcing the ship to deviate. Expenses were incurred for repairs. The cargo interests refused to pay the carrier's general average claim on the grounds that the ship was unseaworthy due to lack of due diligence. This was refuted by the carrier who could state facts showing that due diligence was exercised. The Amsterdam District Court then ordered the cargo interest to disprove the carrier's proof of due diligence.[353]

5.1.2.3 *U.S. law*

232. The division of the burden of proof must have been unclear at the time of the framing of the Hague Rules because, under the ancestor of the Hague Rules, the Harter Act[354], the carrier had to prove due diligence before he could invoke an exception, even if there was no causal connection between the unseaworthiness and the exception.[355]

---

346. Royer 1959, p. 401 and Cleveringa 1961, p. 453.
347. Boonk 1993, p. 215.
348. Arbitral decision, 25 July 2005, S&S 2006, 77 (Frio Espana), District Court Rotterdam 25 October 2001, S&S 2004, 106 (Oasis), District Court Amsterdam 5 February 2003, S&S 2003, 87 (Pauwgracht).
349. Von Ziegler 2000, p. 217.
350. Rotterdam District Court 23 May 1996, S&S 1998, 105 (Singapore Jaya).
351. Amsterdam Court of Appeal 18 February 1999, S&S 1999, 106 (Barentzgracht).
352. The Hague Court of Appeal 23 November 1999, S&S 2000, 107 (Bothniaborg).
353. Amsterdam District Court 8 January 2003, S&S 2003, 76 (Hea).
354. 46 U.S.C. App. § 190 etc.
355. The Isis, 290 U.S. 333.

The U.S. Supreme Court called the provision of a seaworthy ship 'a condition of exemption' under the Harter Act.

Art. IV(1) was introduced to make it clear that under the Hague Rules it is no longer required to prove due diligence before an exception can be relied upon. In *Damodar Bulk Carriers* the 9th Circuit explained that the history of the provision made it clear that art. IV(1) was meant as a division of the burden of proof:

> '[w]hen Congress considered the legislation that became COGSA from 1923 to its eventual enactment in 1936, it exhaustively questioned persons who had served as members of the American delegation to the European conventions that led to the promulgation of the Hague Rules at the Brussels Convention of 1924. To a man, these experts testified year after year that the provision that became 46 U.S.C.App. § 1304 was intended to change the existing law under the Harter Act, 46 U.S.C.App. § 190-95 (Supp. V 1987), to make it more favorable to shipowners. Indeed, the change contemplated and eventually enacted was the *only* benefit carriers received under COGSA that was a change from existing law.
>
> In the first hearing on COGSA, Mr. Norman Beecher, the special admiralty counsel of the United States Shipping Board and a United States representative to the Brussels Conventions of 1922 and 1923, testified to this effect:
>
> 'This section [§ 1304] constitutes a modification of the Harter Act, in that it does not make it a condition precedent to the carrier receiving the benefit of these exceptions that he shall have exercised due diligence to make the ship in all respects seaworthy-properly manned, equipped, and so forth.'[356]

5.1.2.4 *The intended construction of rule IV(1)*

233. The textual construction of art. IV(1) does indicate that it is an exoneration from liability. This however does not make sense. Reading art. IV(1) with art. III(1) shows that the carrier is only bound to exercise due diligence before and at the beginning of the voyage. He would not be responsible for unseaworthiness which did not result from lack of due diligence even without art. IV(1). As the objective construction leads to an unlikely result I shall apply the rule of subjective construction. What did the framers mean when they conceived art. IV(1)? Using legislative history of the U.S. COGSA as an aid to subjective construction it becomes clear that the intention of the framers was to change the law as it existed under the Harter Act. Since *The Isis* decision which was rendered under that Act the carrier had to prove that he had exercised due diligence before he could invoke an exception. No causal connection between lack of due diligence and damage was required. To change this law art. IV(1) was added as a division of the burden of proof and not as an exception. Art. IV (1) makes it clear that the carrier does not have to prove due diligence before he is allowed to invoke an exception. He will only have to prove due diligence if the loss or damage is caused by unseaworthiness. Indeed, a separate exception for unseaworthiness not caused by a lack of due diligence is unnecessary because of the existence of the q-clause.[357]

---

356. Damodar Bulk Carriers, 903 F.2d 675, 684.
357. See infra § 5.5.

5.2 The 'nautical fault' exception[358]

5.2.1 Introduction

234. The 'nautical fault'[359] exception is the first of 17 exceptions provided by art. IV(2). The exception provides:

Neither the carrier nor the ship shall be responsible for loss or damage arising or resulting from:
a. Act, neglect, or default of the master, mariner, pilot or the servants of the carrier in the navigation or in the management of the ship;

235. This is the carrier's major exception[360] and also one of the most controversial exceptions[361] of the Hague (Visby) Rules. The following questions will be discussed in this paragraph:

1. What is 'navigation of the ship'?
2. What is 'management of the ship'?

236. These questions have been discussed in a number of cases.[362] Because of the history of the exception early English and U.S. judgements from before the Harter Act are also relevant for the construction of the exception. Before the Harter Act came into force the exemption clause excusing the carrier for loss or damage caused by errors in the navigation of the ship was used on bills of lading. That clause was adapted by the Liverpool Steamship Owner's Association in 1885 to also exclude liability for damage caused by acts or faults in the management of the ship. Eight years later this exception was included in the Harter Act.[363]

5.2.2 What is meant by 'navigation of the ship'?

237. At the end of the nineteenth century and the beginning of the twentieth there was some discussion about the meaning of this expression.[364] In some pre-Hague Rules cases the meaning was sometimes extended under differently worded exceptions, and in other contexts, particularly insurance, to matters connected with loading and unloading. For that reason Carver considers such cases of little value where the Rules apply.[365] An exception is the *Canada Shipping* in which Bowen L.J. held:

---

358. See Hendrikse & Margetson 2005a for an earlier version of this chapter.
359. As Boonk correctly remarks the expression 'nautical fault' which is used in practice is strictly speaking not correct. All damage due to management of the ship is covered by the exception. A fault is not required (Boonk 1993, p. 172). I shall however use the expression in this chapter because it is convenient.
360. Carver 2005, p. 605, Tetley 1988, p. 397.
361. See e.g. Hare 1999, p. 630 and Aikens et al 2006, p. 270.
362. See infra.
363. See Royer 1959, p. 460.
364. See e.g. The Ferro, [1893] P. 38 and The Glenochil, [1896] P. 10 and The Renée Hyaffil, (1916) 32 T.L.R. 660.
365. Carver 2005, p. 605.

'Navigation must mean something having to do with the sailing of the ship; that is, of course the sailing of the ship having regard to the fact that she is a cargo-carrying ship.'[366]

238. Navigation involves decisions taken at sea, but can also involve decisions taken in port.[367] The aspects of navigation meant in the nautical fault exception concern acts of navigation taken on board the vessel relying on the exception.[368] The word 'navigation' refers to the maritime aspects of navigation and not commercial, economic or legal aspects of the management of the ship.[369] So, if for example, the captain misinterprets the contract of carriage and sails to the wrong port the exception will not apply because the error is not an act of navigation in the sense of the exception.

239. It is not always easy to distinguish between 'navigation' in the sense of the exception and 'navigation' which is related to economic aspects of the management of the ship. It used to be thought that the period in which the exception applies was restricted by time.[370] The period wherein the exception applied was from the moment of departure until the moment of arrival, unless the ship was to depart to a following port after arrival. In other words: the period was the moment of departure from the first port until the moment of arrival at the last port. This would however mean that an error in navigation (e.g. the calculation of an incorrect course) made before departure from the first port, would not be considered an error in the navigation of the ship in the sense of the nautical fault exception. In *The Hill Harmony* the House of Lords however decided that such a restriction of the period of application was not correct, or at least too broadly or confusingly stated, because the moment at which an error in navigation is made is not relevant for the sort of error and for the consequences of the error.

240. Lord Bingham of Cornhill said:

'In Lord (Owners of the Steamship) v. Newsum Sons and Co. Ltd., (1920) 2 Ll.L.Rep. 276; [1920] 1 K.B. 846 the dispute was between owner and charterer. The master had decided to remain in port for some time, despite advice to continue the voyage by a prescribed route. Mr. Justice Bailhache held that the master's deliberate choice, while in harbour, of one or two routes to be pursued could not be an error in the management or navigation of the ship within the meaning of an exception in the charter-party. While the Judge, in my opinion, erred in his formulation of principle, I would not question his conclusion. The decision is inconsistent with the view that the choice of route from one port to another is a navigational matter within the sole discretion of the master.'[371]

241. And Lord Hobhouse of Westborough:

---

366. Canada Shipping Co. v. British Shipowners' Mutual Protection Assn. (1889) 23 Q.B.D. 342, 344.
367. The Hill Harmony, [2001] 1 Lloyd's Rep. 147. See also Carver 2005, p. 605 and Gaskell 2000, p. 278.
368. If a fault in the navigation of a ship causes cargo damage on board another ship that other ship can rely on the perils of the sea exception (art. IV(2)c H(V)R). See e.g. The Xantho, (1887) 12 A.C. 503. See also Cooke e.a. 2007, p. 1022.
369. The Hill Harmony, [2001] 1 Lloyd's Rep. 147.
370. The Carron Park, (1890) 15 P.D. 203 and The Accomac, (1890) 15 P.D. 208. See also Cooke et al 2007, p. 1022.
371. The Hill Harmony, [2001] 1 Lloyd's Rep. 147, 151.

> 'In Lord v. Newsum, the vessel was under a six month time charter made in 1916. She was ordered on a laden voyage to Archangel but had to abandon the voyage because the master chose to proceed by a route close to the coast of Norway and was held up by the presence of German submarines. If he had proceeded by a route further from the coast, as prescribed by the British Admiralty and by the Norwegian war risk insurers, she would have been able to complete the voyage. The owners were held liable under the "utmost despatch" clause. The "navigation and management" clause was held to provide no defence. Mr. Justice Bailhache said at p. 279; p. 849:
> "The decision was no doubt correct but the reasoning is certainly confusing. The character of the decision cannot be determined by where the decision is made. A master, while his vessel is still at the berth, may, on the one hand, decide whether he needs the assistance of a tug to execute a manoeuvre while leaving or whether the vessel's draft will permit safe departure on a certain state of the tide and, on the other hand, what ocean route is consistent with his owners' obligation to execute the coming voyage with the utmost despatch. The former come within the exception; the latter does not. Where the decision is made does not alter either conclusion."'[372]

242. In the Dutch *Poeldijk* case the captain was criticised because he should have slowed down and changed course sooner and the change of course should have been more pronounced. The court of appeal decided that these errors of navigation were not errors in the sense of the exception because if the error had not been made only part of the cargo damage would have been prevented.[373]
In this judgement the word 'navigation' in the exception has the same meaning as it does in ordinary speech. Navigation means conducting the ship from one position to another along to the safest, fastest and most economical route according to the techniques of theoretical and practical seamanship.[374] During such navigation cargo damage may occur due to the ships motion. Safe navigation does not mean a guarantee against cargo damage. Such damage can be prevented by taking account of the obligation contained in art. III(2). If the cargo was treated in accordance with art. III(2) and damage still occurred due to the ships motion then the carrier can invoke the perils of the sea exception provided by art. IV(2)c.[375]

243. In 1959 Royer wrote that 'navigation' entails acts at sea and 'management' entails acts at sea and in port.[376] According to Royer this distinction should be taken into account when construing the words 'management' and 'navigation'. As was seen above the *Hill Harmony* decision has rendered this point of view out of date.
Royer is of the opinion that it is difficult to define the words 'navigation' and 'management' and that it is better to give examples of acts of navigation to get an idea of the

---

372. The Hill Harmony, [2001] 1 Lloyd's Rep. 147, 159.
373. Poeldijk, The Hague Court of Appeal 3 October 1980, S&S 1981, 1.
374. Rough translation from J. van Beylen et al, Maritieme Encyclopedie, Bussem: Uitgeverij C. de Boer Jr. 1972.
375. See § 5.4. Tetley seems to be of the same opinion. He writes: 'On occasion a master will force his ship through a storm, instead of heading at slow speed into the wind, with the result that the cargo is damaged. This is really an error in the management of the cargo because the master has disregarded possible damage to cargo in favour of arriving in port a day or two early (Tetley 1988, p. 402).
376. Royer 1959, p. 483-485.

meaning.[377] By doing so the word 'management' will need no definition because that word will entail all nautical acts which can not be qualified as 'navigation'.
Royer gives the following examples of errors in the navigation of the ship:
- neglecting to run into a port to repair damage to the engines;
- the commencement of a voyage regardless of forecasted storms;
- neglecting to employ a pilot where a pilot it is obligatory to employ one or where one is required;
- neglecting to keep the charts up to date;
- the incorrect choice of an anchorage;
- grounding and collision which is not due to unseaworthiness;
- errors made in the art of steering and or manoeuvring the ship.[378]

244. Blussé van Oud Alblas defines the word as 'acts concerning seamanship in the strict sense of the word.' He gives similar examples to those mentioned by Royer.[379]

245. Royer's conclusion is that an error in 'navigation' can roughly be said to mean a shortcoming on the bridge of the ship in the navigation of the ship and that an error in the management of the ship is an error made in another part of the ship.[380] Cleveringa defines a navigation error as a shortcoming in the art of pilotage and mentions the following examples:
- decisions and acts of pilotage;
- neglecting to take a radio bearing;
- neglecting to consult the available charts.[381]

246. Stevens correctly concludes that there is little doubt about the meaning of the word.[382]
The meaning of the word 'navigation' in the exception is comparable to the meaning of the word in everyday speech. 'Navigation' means the art to sail a ship safely from a known position to the required position along a predetermined route.

5.2.3 What is meant by 'management of the ship'?

247. The construction of the word 'management' has led to many disputes and the use of such a vague expression in the Hague (Visby) Rules has generated a lot of criticism.[383]
Pre Hague Rules judgements are also relevant for the interpretation of the expres-

---

377. Royer uses the Dutch translation of the words 'navigation' and 'management'.
378. Royer 1959, p. 484.
379. Blussé van Oud Alblas 1929, p. 155.
380. Royer 1959, p. 485.
381. Cleveringa 1961, p. 490.
382. Stevens 2001, p. 221.
383. For example Royer 1959, p. 463-464. Blussé van Oud Alblas 1929, p. 153: 'It is not in keeping with the requirements of a national statute, let alone an international convention, to use an expression like this one. Where that expression has led to uncertain judgements the convention has assisted to create unwanted uncertainty.'.

sion.³⁸⁴ In *The Glenochil*, a decision rendered under the Harter Act, the Divisional Court held that damage caused by negligent ballasting was an error in the management of the ship and that the operation of the exception as to 'management' was not limited to the period during which the vessel was at sea, but extended to the period during which the cargo was being discharged.³⁸⁵ Tetley defines an error in the management of the ship in conjunction with an error in the navigation of the ship as 'an erroneous act or omission, the original purpose of which was primarily directed towards the ship, her safety and well-being and towards the common venture generally.'³⁸⁶

248. It is important to distinguish management of the ship from care of the cargo. An error made in the care of the cargo will cause the carrier to be liable for the damage caused by that error because it is a breach of the duty contained in art. III(2) which is not covered by the nautical fault exception.

249. In his dissenting judgement in the *Canadian Highlander* case which was approved in the House of Lords³⁸⁷ Lord Justice Greer correctly summarised the meaning of the expression as follows:

> '..., if the cause of the damage is solely, or even primarily, a neglect to take reasonable care of the cargo, the ship is liable, but if the cause of the damage is a neglect to take reasonable care of the ship, *or some part of it*, as distinct from the cargo, the ship is relieved from liability; but if the negligence is not negligence towards the ship, but only negligent failure to use the apparatus of the ship for the protection of the cargo, the ship is not so relieved.'³⁸⁸ (emphasis added, NJM)

250. In the House of Lords Viscount Sumner said:

> 'If the navigation is of the entire ship, so must the management be. Of course, in both cases alike some one and perhaps very subordinate part of the ship or its equipment may be the object which is immediately dealt with negligently, but neglect in regard to that object must still be neglect in the management of the ship, if it is to avail the ship-owner as a defence. (...) There is no evidence that an amount of water entered that would have done any harm to an empty hold or to the ship as a ship. Water sufficient when soaked into the wood of the boxes to rust the tinplates in the course of a voyage through the tropics, might well have been harmless if it merely ran into the bilges. There is neither fact nor finding to the contrary. *I think it quite plain that the particular use of the tarpau-*

---

384. Carver 2005, p. 609. See also Cooke e.a. 2007, p. 1023 where it is remarked that judgements from the period before the Hague Rules regarding the word 'mangement' still apply. On the other hand judgements concerning the word 'navigation' do not still apply, because that word is used in different contexts. The authors of Cooke e.a. refer to the Canadian Highlander case (see above) to add weight to this point of view.
385. The Glenochil. [1896] P. 10.
386. Tetley 1988, p. 398.
387. Gosse Millard Ltd. v. Canadian Government Merchant Marine Ltd. (The Canadian Highlander), 32 LL.L.L.R 91. In the House of Lords report the name is spelt 'Millerd' whereas in the lower courts it is spelt 'Millard'.
388. Gosse Millard Ltd. v. Canadian Government Merchant Marine Ltd. (The Canadian Highlander), 29 LL.L.L.R 190.

lin, which was neglected, was a precaution solely in the interest of the cargo. While the ship's work was going on these special precautions were required as cargo operations. They were no part of the operations of shifting the liner of the tail shaft or of scraping the 'tween decks'.[389] (emphasis added, NJM)

251. Tetley remarks that '[i]f both ship and cargo have been affected by the same error then the carrier is usually exculpated, because the whole venture is implicated, but each case must be decided on its own facts.'[390] He writes that the House of Lords upheld Greer L.J. in the *Canadian Highlander* case, declaring the error was in management of the cargo because the act, although made by persons directing their attention to the ship, was one which affected cargo alone.[391] This point of view can indeed be derived from the above quoted passage of Sumner's speech. Another test can also be derived from that passage. The so called 'primary purpose test' which is discussed below. The purpose of the tarpaulin was solely (and so *primarily*) for the protection of the cargo. Neglecting to use the tarpaulin caused the damage to the cargo. The neglect was therefore an error in the management of the cargo, and not of the ship. Therefore the carrier cannot rely on the nautical fault exception.

252. Carver cites a number of cases from which the following examples of 'management' are derived. In *The Hector* negligent failure to use locking bars on board to secure tarpaulins in rough conditions.[392] In that case the failure to use locking bars before the beginning of the voyage was not considered to be a breach of the duty to use due diligence to make the ship seaworthy. McNair said:

> 'I am satisfied that this forecast in these waters indicated a prospect of improving weather conditions, and that prudent seamanship did not require on that forecast that locking bars should be fitted in position on leaving Melbourne, even though this involved a winter voyage across the Australian Bight, in which, according to the master of the *Hector*, conditions may be expected to change very quickly. Though the Australian Bight has a bad reputation, the voyage to Fremantle traverses a part of the Australian Bight which was just within the permanent summer zone under the Load Line Rules.
> I therefore hold that there was no lack of due diligence in this respect.'[393]

253. Other examples are the negligent taking in of fresh water[394] and negligent control of a refrigeration apparatus which cooled not only the cargo but also other chambers in the ship.[395]
Theft of ship's parts or of goods by employees of stevedores unloading the ship is not covered by the exception.[396] Regarding this point Mr. Justice McNair said:

---

389. Gosse Millard Ltd. v. Canadian Government Merchant Marine Ltd. (The Canadian Highlander), 32 Ll.L.L.R 91.
390. Tetley 1988, p. 398.
391. Tetely 1988, p. 399.
392. International Packers London Ltd v. Ocean SS Co. Ltd (The Hector), [1955] 2 Lloyd's Rep. 218.
393. Ibid.
394. Minnesota Mining and Manufacturing (Australia) Pty Ltd. v. Ship Novoaltaisk (1972) 2 N.S.W.L.R. 476.
395. Rowson v. Atlantic Transport Co. Ltd., [1903] K.B. 666 (A case governed by the Harter Act.).
396. Hourani v. T. & J. Harrison [1927] 28 Ll.L.L.Rep. and Leesh River Tea Co. Ltd v. British India S.N. Co. Ltd., [1966] 1 Lloyd's Rep. 450.

'Admittedly, the felonious act of the stevedores in removing the cover plate was not an act done in the navigation of the ship, and I am equally certain that it was not an act done in the management of the ship. The authorities on the meaning of this phrase are set out in Scrutton on Charterparties, 17th ed. (1964), at p. 243, and none of them covers this particular form of activity by the crew. See in particular Hourani v. T. & J. Harrison,(1927) 28 Ll.L.Rep. 120; (1927) 32 Com. Cas. 305 (C.A.), to which I shall have to refer later. In my judgement, this point fails.'[397]

254. Other examples are the entry of rain through hatches negligently left uncovered to facilitate repairs while the ship was in port[398] and mismanagement of refrigeration machinery by the chief engineer.[399] Tetley remarks that carriers most often invoke the nautical fault exception as a defence against claims for damage to cargo due to improper ballasting. He correctly points out that the error must not have taken place before the beginning of the voyage because the error would be a breach of the duty contained in art. III(1) and that cargo damage due to water entering through defective valves will only be covered by the nautical fault exception if the carrier can prove that he exercised due diligence before the beginning of the voyage to check the valves.[400]

255. According to Carver because the words of art. IV(2)a do not refer to negligence, but to 'act, neglect or default' it seems that the exception would even cover a wilful or reckless act.[401] However, no authority regarding this point is cited. In the Dutch case *Quo Vadis* the court of Appeal in The Hague held that: ',... Kroezen [the Captain and owner of the *Quo Vadis*, NJM] can also invoke his contractual defence (error in the management of the ship) to parry the claim based on tort even if he is reproached for making a severe error, *as long as there was no default verging onto wilful misconduct*.'[402, 403] (emphasis added, NJM)

256. As was made clear by Lord Justice Greer in *The Canadian Highlander*[404] the principal inquiry, therefore, is whether the act or default which caused loss or damage was done (or left undone) as part of the care of the cargo or as part of the running of the ship, not specifically related to the cargo.[405] This question is not always easy to answer. In *Rowson v. Atlantic Transport Co.* (Court of Appeal) for example it was held that an error in the use of refrigeration machinery was an error in the management of the ship because the refrigeration machinery was used to cool the ship's stores as well as the cargo.[406] This decision does seem strange. I would sooner agree with Wright J. in *Foreman and Ellams v. Federal Steam Navigation Co.* (KBD). Wright J. said:

---

397. [1961] 1 Lloyd's Rep. 450, 458.
398. Canadian Highlander (see supra).
399. Foreman & Ellams Ltd. v. Federal S.N. Co. Ltd., [1928] 2 K.B. 424.
400. Tetley 1988, p. 404.
401. See Carver 2005, p. 607.
402. The Dutch expression is: 'aan opzet grenzende schuld'.
403. Quo Vadis, Hof 's-Gravenhage 13 maart 2001, S&S 2002, 82.
404. See above.
405. See also Cooke e.a. 2007, p. 1024.
406. Rowson v. Atlantic Transport Co., [1903] 2 K.B. 666 (a case governed by the Harter Act).

> 'A negligence or exception clause in a statute, as in a contract, ought, I think, to be strictly construed. The words of Art. IV., r. 2 (a), appear to be connected with matters directly affecting the ship as a ship, and not with matters affecting exclusively, or even primarily, the cargo, even though such latter matters involve the user of parts of the ship. The word "navigation" is clearly only applicable to the ship as such, and I think the more general word "management" should be read as ejusdem generis, and the word "ship" should receive the same connotation with each of the substantives on which it is dependent, the word "management" covering many acts directly affecting the ship which could not well be covered by "navigation". The words of the exception are not "in the navigation or in the management of the ship or in the management of any part of the ship necessary for the proper and due care of the cargo", nor are the words, to put it differently, "in the management of the cargo by the use of the ship's parts or appliances".'[407]

257. Wright J. points out that Rowson's case was not followed in the USA:

> 'The limitation in question has not been approved in the United States: see The Samland, where it was held that failure properly to control the refrigerating appliances was not a fault in the management of the vessel. The judge said of Rowson's case: This case, however, was not followed by Judge Dietrich in The Jean Bart, and the Circuit Court of Appeals in this [New York] Circuit in Andean Trading Co. v. Pacific Steam Navigation Co., has expressly approved and followed Judge Dietrich's decision. It is clearly established that s. 3 of the Harter Act is limited in its application to faults "primarily connected with the management of the vessel, and not with the cargo." I may add that even if the provision of refrigerated food for the crew is equated with the provision of fuel for the propulsion of the ship, so that the refrigeration of the ship's chamber forms part of the management of the ship, and the same refrigerating machinery is used for the crew's food and for the cargo, these facts ought not to affect the conclusion that, quoad the refrigeration of the cargo holds, it is the management of the cargo and not of the ship which is involved. But the point does not arise in this case.'[408] (citations omitted, NJM)

258. Some machinery on board is exclusively intended for the management of the cargo. For example refrigeration equipment used to cool the cargo holds. Some parts of the engine room are exclusively related to the management of the ship, such as the main engines used for the propulsion of the ship. Other parts of the ship may relate to either, according to the situation, so that hatch covers are part of the vessel's outer skin in bad weather but for the protection of cargo in port or in calm weather.[409]
In the *Canadian Highlander* cargo was damaged because rain could enter through the hatches which were open to facilitate repairs in port. The carrier invoked the nautical fault exception to escape liability. The House of Lords held that there is a difference between lack of care for the cargo and lack of care for the ship which causes cargo damage. Only the last instance is covered by the exception. Although the hatches were

---
407. Foreman and Ellams v. Federal Steam Navigation Co., [1928] 2 KB 424.
408. Ibid.
409. Per Wright J. in Foreman and Ellams v. Federal Steam Navigation Co., (1928) K.B. 424.

open to facilitate the repair of the ship, tarpaulins were rigged to protect the cargo. The purpose of the tarpaulins was protection of the cargo. Neglect to use the tarpaulins constituted lack of care for the cargo so that the carrier could not rely on the exception.[410]

Conclusion

259. Management of the ship should be distinguished from management of the cargo. The carrier is responsible for damage caused by mismanagement of the cargo. The carrier can rely on exception IV(2)a to escape liability for damage caused by an act or omission concerning the management of the ship but not for mismanagement of the cargo. It can sometimes be hard to qualify an act (or omission) as management of the ship or as care of the cargo. This problem is discussed below.

5.2.3.1 *The primary purpose test*

260. Because an act or omission can influence the ship and the cargo the question will arise how to qualify that act or omission. The US Supreme Court considered this question in *The Germanic*, a case governed by the Harter Act.[411] That case has been the leading case in the US for almost a century.[412] *The Germanic* arrived in port 36 hours behind schedule and coated with ice (approximately 213 tons). This weight was increased by a heavy fall of snow after her arrival. In order to sail at her regular time on the following Wednesday, cargo was discharged from all of the five hatches at once. At the same time coal was being bunkered from coal barges on both sides. Due to the high centre of gravity and the manner of loading and bunkering of coal the ship eventually listed beyond control and sunk.
The defence of the carrier was that the ship had sunk due to an error in the management of the ship (loading fuel in the form of coal).[413] On the other side the cargo interests stated that the damage was a result of mismanagement of the cargo. The U.S. Supreme Court held:

> 'The question is whether the damage to the cargo was "damage or loss resulting from faults or errors in navigation or in the management of said vessel", as was set up in the answers, in which case the owner was exempted from liability by § 3 of the Harter act, or whether it was "loss or damage arising from negligence, fault, or failure in proper loading, storage, custody, care, or proper delivery" of merchandise under § 1 of the same, in which case he could not stipulate to be exempt. The second section also recognizes and affirms the "obligations" to carefully handle and store her cargo, and to care for and properly deliver the same.
> (...)

---

410. Gosse Millard v. Canadian Government Merchant Marine, 32 Ll.L.L.Rep. 91. This case is also discussed infra in § 5.2.3.2.
411. Oceanic Steam Nav. Co. v. Aitkin (The Germanic), 196 U.S. 589 (1905). See also Sturley 1997, p. 307.
412. Sturley 1997, p. 307.
413. The decision is from 1905 when ships still burned coal as fuel. Therefore the loading of coal is an act in the management of the ship. The coal is not cargo but fuel.

If the primary purpose is to affect the ballast of the ship, the change is management of the vessel; but if (...) the primary purpose is to get the cargo ashore, the fact that it also affects the trim of the vessel does not make it the less *a fault of the class which the first section removes from the operation of the third*. We think it plain that a case may occur which, in different aspects falls within both sections; and if that be true, the question which section is to govern must be determined by the primary nature and object of the acts which cause the loss.' (emphasis added, NJM)

261. This test is known as the 'primary purpose test'.[414] Although the *Germanic* case was governed by the Harter Act the test is also used under the H(V)R.[415]

262. In the *Iron Gippsland* case[416] damage (vapour contamination) occurred to a cargo of 'Singapore Gas Oil' (also known as 'ADO'). ADO is an inflammable product. To prevent ignition of explosive gases which develop in the tanks containing ADO the tanks are first filled with inert gas.
In the *Iron Gippsland* case the ADO was contaminated via the inert gas system and its flashpoint reduced to an unacceptable level. The question to be answered was whether the contamination of the ADO was failure to care for the cargo in accordance with art. III(2) or if it was an act covered by the nautical fault exception. The Australia Supreme Court of New South Wales (Carruthers, J.) said that:

'It is true that inert gas systems were installed on tankers fundamentally for the protection of the vessel. However, *the purpose of the inert gas system is primarily to manage the cargo*, not only for the protection of the cargo but for the ultimate protection of the vessel from adverse consequences associated with that cargo and, in my view, damage occasioned to cargo by mismanagement of the inert gas system cannot be categorized as neglect or fault in the management of the ship.'[417] (emphasis added, NJM)

263. I agree. This exception should be strictly construed otherwise it could also cover incidents regarding the care of the cargo. If, in those instances, the exception were to be applied in favour of the carrier the duty contained in art. III(2) could be undermined.

5.2.3.2 *The author's opinion*

264. As was noted above old decisions rendered before the enactment of the Hague Rules are still relevant for the construction of the expression 'management of the ship'. The first English judgement in which the expression was interpreted was the *Ferro* case.[418] In that decision it was held that stowing of the cargo was not an act covered by the expression 'management of the ship'. Gorell Barnes, J. said:

---
414. See Von Ziegler 2002, p. 224-225 and p. 231-232; Schoenbaum 2001, p. 608 and Hare 1999, p. 631.
415. See e.g. the Isla Fernadina case, [2000] 2 Lloyd's Rep. 15, 35.
416. The Iron Gippsland, [1994] 1 Lloyd's Rep. 335.
417. The Iron Gippsland, [1994] 1 Lloyd's Rep. 335, 358.
418. Ferro, [1893] P. 38. See also the reference made to this case by Bankes J. in Hourani v. Harrison, 28 Ll.L.L.Rep. 120, 122.

> 'It seems to me a perversion of terms to say that the management of a ship has anything to do with the stowage of the cargo.'

265. In the *Glenochil* case a clear distinction was made between acts concerning the management of the ship and acts not concerning management. Regarding that distinction it was held:

> '..., but the distinction, (...), is one between want of care of cargo and want of care of vessel indirectly affecting the cargo.'

In the same judgement Gorell Barnes J. said:

> '..., and I think that where the act done in the management of the ship is one which is necessarily done in the proper handling of the vessel, though in the particular case the handling is not properly done, but is done for the safety of the ship herself, and is not primarily done at all in connection with the cargo, that must be a matter which falls within the words "management of the said vessel".'[419]

266. As was said above the U.S. Supreme court developed the 'primary purpose test' under the Harter Act in *The Germanic*[420] and this is still the test used under the H(V)R and the COGSA statutes which are based on the Hague Rules.

267. In *Rowson v. Atlantic Transport Company*[421] Kennedy J. quoted the following consideration from the *Rodney* case:

> '..., the words "faults or errors in the management of the vessel" include improper *handling of the ship as a ship*, which affects the safety of the cargo, ...' [422] (emphasis added, NJM)

268. The emphasised passage shows that the act should be an act committed for the sake of the ship, so that an act committed for the sake of the cargo is not an act in the management of the ship.

269. Often the problem in cases concerning the nautical fault exception is the qualification of an act. The question will then be whether the act is an act primarily for the sake of the ship or an act primarily for the sake of the cargo. See e.g. the differences in qualifying the act which caused the damage in the *Canadian Highlander* case.[423] In the court of appeal Lord Scrutton found that leaving the hatches open (allowing rain to enter which damaged the cargo) was an act for the sake of the ship. The hatches were indeed open because it was necessary for the repair of the ship. On the other hand Greer J. (one of the other three judges of the court of appeal) said with regard to leaving the hatches open:

---

419. Glenochil, (1896) P. 10.
420. See supra.
421. Rowson v. Atlantic Transport Company, (1903) 1 K.B. 114.
422. Rodney, [1900] P. 112.
423. Canadian Highlander, 29 Ll.L.L.Rep. 190.

'... the evidence in this case failed to establish any want of care of the vessel, but only want of care of the cargo, consisting of a failure to use the hatch covers and tarpaulins sufficiently to afford adequate protection of the cargo.'[424]

270. If the act which caused cargo damage can be qualified as an act equally well for the sake of the ship as for the sake of the cargo then the exception should be interpreted strictly. It is a strong defence and if the scope of it's application were not restricted the exception could undermine the obligation contained in art. III(2).[425] A good example is the *Iron Gippsland* case.[426] The inert gas is used to contain the cargo so it could be seen as an application primarily for the sake of the cargo. On the other hand the application of inert gas could also be qualified as an act in the management of the ship because if the cargo explodes the ship will be damaged. In such a case strict interpretation of the expression will lead to the result that the act is to qualified as an act primarily for the sake of the cargo.

5.2.3.3 *An alternative for the primary purpose test?*

271. Stevens discusses an alternative for the primary purpose test.[427] That alternative test is two staged. Firstly the question should be answered whether the act would also have been committed if there were no cargo on board. If the answer is 'no' then it is an act concerning the management of the cargo. If the answer is 'yes' then the second question is: where will the greatest damage occur? If the cargo will suffer the greatest damage the act is qualified as management of the cargo.
In the *Iron Gippsland*[428] case a strict interpretation of the expression led to the decision that the application of inert gas was primarily for the purpose of controlling the cargo. Using the alternative test the answer to the first question would probably have been 'no, the inert gas would not have been applied if no potentially explosive cargo was carried'.[429] That answer leads to the conclusion that, as inert gas is only applied when cargo is carried, the use of inert gas is therefore an act primarily for the care of the cargo and not an act in the management of the ship. In this instance the alternative method leads to the same solution as the primary purpose test.
If the act would also have been committed with cargo on board it does not necessarily mean that the act is an act in the management of the ship. As was said above, the decisive factor is where the greatest risk of damage is created.[430] If the act (or omission) primarily or exclusively causes damage to the cargo then the act or omission is management of the cargo and not management of the ship. An example is the pumping out of the bilges. If the bilges are not properly pumped out an amount of the remaining bilge water will primarily cause damage to the cargo if it enters the hold. On the other hand some bilge water in the hold will not affect the safety of the ship and will also not cause damage to the ship. This leads to the result that the carrier will be liable for the cargo damage caused by the bilge water.

---

424. Ibid.
425. See infra § 3.8.
426. See supra.
427. See Stevens 2001, p. 222-223.
428. See supra.
429. This answer does however depend on the facts. Empty tanks may contain volatile vapours depending on the previous cargo. In that case inert gas would be used to contain those vapours.
430. Supreme Court of Belgium 21 March 1985, R.W. 1985-1986, 112.

However, if the act or omission primarily endangers or damages the ship then the exception will apply because the act or omission is to considered 'management of the ship'.

272. The alternative method discussed by Stevens can lead to different solutions than the primary purpose test.[431] Stevens discusses a decision of the Antwerp court of Appeal of 5 October 1982. In that case bunkers were overheated causing damage to the cargo. Overheated bunkers will create hardly any risk for the ship, but can damage the cargo due to overheating of the holds. Under the primary purpose test overheating the bunkers would clearly have been an act of management of the ship and thus an exclusion from liability for the owners. Under the alternative test the answer to the first question (would the bunkers have been heated without cargo on board?) is 'possibly'. The second stage is: where did most damage occur?

273. The answer is 'damage occurred to the cargo'. Therefore, according to the alternative test, the carrier is liable for mismanaging the cargo. Another example is a decision of the Brussels court of appeal of 22 February 1973. Bunker hoses were connected to the wrong pipe causing fuel oil to access the cargo. No danger or damage existed for the ship but the cargo was damaged, leading to liability of the carrier.

274. In my opinion the last two examples lead to incorrect decisions. The heating of fuel oil and the bunkering of fuel oil are beyond doubt acts of management of the ship. There is no reason to apply rules of construction or interpretation to a case which is clear. Objective reading of the expression 'management of the ship' and the purpose of the exception – no liability for damage caused by acts regarding the management of the ship – can only lead to the conclusion that bunkering and heating fuel oil are acts of management of the ship. Fuel oil is required for the propulsion of the ship. Only the hypothetical case of damage caused by loading fuel which is exclusively intended to run machinery required to condition the cargo could be an error in the treatment of the cargo.
The last two examples show that the alternative test should be applied with care.

5.2.4 The intended construction of art. IV(2)a

275. There seem to be consensus on the construction and application of art. IV(2)a, i.e. there is no obvious lack of uniformity. Therefore there is no need to establish the intended construction and application of art. IV(2)a.

5.3 The fire exception

5.3.1 Introduction

276. Art. IV(2)b H(V)R provides:
Neither the carrier nor the ship shall be responsible for loss or damage arising or resulting from:

---

431. See Stevens 2001, p. 222. He refers to an unpublished decision of the Antwerp Court of Appeal 5 October 1982 and a decision of the Court of Appeal Brussels of 22 February 1973, Rechtspr. Ant. 1974, 48.

(...)
b. Fire, *unless caused by the actual fault or privity of the carrier* (emphasis added, NJM).

277. The following questions will be discussed below.

(i) Why is there a proviso added to the exception?
(ii) What is meant by 'fire'?
(iii) What is meant by 'actual fault or privity'?
(iv) Which persons can be seen as 'the carrier'?
(v) How is the burden of proof divided?

278. Before studying these questions, or rather, the possible answers to those questions, some additional information on the Fire Statutes of England and America is required.

5.3.2 The Fire Statutes and the fire exception

5.3.2.1 *Introduction*

279. When comparing the application of the fire exception of the H(V)R under different legal systems it is important to bear in mind that under American and English law other statutes exonerating the carrier from damage caused by fire apply: the so called 'Fire Statutes'. The name 'Fire Statute' is confusing because the name does not make clear that no more is meant than an article of statutory law. The English Fire Statute is contained in section 186(1) of the Merchant Shipping Act 1995. The American Fire Statute is contained in 46 U.S.C. App. § 182. The Fire Statutes provide the carrier with a fire defence independent of the H(V)R. It is possible that a Fire Statute applies besides the fire exception of the H(V)R.

280. The present English Fire Statute provides:
'Subject to subsection (3) below, the owner of a United Kingdom ship shall not be liable for any loss or damage in the following cases, namely
(a) where any property on board the ship is lost or damaged by reason of fire on board the ship.'[432]

281. The American statute is contained in section 182 of the Limitation of Ship-owners' Liability Act of 1851 and it provides:

> 'No owner of any vessel shall be liable to answer for or make good to any person any loss or damage, which may happen to any merchandise whatsoever, which shall be shipped, taken in, or put on board any such vessel, by reason or by

---

[432] S. 186(1) sub a of the Merchant Shipping Act 1995. Section 502 of the Merchant Shipping Act 1894 contained an earlier version of the Fire Statute. That section provided: 'The owner of a British sea-going ship, or any share therein, shall not be liable to make good to any extent whatever any loss or damage happening without his actual fault or privity in the following cases; namely, (a) Where any goods, merchandise, or other things whatsoever taken in or put on board his ship are lost or damaged by reason of fire on board the ship, ...'.

means of any fire happening to or on board the vessel, unless such fire is caused by the design or neglect of such owner'.[433]

282. For the sake of simplicity I shall refer to the fire exception of the H(V)R as 'the fire exception'. The expression 'fire defences' means the Fire Statute (English or American) and the fire exception jointly.

283. In cases concerning loss or damage of goods by fire the question is which fire defence applies (Fire Statute of fire exception). Another question is if the carrier can rely on the fire defences if the loss or damage was caused by lack of due diligence to make the ship seaworthy. One view is that the carrier can rely on the Fire Statute even if the loss or damage was caused by lack of due diligence. Another view is that the duty to exercise due diligence is an overriding obligation and failure to fulfil that duty will lead to liability of the carrier if that failure caused the loss or damage by fire.

284. Before going in to these points I shall discuss the historical background of the Fire Statutes.

5.3.2.2 *The historical background of the Fire Statutes*

285. The exoneration for damage by fire provided by the English Fire Statute is based on the principle in the maritime law states that a carrier is not responsible for loss or damage caused by fire unless caused by his actual fault or privity.[434] The reasons are that fire can easily start on board a ship and that the potential danger posed to cargo, vessel and crew that may result from fire is serious. Moreover because of the nature of fire and the destruction that results, the causes of a fire are often difficult to determine.[435] Because of the risk of fire and the destructive consequences of fire the English legislator found it necessary to protect the carrier against liability for damage caused by fire at sea. After the English Fire Statute was established the Americans found themselves bound to follow the English example in the interest of American carriers.

286. In *Consumers Import Co. v. Zosenjo* (1943) the U.S. Supreme Court explained the historical background of the Fire Statute Justice Jackson said:

> 'At common law, the shipowner was liable as an insurer for fire damage to cargo (...) We may be sure that this legal policy of annexing an insurer's liability to the contract of carriage loaded the transportation rates of prudent carriers to compensate the risk. Long before Congress did so, England had separated the insurance liability from the carrier's duty (...). To enable our merchant marine to compete, Congress enacted this statute [the Fire Statute, NJM]. It was a sharp departure from the concepts that had usually governed the common carrier relation, but it is not to be judged as if applied to land carriage, where shipments are relatively multitudinous and small and where it might well work injustice and hardship. The change on sea transport seems less drastic in economic ef-

---
433. 46 U.S.C.App. § 182.
434. Von Ziegler 2002, p. 239. See on limitation of shipowners; liability in general: Donovan 1979.
435. UNCITRAL WP.21, p. 27 and Aikens et al, p. 271-272. See also Nissan Fire & Marine Insurance v. M/V Hyundai Explorer (Hyundai Explorer), 93 F.3d 641, 646.

fects than in terms of doctrine. It enabled the carrier to compete by offering a carriage rate that paid for carriage only, without loading it for fire liability. The shipper was free to carry his own fire risk, but if he did not care to do so it was well-known that those who made a business of risk-taking would issue him a separate contract of fire insurance. Congress had simply severed the insurance features from the carriage features of sea transport and left the shipper to buy each separately. While it does not often come to the surface of the record in admiralty proceedings, we are not unaware that in commercial practice the shipper who buys carriage from the shipowner usually buys fire protection from an insurance company, thus obtaining in two contracts what once might have been embodied in one. The purpose of the statute to relieve carriage rates of the insurance burden would be largely defeated if we were to adopt an interpretation which would enable cargo claimants and their subrogees to shift to the ship the risk of which Congress relieved the owner. This would restore the insurance burden at least in large part to the cost of carriage and hamper the competitive opportunity it was purposed to foster by putting our law on an equal basis with that of England.'[436]

287. The Supreme Court quoted Senator Hamlin where he was discussing the bill which led to the Fire Statute:

'This bill is predicated on what is now the English law, and it is deemed advisable by the Committee on Commerce that the American marine should stand at home and abroad as well as the English marine.'[437] (...)

288. In *Consumers Import Co. v. Zosenjo* the U.S. Supreme Court continued to discuss the legislative history.

289. On February 26, 1851, speaking to the bill, Senator Hamlin said:

'These are the provisions of the bill. It is true that the changes are most radical from the common law upon the subject; but they are rendered necessary first, from the fact that the English common law system really never had an application to this country, and second, that the English Government has changed the law, which is a very strong and established reason why we should place our commercial marine upon an equal footing with hers. Why not give to those who navigate the ocean as many inducements to do so as England has done? Why not place them upon that great theatre where we are to have the great contest for the supremacy of the commerce of the world? That is what this bill seeks to do, and it asks no more.'[438]

290. The above makes it clear that the statutory defences against fire were given to carriers for commercial reasons. The reasons mentioned above are that fire can easily start on board a ship and the potential danger posed to cargo, vessel and crew is great. Because of the nature of fire and the destruction that results, the causes of a fire are of-

---
436. Consumers Import Co. v. Zosenjo, 320 U.S. 249.
437. Senator Hamlin reported the bill from the Committee on Commerce on January 25, 1851.
438. Consumers Import v. Kabushiki Kaisha Kawasaki Zosenjo, 320 U.S. 249.

ten difficult to determine.[439] For these reasons English and American legislators provided carriers with a statutory protection against responsibility for damage caused by fire. This allowed the carriers to lower their freight rates.

5.3.2.3 The English Fire Statute[440]

291. The English Fire Statute only applies to ships of the United Kingdom.[441] Because of art. VIII of the Hague Rules the English Fire Statute also applies when the fire exception applies.[442] This means that the carrier can invoke the Fire Statute instead of the fire exception of the H(V)R. The reason for the carrier to do so is that the Fire Statute offers the carrier more protection than the fire exception of the H(V)R. Contrary to the fire exception the English Fire Statute also applies in case of a proven failure to fulfil the duty of art. III(1) H(V)R (the duty to exercise due diligence to furnish a seaworthy ship) unless the shipowner could be proved to have been personally wilful or reckless.[443] This was also the construction of section 502 of the Merchant Shipping Act 1894 (the older version of the English Fire Statute). E.g. in *Virginia Carolina Chemical Company v. Norfolk and North American Steam Shipping Company* the Court of Appeal held that a shipowner is not deprived of the protection of s. 502 merely by reason of the fact that the fire is caused by the unseaworthiness of the ship. Buckley L.J. said:

> 'The first question is as regards the true construction of s. 502 of the Merchant Shipping Act, 1894. Apart from statute a shipowner was at common law under two liabilities, the one that of an insurer arising from the fact that he was a carrier, and therefore bound to produce the goods which had been entrusted to him for carriage, and the other under an implied warranty of seaworthiness. The statute in the case of fire, if I rightly understand it, relieves him from both the first and the second of those liabilities, if the fire happens without his actual fault or privity. It relieves him not only from the liability as an insurer but also from the liability under an implied warranty of seaworthiness. To express the same thing in other words, the section is not to be read as if it said "the owner of a seaworthy British sea-going ship"; it is, *"the owner of any British sea-going ship," be it seaworthy or unseaworthy, "shall not be liable" for damage by fire unless it happens with his actual fault or privity.* That is the construction which I place upon the statute. If there is no special contract, the defendants can rely on the statute construed as I have construed it.'[444] (emphasis added, NJM)

---

439. Aikens et al 2006, p. 271-272.
440. See § 5.3.2.1 for the text of the English Fire Statute.
441. Section 1(3) Merchant Shipping Act defines 'A United Kingdom Ship' as 'A ship is a "United Kingdom ship" for the purposes of this Act (except section 85 and 144(3)) if the ship is registered in the United Kingdom under Part II (and in Part V "United Kingdom fishing vessel" has a corresponding meaning)'.
442. That article reads: The provisions of these Rules shall not affect the rights and obligations of the carrier under any statute for the time being in force relating to the limitation of the liability of owners of sea-going vessels.
    The Fire Statute is expressly designated as a limitation provision for the purposes of art. VIII by section 6(4) of the Carriage of Goods by Sea Act 1971 (as amended by the 1995 Act).
443. Carver 2005, p. 608.
444. Virginia Carolina Chemical Company v. Norfolk and North American Steam Shipping Company (The West Point), [1912] 1 KB 229, 240-241.

THE FIRE EXCEPTION 5.3

292. Depending on the circumstances either the English Fire Statute or the fire exception will apply. The existence of the two regimes (Fire Statute and fire exception) relating to the same issue (damage caused to cargo by fire) does not lead to problems in English courts. The same cannot, however, be said for American courts.

5.3.2.4 *The American Fire Statute*[445]

293. The words 'No owner of any vessel, ...' indicate that the American Fire Statute can also apply to foreign vessels. There is no explicit restriction that the rule can only apply to American ships. See e.g. *The Pocone* case concerning a Brazilian carrier.[446]

294. Although the proviso 'unless such fire, ...' is worded differently than the fire exception, American courts have held that the words '*actual fault or privity*' of the fire exception, and the words '*design or neglect*' have the same meaning.[447]

295. The USA have been party to the Hague Rules since 1936.[448] The American codification of the Hague Rules is the US 'Carriage of Goods by Sea Act' (US COGSA). The fire exception of the Hague Rules is codified by art. 4(2)b COGSA. Art. 8 of the US COGSA should cause the American Fire Statute to prevail above the fire exception.[449] However, the existence of two statutory provisions dealing with the same issue (fire causing damage to cargo) has led to two different lines of reasoning in the American courts.

5.3.3 **American decisions**

296. If the American Fire Statute applies on its own there is no statutory legal obligation for the carrier to exercise due diligence to provide a seaworthy ship. There is however an implied warranty to provide a seaworthy ship. In *Earle & Stoddart, Inc et al. v. Ellerman's Wilson Line, Ltd.* the U.S. Supreme Court held:

> '..., in every contract of affreightment there is, unless otherwise expressly stipulated, *an implied warranty of seaworthiness at the commencement of the voyage. The warranty is absolute that the ship is in fact seaworthy at that time*, and the liability does not depend upon the knowledge or ignorance, the care or negligence, of the shipowner or charterer.'[450] (emphasis added, NJM)

297. This means that a contract for the carriage of goods by sea contains the implied warranty that the ship be seaworthy when she commences the voyage. The 9th Circuit follows a different line of reasoning than the other circuits regarding the relationship

---

445. See § 5.3.2.1 for the text of the American Fire Statute.
446. Great A. & P. Co. v. Lloyd Brasileiro (The Pocone), 1947 A.M.C. 306 (2nd Circuit).
447. See e.g. Damodar Bulk Carriers, Ltd. v. People's Insurance Company of China, 903 F.2d 675, 681.
448. 46 U.S.C. app. sections 1300 etc (COGSA). The USA did not ratify the Visby protocol.
449. 46 USC app. section 1308 is referred to (also referred to as section 8 US COGSA). That section provides: The provisions of this chapter shall not affect the rights and obligations of the carrier under the provisions of the Shipping Act, 1916 [46 App. U.S.C. 801 et seq.], or under the provisions of sections 4281 to 4289, inclusive, of the Revised Statutes of the United States [46 App. 181-188] or of any amendments thereto; or under the provisions of any other enactment for the time being in force relating to the limitation of the liability of the owners of seagoing vessels.
450. Earle & Stoddart, Inc et al. v. Ellerman's Wilson Line, Ltd., 287 U.S. 420.

that exist between the American Fire Statute, the implied warranty that the ship be seaworthy and the COGSA obligation to exercise due diligence to furnish a seaworthy ship.

5.3.3.1 *Application of the Fire Statute on its own: breach of non delegable duty by others than owner is not to be considered 'design or neglect of the owner'*

Earle & Stoddart v. Ellerman's Wilson Line

298. In *Earle & Stoddart v. Ellerman's Wilson Line* the U.S. Supreme Court held that the owner's failure to diligently determine whether the vessel was seaworthy was not 'neglect of such owner' within the Fire Statute so that the owner could rely on the Fire Statute. The U.S. Supreme Court said that the purpose[451] of the Fire Statute would be thwarted if the Fire Statute would be construed in such a way that the carrier would have to bear a risk which the legislator aimed to take away from him. The breach of a non delegable duty by others than those who could be considered to be the carrier personally is not to be considered 'design or neglect of the owner'.[452] The US Supreme Court followed earlier English decisions.[453]

A/s J. Mowinckels Rederi v. Accinanto (The Ocean Liberty)

299. The *Earle & Stoddart*-reasoning was applied under COGSA in *A/s J. Mowinckels Rederi v. Accinanto (The Ocean Liberty)*. The Court of Appeal (4th Circuit) held:

> '[w]e do not think that the carrier can be held liable on the theory that stowage of cargo was a non-delegable duty negligence in performance of which should be imputed to the carrier in determining whether it had exercised due care to make the vessel seaworthy. Directly in point is the case of Earle & Stoddart v. Ellerman's Wilson Line, supra, 287 U.S. 420, 53 S.Ct. 200, in which a vessel was held to be exempted from liability by reason of the fire statute, although she was rendered unseaworthy before leaving port as the result of the negligent stowage of coal in her bunkers by her chief engineer. The exemption of the fire statute is admittedly the same as that provided by the Carriage of Goods by Sea Act. The Supreme Court, speaking through Justice Brandeis, thus dealt with the questions which seem to be crucial here:
> "The contention is that the statute does not confer immunity where the fire resulted from unseaworthiness existing at the commencement of the voyage and discoverable by the exercise of ordinary care; (...) The first statute, in terms, relieves the owners from liability 'unless such fire is caused by the design or neglect of such owner.' The statute makes no other exception from the complete immunity granted. The cargo owners do not make the broad contention that the statute affords no protection to the vessel owner if the fire was caused by unseaworthiness existing at the commencement of the voyage. Their conten-

---

451. See supra. The purpose was to allow American carriers to compete on an equal footing with English carriers.
452. Earle & Stoddart v. Ellerman's Wilson Line, 287 U.S. 420.
453. See e.g. Louis Dreyfus & Co. v. Tempus Shipping Co., [1931] A.C. 726 en Virginia Carolina Chemical Co. v. Norfolk & N.A. Steam Shipping Co., [1912] 1 K.B. 229.

tion is that it does not relieve the owner if the unseaworthiness was discoverable by due diligence. The argument is that the duty of the owner to make the ship seaworthy before starting on her voyage is non-delegable, and if the unseaworthiness could have been discovered by due diligence there was necessarily neglect of the vessel owner. (...) *The courts have been careful not to thwart the purpose of the fire statute by interpreting as 'neglect' of the owners the breach of what in other connections is held to be a non-delegable duty.*"[454] (emphasis added, NJM)

300. The above shows that where the Fire Statute applies on its own (so not besides COGSA) there is no problem. Even if the fire was caused by lack of due diligence to make the ship seaworthy the carrier can still rely on the Fire statute, unless the lack of due diligence qualifies as design or neglect of the owner.

5.3.3.2 *When both the Fire Statute and COGSA apply: the 9th Circuit contrary to the other circuits?*

301. When the Fire Statute and COGSA both apply in the same case the court of appeal of the 9th Circuit tends to hold that the carrier cannot assert the fire defences if lack of due diligence to make the ship seaworthy caused the fire.[455] The courts of appeal of 2nd, 5th and 11th Circuits apply the law differently i.e. if the Fire Statue and the fire exception are both applicable then the Fire Statute will prevail ex section 8 COGSA which provides:

> 'The provisions of this chapter shall not affect the rights and obligations of the carrier under the provisions of the Shipping Act, 1916 [46 App. U.S.C. 801 et seq.], or under the provisions of sections 4281 to 4289, inclusive, of the Revised Statutes of the United States [46 App. 181-188] or of any amendments thereto; or under the provisions of any other enactment for the time being in force relating to the limitation of the liability of the owners of seagoing vessels.'

302. Therefore if the fire exception of COGSA applies as well as the Fire Statute, the fire exception should be ignored and the Fire Statute should be applied. That means that the carrier can only be responsible for damage by fire if the fire was caused by the owners design or neglect.[456]

303. Below relevant American decisions are discussed to illustrate the different lines of reasoning discussed above.

Asbestos Corp v. Compagnie de Navigation Fraissinet et Cyprien Fabre (2nd Cir. 1972)[457]

304. This is the first judgement of the 2nd Circuit in a case concerning damage by fire in a case in which both the Fire Statute and the fire exception of COGSA applied. In that case fire in the engine room could not be extinguished because all fire fighting

---

454. A/s J. Mowinckels Rederi v. Accinanto (The Ocean Liberty),199 F.2d 134, 143-144.
455. See e.g. Sunkist Growers Inv v. Adelaide Shipping Lines Ltd., 603 F.2d 1327.
456. See e.g. Louis Dreyfus & Co. v. Tempus Shipping Co., [1931] A.C. 726 en Virginia Carolina Chemical Co. v. Norfolk & N.A. Steam Shipping Co., [1912] 1 K.B. 229.
457. Asbestos Corp v. Compagnie de Navigation Fraissinet et Cyprien Fabre, (1973) A.M.C. 1683 (2nd Cir. 1973).

equipment was in the engine room and thus could not be reached. It was held that the ship was unseaworthy due to the absence of fire fighting equipment. The question to be answered was if the unseaworthiness should preclude application of the fire exception / Fire Statute. The court of appeal (2nd Circuit) affirmed the decision of the district court (SDNY) in which Judge Levet said that an inexcusable condition of unseaworthiness of a vessel, which in fact causes the damage – either by starting a fire or by preventing the fire to be extinguished – will exclude the shipowners form the exemption of the Fire Statute and COGSA. Judge Levet of the district court had said:

> 'The owners of the Marquette through their "design or neglect" and "privity or knowledge" were negligent in placing all fire fighting equipment inside the engine room and failing to provide an emergency pump or fire system located or controlled from outside the engine room. This negligence on the part of the shipowners displays a total disregard for minimal protection of cargo and rendered the Marquette unseaworthy. Under the circumstances this court concludes that the defendant-shipowners are not exempt from liability under COGSA § 1304(2) (b) or the Fire Statute.'[458]

Liberty Shipping (9th Cir. 1975)

305. In this case the Fire Statute and COGSA applied. In a short judgement the 9th Cir. agreed with the consideration in the *Asbestos Corp*[459] case where the 2nd Circuit (1973) held that an inexcusable condition of unseaworthiness of a vessel, which in fact causes the damage will exclude the shipowners form the exemption of the Fire Statute and COGSA. The 9th Circuit also held that:

> 'The statutory exemptions, it is contended, do not permit the imposition of liability by non-delegable duty. Appellant relies on *Earle & Stoddart, Inc. v. Ellerman's Wilson Line, Ltd.*, 287 U.S. 420, 53 S.Ct. 200, 77 L.Ed. 403 (1932), where it was held that owner liability for loss attributable to unseaworthiness cannot be imposed on the theory of a non delegable duty created by implied warranty; and that the statutory requirement that there be design or neglect on the part of the owner precludes such a result.
> However, the district court's holding here was entirely consistent with Earle & Stoddart. COGSA provides, 46 U.S.C. s 1303(1):
> The carrier shall be bound, before and at the beginning of the voyage, to exercise due diligence to
> (a) Make the ship seaworthy, ...
> In the case before us liability was not based on the traditional elements by which an owner is held liable for unseaworthiness of his vessel – those related to warranty and non delegable duty. Here there was owner neglect and actual fault constituting failure to exercise the due diligence required by COGSA through permitting the vessel to put to sea without having properly trained the master and crew in the use of fire-fighting equipment and without having

---
458. Asbestos Corp v. Compagnie de Navigation Fraissinet et Cyprien Fabre, 345 F.Supp 814 (S.D.N.Y. 1972) per Judge Levet.
459. Asbestos Corp v Compagnie de Navigation Fraissinet et Cyprien Fabre, (1973) A.M.C. 1683 (2nd Cir. 1973). See supra.

remedied deficiencies in the vent closing devices. Where the unseaworthy conditions that were the cause of the fire damage existed by reason of owner neglect or actual fault, the exemptions created by the Fire Statute and COGSA do not apply.'[460]

306. This case makes clear that COGSA is applied by the 9th Circuit regardless of art. 8 COGSA through which the Fire Statute should prevail. In the next case, *Sunkist*, the line of reasoning of the 9th Circuit was clarified.

Sunkist (9th Cir. 1979)[461]

307. In this case the Fire Statute and COGSA applied. Fire broke out in the engine room and spread via the bilge. A break in the fuel line and oil splashing onto the hot exhaust turbo chargers of the numbers 1 and 2 generators was the cause of the fire. Due to errors of the crew the fire could spread resulting in failure of refrigeration machinery causing loss of the cargo of fruit. The vessel owner and charterer were in violation of COGSA both in their failure to provide a proper compression or flange joint in the fuel line to a generator and in failing to properly man and equip the crew properly trained in engine room fire-fighting. The 9th Circuit held that if a ship is unseaworthy due to lack of due diligence the carrier could not rely on the fire exception or Fire Statute. The 9th Circuit did make clear that 'neglect of the owner' under the Fire Statute refers to 'the neglect of managing officers and agents as distinguished from that of the master or other members of the crew or subordinate employees.' In other words the neglect of the employees is not imputed to the carrier.

308. The court of appeal (9th Circuit) cited the Canadian case *Maxine Footwear (The Maurienne)*[462] and concluded that if there was a breach of the duty contained in art. 3(1) COGSA which caused the loss, the carrier is responsible for the damage. Regarding art. 8 COGSA the court held:

> 'we do not believe the provisions of Section 8 of the original COGSA, 46 U.S.C. s 1308, invalidates or in any manner affects COGSA's requirements that the carrier shall be bound to exercise due diligence to make the ship seaworthy. Section 1308 provides that the provisions of the legislation shall not affect the rights and obligations of the carrier under the Fire Statute and other legislation. As we have already said, the Fire Statute must be read in the light of COGSA, the more recent legislation.'[463]

---

460. Liberty Shipping, 509 F.2d 1249.
461. Sunkist Growers Inv v. Adelaide Shipping Lines Ltd., 603 F.2d 1327.
462. Maxine Footwear Co. Ltd v. Canadian Government Merchant Marine Ltd., [1959] 2 Lloyd's Rep. 105 (The Maurienne).
463. Sunkist Growers Inv v. Adelaide Shipping Lines Ltd., 603 F.2d 1327.

309. This is an unrealistic construction of section 8 COGSA because that construction reaches a solution which is contrary to the intention of section 8. That intention is that older legislation should prevail.[464]

310. The court of appeal of the 9th Circuit emphasised the importance of uniformity. The court held:

> 'If not in conflict with our decisions, and they are not, we should follow the decisions of the Canadian authorities that have already interpreted The Hague Rules. See Foscolo, Mango & Co., Ltd. v. Stag Line (1932) A.C. 328; (1931) 41 Lloyd's List L.R. 165 (1931). It is there said "As these rules must come under the consideration of foreign courts, it is desirable in the interests of uniformity that their interpretation should not be rigidly controlled by domestic precedents of antecedent date, but rather that the language of the Rules should be construed on broad principles of general acceptance."'[465]

311. The attempted uniformity is however not achieved. The 9th Circuit applies the *Maxine Footwear* (*The Maurienne*) decision of the Privy Council differently than the Privy Council does. In *The Maurienne* it was made clear that the duty to exercise due diligence to make the ship seaworthy before and at the beginning of the voyage is an overriding obligation and that failure to fulfil that obligation by employees of the carrier will be imputed to the carrier and cause the fire exception to fail. In the decisions of the 9th Circuit however, only lack of due diligence by the carrier *personally* will cause the fire exception to fail. Lack of due diligence by employees or agents is not imputed to the carrier. Furthermore the Privy Council based its decision that art. III(1) was an overriding obligation on the words 'Subject to the provisions of article 4' in art. III(2). These words were however omitted from the U.S. COGSA. This indicates that the American legislator did not intend to differentiate between the strictness of the duty contained in art. III(1) and art. III(2) as the 9th Circuit does.

Another obstacle to uniformity is the existence of the Fire Statutes. Because England and America have the Fire Statutes it is impossible to reach uniformity with nations who do not have such legislation as the Fire Statutes, without ignoring art. 8 COGSA (or art. VIII of the Hague Rules). The *Maurienne* is based on the Canadian Water Carriage of Goods Act, 1936. There is no fire statute in Canadian law. If there had been a Canadian fire statute the *Maurienne* would have had a different outcome because the carrier would have been able to rely on the fire statute.

312. In the *Sunkist* case the court of appeal of the 9th Circuit made clear that the failure of the carrier *personally*[466] to use due diligence to make the ship seaworthy will deny the carrier of the fire exception if the failure to exercise due diligence led to an

---

464. Art. 8 COGSA provides: 'The provisions of this chapter shall not affect the rights and obligations of the carrier under the provisions of the Shipping Act, 1916 [46 App. U.S.C. 801 et seq.], or under the provisions of sections 4281 to 4289, inclusive, of the Revised Statutes of the United States [46 App. 181-188] or of any amendments thereto; or under the provisions of any other enactment for the time being in force relating to the limitation of the liability of the owners of seagoing vessels.'
465. Sunkist Growers Inv v. Adelaide Shipping Lines Ltd., 603 F.2d 1327, 1338.
466. In this case the 9th Circuit recognises that for the application of the fire exception a failure of the carrier's employees to exercise due diligence will not be imputed to the carrier (at p. 1336).

inexcusable condition of unseaworthiness.[467] An inexcusable condition of unseaworthiness is a condition of unseaworthiness that existed because of the carrier's lack of due diligence.[468] At first glance the court of appeal seems to be adding a reason to the statutory proviso of the defence:[469] an inexcusable condition of unseaworthiness. Lack of due diligence by the carrier personally to make the ship seaworthy will, however, only be an addition to the proviso if that lack of due diligence cannot be considered equal to 'actual fault or privity' of the carrier. It seems to me, however, that the two reasons to deny the fire defence, are the same. Lack of due diligence by the carrier personally to make the ship seaworthy is equal to actual fault or privity (or design or neglect) of the carrier. Indeed the *Sunkist* court held:

> 'Here, the design or neglect was that of managing officers or supervisory employees, not that of the master or crew or subordinate employees. The "design or neglect" being the failure to provide a proper compression or flange joint and to properly man and equip a trained crew prior to the commencement of the voyage.'[470]

313. The 9th Circuit denied the carrier the benefit of the Fire Statute because the carrier personally failed to exercise due diligence to make the ship seaworthy. This failure is equal to 'design or neglect' of the Fire Statute and therefore the carrier cannot rely on the defence. The result is correct but the reasoning could have been clearer.

Ta Chi Navigation (2nd Cir. 1982)[471]

314. This was the second opportunity the 2nd Circuit had to decide a case concerning cargo damaged by fire. The fire was caused by an explosion which was caused by a gas leak.
Van Graafeiland, Circuit Judge said:

> 'The shipper can prove that the carrier caused the damage either by proving that a negligent act of the carrier caused the fire or that such an act prevented the fire's extinguishment. Asbestos Corp. Ltd., supra, 480 F.2d at 672.
> This delineation of the carrier's liability did not change with the 1936 enactment of the Carriage of Goods by Sea Act (COGSA) (...) *Congress specifically provided that COGSA shall not affect the rights and obligations of the carrier under the Fire Statute.* 46 U.S.C. s 1308. Congress also included in COGSA a provision that the carrier shall not be responsible for fire damage resulting from fire "unless caused by the actual fault or privity of the carrier". 46 U.S.C. s 1304(2)(b) (...) We disagree (...) with the 9th Circuit's interpretation of the interrelation between the Fire Statute and COGSA, an interpretation that is concurred in by no other Circuit. (...) In American Tobacco Co. v. The Katingo Hadjipatera (...) Judge Frank, writing for himself, Judge Swan, and Judge Learned Hand, said that, once a shipowner

---

467. Ibid. at p. 1335.
468. Hyundai Explorer, 93 F.3d 641, 647.
469. That proviso provides that the defence will fail if the fire was caused by the actual fault or privity of the carrier.
470. Ibid.
471. Complaint of Ta Chi Navigation (Panama) Corp S.A, 677 F.2d 225.

established loss by fire, "*(n)o liability could be imposed unless the owners of (cargo) carried the burden of proving that the fire was caused by the shipowner's design or negligence or the carriers' actual fault or privity.*" (...) When Congress wanted to put the burden of proving freedom from fault on a shipowner claiming the benefit of an exemption, it specifically said so. See 46 U.S.C. s 1304(2)(q). The Sunkist court would read the language of subsection (q) into subsection (b), "although Congress did not put it there". (...) This Court has not put it there either. We adhere to our prior holdings that, *if the carrier shows that the damage was caused by fire, the shipper must prove that the carrier's negligence caused the fire or prevented its extinguishment. If on remand the shipper fails to meet this burden, the action must be dismissed. Only if the shipper sustained the burden would the carrier have the obligation to establish what portion of the damage was not attributable to its fault.*' [472] (emphasis added, NJM)

315. The above decision was followed by the 5th Circuit in *Westinghouse Electric*[473] and the 11th Circuit in *Banana Services v M/V Tasman Star*.[474]

> *Damodar Bulk Carriers, Ltd. v. People's Insurance Company of China (9th Cir. 1990)*

316. The 9th Circuit clarified its previous decisions in the *Damodar Tanabe* case. In that case the COGSA fire exception applied and the US Fire Statute applied by its incorporation in the bill of lading. The 9th Circuit repeated that under the *Sunkist* rules the carrier has an

> 'overriding obligation to make the ship seaworthy [sic, NJM][475] and if that obligation is not fulfilled and the non-fulfillment causes the damage, the fire immunity of Section 4, Paragraph 2(b), cannot be relied upon.'[476]

317. The 9th Circuit explained that none of its earlier cases presented facts that pose the problem of the burden of proving the cause of the fire. That problem did not arise in the earlier cases because in those cases unseaworthiness was the cause of the damage.[477]

318. Sneed (Circuit Judge) said:

> 'Section 1304(2)(b) excuses the carrier or the ship from responsibility "for loss or damage arising or resulting from (...) [f]ire, unless caused by the actual fault or privity of the carrier." The provision itself does not state on which party the burden of proof lies when the cause of the fire is unknown. None of our earlier cases present facts that pose this specific problem. In earlier cases unseaworthiness *was* the cause of the damage. See, e.g., Sunkist Growers, Inc. v. Adelaide Shipping Lines, 603 F.2d 1327, 1341 (9th Cir.1979), cert. denied, 444 U.S. 1012, 100 S.Ct. 659,

---

472. Complaint of Ta Chi Navigation (Panama) Corp S.A, 677 F.2d 225.
473. Westinghouse Electric Corp v. M/V Leslie Lykes,734 F.2d 199 (5th Cir. 1984).
474. Banana Services v. M/V Tasman Star 68 F.3d 418 (11th Cir. 1995).
475. The obligation is to exercise due diligence to make the ship seaworthy.
476. Damodar Bulk Carriers, Ltd v. People's Insurance Company of China, (Damodar Tanabe), 903 F.2d 675.
477. Ibid. at page 686.

62 L.Ed.2d 640 (1980) (holding that carrier could not invoke the fire exemption if it failed to carry the burden of showing due diligence to make the ship seaworthy and the unseaworthiness caused the cargo damage); *In re Liberty Shipping Corp.*, 509 F.2d 1249, 1252 (9th Cir.1975) (holding that carrier could not invoke COGSA and Fire Statute exemptions where the "unseaworthy conditions that were the cause of the fire damage existed by reason of owner neglect or actual fault"). Here unseaworthiness has not been established as the cause of the damage.

When that is the case, the shifting burdens of proof take a slightly different focus. First, the carrier has the burden to show that the loss was caused by one of the section 1304(2) exemptions, in this case, fire. 46 U.S.C. § 1304(2)(b). That burden has been successfully borne in this case. At this point the burden returns to the shipper to prove that the fire was "caused by the actual fault or privity of the carrier." Id.[478] *See In re Ta Chi Navigation (Pan.) Corp., S.A.*, 677 F.2d 225, 228 (2d Cir.1982) ("If the carrier shows that the damage was caused by fire, the shipper must prove that the carrier's negligence caused' the fire or prevented its extinguishment.") (quoting *Asbestos Corp. v. Compagnie De Navigation Fraissinet et Cyprien Fabre*, 480 F.2d 669, 673 (2d Cir.1973)).'[479]

319. To summarise: Here the cause of the damage was not unseaworthiness. This means that once the carrier has proved damage by fire the cargo interests have to prove that fire was caused by the actual fault or privity to beat the fire exception defence.

320. The 9th Circuit then went on to explain that:

> 'Sunkist, 603 F.2d at 1327, does not alter this analysis. In Sunkist, the court did not reach the question before us. The Sunkist court merely reasoned that because the ship's unseaworthiness caused the loss, the carrier could not invoke the fire exception. Id. at 1336. A different issue arises in this case. Here the cargo interests have failed to carry their burden of proof to show that unseaworthiness had caused the loss and now insist that they need not show that the carriers' negligence caused the fire. This would weight the scales too heavily in favor of the cargo interests.'[480]

321. It can be concluded that if the damage was not caused by unseaworthiness the law of the 9th Circuit is the same as that of the 2nd, 5th and 11th. However if the Fire Statute and COGSA apply and if unseaworthiness caused the fire and the cause of the unseaworthiness was due to the failure to exercise due diligence to make the ship seaworthy, the 9th Circuit applies the law as if the Fire Statute does not exist. The 9th Circuit considers the duty to exercise due diligence to make the ship seaworthy an overriding

---

478. Footnote quoted: 'The existence of the Fire Statute, 46 U.S.C.App. § 182, as a contractual term in the bill of lading does not change this analysis. Under that statute, the carrier must prove that the loss was caused by fire, and then the shipper must prove that the fire was "caused by the design or neglect of such owner." (...) We agree with the Second Circuit that "design or neglect" is functionally equivalent to "actual fault or privity." Asbestos Corp. v. Compagnie De Navigation Fraissinet et Cyprien Fabre, 480 F.2d 669, 672 (2d Cir.1973).'
479. Damodar Tanabe, 903 F.2d 675, 686.
480. Ibid. at p. 686-687.

obligation.[481] Under the law of the 9th Circuit this means that if lack of due diligence *by the carrier personally* to make the ship seaworthy caused the fire, the carrier cannot rely on the Fire Statute. In the *Hyundai Explorer* case the 9th Circuit repeated its rule that, when applying the fire exception, the negligence of employees of the carrier is not to be imputed to the carrier.[482]

Hyundai Explorer (9th Cir., 1996)

322. In this case fire was caused by a faulty repair job in the engine room. The fault was not discoverable by due diligence and it was not possible to determine who was responsible for the repair job. Both the Fire Statute and the fire exception applied. The cargo interests argued that the duty to exercise due diligence to make the ship seaworthy was a non-delegable duty, meaning that the fault of an employee was to be regarded as a fault of the carrier. The 9th Circuit did not agree and held:

> 'This claim is without merit and manifests Cargo Interests' failure to recognize the different standards of due diligence that apply in the fire defences and other COGSA exemptions. While the carrier's duty of due diligence is non-delegable for exoneration under the non-fire COGSA exemptions, a different standard of due diligence, one derived from the Fire Statute, governs fire cases and eliminates vicarious liability imputed to the carrier. Under the fire defenses, a carrier is liable only for "his personal negligence, or in case of a corporate owner, negligence of its managing officers and agents as distinguished from that of the master or subordinates." *Consumers Import Co. v. Kabushiki Kaisha*, 320 U.S. 249, 252, 64 S.Ct. 15, 16, 88 L.Ed. 30 (1943); *see also Earle & Stoddart v. Ellerman's Wilson Line*, 287 U.S. 420, 427, 53 S.Ct. 200, 201, 77 L.Ed. 403 (1932) ("The courts have been careful not to thwart the purpose of the fire statute by interpreting as 'neglect' of the owners the breach of what in other connections is held to be a non-delegable duty."); *Westinghouse Elec. Corp. v. M/V "LESLIE LYKES"*, 734 F.2d 199, 209 (5th Cir.), *cert. denied,* 469 U.S. 1077, 105 S.Ct. 577, 83 L.Ed.2d 516 (1984); *Hasbro Indus. v. M/S St. Constantine*, 705 F.2d 339, 342 (9th Cir.1983) (holding that the negligence of the "shipowner's supervisory or managing employees" was sufficient to find personal negligence); *In re Ta Chi Navigation Corp., S.A.*, 677 F.2d 225, 228 (2d Cir.1982) ("'Neglect' ... means negligence, not the breach of a non-delegable duty."); *Sunkist,* 603 F.2d at 1336 (stating that "'neglect of the owner' under the Fire Statute refers to 'the neglect of the managing officers and agents as distinguished from that of the master or other members of the crew'") (quoting *Albina Engine & Machine Works v. Hershey Chocolate Corp.*, 295 F.2d 619, 621 (9th Cir.1961)); *In re Liberty Shipping Corp.,* 509 F.2d 1249, 1252 (9th Cir.1975); *Asbestos Corp. Ltd. v. Compagnie De Navigation Fraissinet et Cyprien Fabre et al.*, 480 F.2d 669, 673 n. 7 (2d Cir.1973).
>
> Although a carrier generally is not liable for the negligence or lack of due diligence of its crew or other lower level employees, it still may be liable for the actions of an employee responsible for starting the fire or preventing its spread if the carrier was personally negligent, for example, by not adequately training

---

481. See § 5.3.2.
482. Hyundai Explorer, 93 F.3d 641.

the employee or by failing to provide sufficient fire fighting equipment. *See, e.g., Hasbro,* 705 F.2d at 342; *Asbestos Corp.,* 480 F.2d at 672.'[483]

323. The 9th Circuit thus repeated the point of view taken in its previous decisions that the negligence of the carrier's employees is not imputed to the carrier. Regarding the requirement to exercise due diligence to make the ship seaworthy the court of appeal of the 9th Circuit said:

> 'Exoneration under the fire defenses is not voided by an unseaworthy condition, but rather by an "inexcusable" unseaworthy condition, *i.e.,* one that existed because of the carrier's lack of due diligence. *See Hasbro,* 705 F.2d at 341; *Sunkist,* 603 F.2d at 1335 (quoting *Asbestos Corp.,* 480 F.2d at 672). To carry its burden of proving due diligence, HMM had to prove that it had done all that was "proper and reasonable" to make the Vessel seaworthy. *See Martin v. The Southwark,* 191 U.S. 1, 15-16, 24 S.Ct. 1, 5-6, 48 L.Ed. 65 (1903).'[484]

Conclusion: 9th Circuit contra 2nd, 5th and 11th Circuits?

324. It has now become clear that the disagreement between the 9th Circuit and the 2nd, 5th and 11th Circuits is more academic than real. The latter three circuits will allow the fire defences (Fire Statute and probably fire exception) unless the fire was caused by the carrier's actual fault or privity. An inexcusable condition of unseaworthiness due to lack of fire fighting equipment or lack of crew training will constitute such actual fault or privity.
The 9th Circuit seems to reach same result but on different grounds. The 9th Circuit introduces an overriding obligation[485] (based on *Maxine Footwear*) to exercise due diligence to make the ship seaworthy. Failure to fulfil this obligation by the *carrier personally* will deprive him of the fire exception and the fire statute. An inexcusable condition of unseaworthiness caused by the carrier's failure to properly equip the ship with fire fighting equipment and man it with a properly trained crew will prove failure to fulfil the overriding obligation and therefore will deprive the carrier of the benefit of the Fire Statute or the fire exception.
All of the circuits recognise that negligence of the carrier's employees or agents is not imputed to the carrier. The results of the 9th Circuit are however the same as the other circuits only for different reasons. The 9th Circuit will deny the defence because of a breach of an overriding obligation by the carrier personally. In the other circuits the exception will also be denied, but in those circuits the reason would be that the fire was caused by the carrier's design or neglect. The difference in construction does not lead to a difference in application of the fire defences.

---

483. Hyundai Explorer, 93 F.3d 641.
484. Ibid.
485. See § 5.3.2. for a comment on the introduction of an overriding obligation under U.S. COGSA.

5.3.3.3 *What if COGSA applies alone and not besides the Fire Statute?*

325. It can be derived from *Westinghouse Electric*[486] and *Banana Services v. M/V Tasman Star*[487] that if the fire exception would apply on its own (i.e. not additional to the Fire Statute) the decisions of the 2nd, 5th and 11th Circuits would not be different. Schoenbaum also remarks that fire cases are treated *sui generis* under COGSA.[488] This means that the construction of the 2nd, 5th and 11th Circuits of the fire exception on its own would be the same as the construction of the fire exception if it applied with the Fire Statute. This construction makes sense because it is in line with the reasoning that the intention of the framers of the Hague Rules was to incorporate the Fire Statute into the Rules. This view is supported by the fact that the addition of the proviso to the fire exception was added after the proposal of the USA.[489] It would seem that the intention was to make the fire exception similar to the US Fire Statute. It has indeed been said that the fire exception under the Hague Rules could yield a different interpretation from US COGSA, because the Hague Rules do not have the antecedent of the Fire Statute.[490]

5.3.3.4 *Conclusion*

326. In the U.S. only fault or neglect of the carrier personally will cause the fire defences to fail. Failure by the carrier personally to exercise due diligence to make the ship seaworthy qualifies as fault or neglect and will cause the fire defences to fail. However, failure of the carrier's employees or agents to exercise due diligence to make the ship seaworthy will not be imputed to the carrier and will not cause the fire defence to fail. Under English law this is different. Failure of the carrier's employees or agents to exercise due diligence to make the ship seaworthy is imputed to the carrier and is considered a breach of the overriding obligation to exercise due diligence to make the ship

---

486. Westinghouse Electric Corp v. M/V Leslie Lykes, 734 F.2d 199 (5th Cir. 1984).
487. Banana Services v. M/V Tasman Star, 68 F.3d 418 (11th Cir. 1995).
488. Schoenbaum 2003, p. 620.
489. See infra § 5.3.4.
490. Damodar Bulk Carriers Ltd., 903 F.2d 675, 681 (2nd Circuit). Speaking through Circuit Judge Sneed the 9th Circuit Court of Appeal said:
    'COGSA and the Hague Rules are virtually identical in their language. The only possible discrepancy is an interpretive one involving the fire exception in COGSA (...) and the International Convention for the Unification of Certain Rules Relating to Bills of Lading (Hague Rules), art. IV(2)(b) (...) Prior to COGSA's passage, bills of lading under American law were subject to the Fire Statute (...) enacted in 1851. The Fire Statute attempted to free the vessel owner from liability for fires on board unless the fire started because of his "design or neglect". This language differed slightly from COGSA's "actual fault or privity" in the fire exemption (...) Nevertheless, Mr. Cletus Keating, who represented the American Steamship Owners' Association at the 1935 hearings on COGSA, testified that commercial interests viewed these clauses as having the same legal effect:
    I personally do not believe there is any difference between actual fault, privity, design, or neglect. This language here on line 8, page 7, follows the language of the British statute, and, of course, that is the language of the original convention, and I do not believe we ought to put in different words, because that would interfere with the effectivity of the language; and as it is, I do not think it interferes with the uniformity of the substance.
    Carriage of Goods by Sea: Hearing on S. 1152 Before the Senate Comm. on Commerce, 74th Cong., 1st Sess. 60 (1935). Gilmore and Black observe that the courts have interpreted COGSA "to save the Fire Statute from repeal". Gilmore & Black, *supra*, at 161.
    Because the Hague Rules do not have this antecedent, the fire exception under the international version could yield a different interpretation from COGSA.' (emphasis added, NJM)

seaworthy so that the fire exception of the Hague Rules will fail. However, this is not so for the English Fire Statute. The English Fire Statute can relieve the carrier from responsibility even if the duty to exercise due diligence was not fulfilled.

5.3.4 The proviso 'unless caused by the actual fault or privity of the carrier' in the fire exception

327. Under the Hague (Visby) Rules the carrier is not responsible unless the fire was caused by his actual fault or privity. During the Diplomatic Conference of October 1923 Sir Leslie Scott recognised that there was something illogical in including the reservation 'the actual fault or privity of the carrier' in the fire exception, when there was the same provision in the q-exception ('catch all'). But he feared omitting the proviso, which recalled the previous rounds of the compromise finally reached by the interested parties.[491]

It seems to be a proviso added to be sure that it is clear that *the carrier* means *the carrier personally* and e.g. not the fault or privity of the agents of the carrier. The q-exception will apply only if there was no negligence by the carrier or his agents and servants. Therefore the wording of the fire exception is similar to the wording of the Fire Statutes. Furthermore, the fact that they were added on the proposal of the United States[492] increases the likelihood of the intention of similarity with the Fire Statutes. Therefore I do not agree with the remark of Sir Leslie Scott that the proviso is illogical.

328. It has been said that this phrase did not merely denote the fault of someone for whom the carrier was responsible, but required *personal* fault of the carrier, or, where as is usual the carrier is a corporation, its *alter ego* 'directing mind and will'.[493]

329. The question of how to determine whose act or knowledge or state of mind was to be attributed to the company was discussed by the Privy Council in *Meridian Global Funds Management Asia Ltd. v. Securities Commission.*[494] The Privy Council held that a company's rights and obligations were determined by rules whereby the acts of natural persons were attributed to the company normally to be determined by reference to the primary rules of attribution generally contained in the company's constitution and implied by company law and or general rules of agency; but that, in an exceptional case, where application of those principles would defeat the intended application of a particular provision to companies, it was necessary to devise a special rule of attribution to determine whose act or knowledge or state of mind was for the purpose of that provision to be attributed to the company; that, although the description of such a person as the 'directing mind and will' of a company did not have to be apposite in every case, knowledge of an act of a company's duly authorised servant or agent, or the state of mind with which it was done, would be attributed to the company only where a true construction of the relevant substantive provision so required.[495]

---

491. Travaux Préparatoires, p. 401.
492. Travaux Préparatoires, p. 402.
493. See Carver 2005, p. 608. The phrase 'directing mind and will' comes from the speech of Viscount Haldane L.C. in Lennard's Carrying Co. Ltd. v. Asiatic Petroleum Co. Ltd. [1915] A.C. 705, 713.
494. Meridian Global Funds Management Asia Ltd. v. Securities Commission, [1995] 2 A.C. 500.
495. Ibid.

330. The Privy Council held that, having regard to the policy of the applicable rules (the Securities Amendment Act 1988), the appropriate rule of attribution in this case led to the decision that the knowledge of a person was attributable to the company irrespective of whether that person could be described in a general sense as the directing mind and will of the company.

331. Lord Hoffmann, speaking for the Privy Council, said:

> 'Once it is appreciated that the question [of whose act (or knowledge or state of mind) was for this purpose attributable to the company, NJM] is one of construction rather than metaphysics, the answer in this case seems to their Lordships to be (...) straightforward (...) The policy of section 20 of the Securities Amendment Act 1988 is to compel, in fast-moving markets, the immediate disclosure of the identity of persons who become substantial security holders in public issuers. Notice must be given as soon as that person knows that he has become a substantial security holder. In the case of a corporate security holder, what rule should be implied as to the person whose knowledge for this purpose is to count as the knowledge of the company? Surely the person who, with the authority of the company, acquired the relevant interest. Otherwise the policy of the Act would be defeated. Companies would be able to allow employees to acquire interests on their behalf which made them substantial security holders but would not have to report them until the board or someone else in senior management got to know about it. This would put a premium on the board paying as little attention as possible to what its investment managers were doing. Their Lordships would therefore hold that upon the true construction of section 20(4)(e), the company knows that it has become a substantial security holder when that is known to the person who had authority to do the deal. It is then obliged to give notice under section 20(3). The fact that Koo did the deal for a corrupt purpose and did not give such notice because he did not want his employers to find out cannot in their Lordships' view affect the attribution of knowledge and the consequent duty to notify.
> It was therefore not necessary in this case to inquire into whether Koo could have been described in some more general sense as the "directing mind and will" of the company. But their Lordships would wish to guard themselves against being understood to mean that whenever a servant of a company has authority to do an act on its behalf, knowledge of that act will for all purposes be attributed to the company. It is a question of construction in each case as to whether the particular rule requires that the knowledge that an act has been done, or the state of mind with which it was done, should be attributed to the company. Sometimes, as in In re Supply of Ready Mixed Concrete (No. 2) [1995] 1 A.C. 456 and this case, it will be appropriate. Likewise in a case in which a company was required to make a return for revenue purposes and the statute made it an offence to make a false return with intent to deceive, the Divisional Court held that the mens rea of the servant authorised to discharge the duty to make the return should be attributed to the company: see Moore v. I. Bresler Ltd. [1944] 2 All E.R. 515. On the other hand, the fact that a company's employee is authorised to drive a lorry does not in itself lead to the conclusion that if he kills someone by reckless driving, the company will be guilty of manslaugh-

ter. There is no inconsistency. Each is an example of an attribution rule for a particular purpose, tailored as it always must be to the terms and policies of the substantive rule.'[496]

332. In *Lennard's Carrying Co. Ltd. v. Asiatic Petroleum Co. Ltd.* (*The Edward Dawson*) the question was whether the company could invoke the protection of s. 502 of the Merchant Shipping Act 1894 to relieve it from the liability which the respondents sought to impose on it. That section provided:

> 'The owner of a British sea-going ship, or any share therein, shall not be liable to make good to any extent whatever any loss or damage happening without h*is actual fault or privity* in the following cases; namely, (a) Where any goods, merchandise, or other things whatsoever taken in or put on board his ship are lost or damaged by reason of fire on board the ship, ...' (emphasis added, NJM)

333. In the House of Lords Viscount Haldane L.C. said:

> 'It has not been contended at the Bar, and it could not have been successfully contended, that s. 502 is so worded as to exempt a corporation altogether which happens to be the owner of a ship, merely because it happens to be a corporation. It must be upon the true construction of that section in such a case as the present one that the fault or privity is the fault or privity of somebody *who is not merely a servant or agent for whom the company is liable* upon the footing respondeat superior, *but somebody for whom the company is liable because his action is the very action of the company itself*. It is not enough that the fault should be the fault of a servant in order to exonerate the owner, the fault must also be one which is not the fault of the owner, or a fault to which the owner is privy; and I take the view that when anybody sets up that section to excuse himself from the normal consequences of the maxim respondeat superior the burden lies upon him to do so.'[497] (emphasis added, NJM)

334. This makes it clear that the proviso contained in the fire exception is of true value because it limits the group if people who's 'fault or privity' should be taken into account to the people who can be considered to be the company itself. This group of people is smaller than the group whose actions are taken into account when construing the other exceptions. If, for example, the ship's officers who are responsible for the stowing of the cargo, are negligent in supervising and directing that work, and cargo damage occurs during rough weather which would not have occurred if the cargo had been stowed properly, then the carrier will not be able to rely on the 'perils of the sea' exception. The negligence of the ship's officers is negligence of the carrier.[498] Another example is the duty of the carrier to exercise due diligence to make the ship seaworthy. The English cases *The Muncaster Castle*[499] and *The Happy Ranger*[500] show that a carrier will

---
496. *Meridian Global Funds Management Asia Ltd. v. Securities Commission*, [1995] 2 A.C. 500, 511-512.
497. Lennard's Carrying Co. Ltd v. Asiatic Petroleum Co. Ltd (The Edward Dawson), [1915] A.C. 705, 713-714.
498. See § 5.4 about the perils of the sea exception. The carrier has the duty to load and stow the cargo properly and carefully. If his employees or agents fail to do so that failure is imputed to the carrier.
499. [1961] 1 Lloyd's Rep. 57.
500. [2006] 1 Lloyd's Rep. 649.

not be able to escape from liability if the unseaworthiness was due to an error of the carrier's servants, agents or independent contractors. This will even be the case if the servants, agents and or contractors of the carrier are well-known, experienced and respected so that one should be allowed to trust that the work delegated to such entities would be sound.[501]

The result of the proviso of the fire exception is that the carrier will only be responsible for damage caused by fire if it can be proved that the cause of the damage was a result of the *actual fault or privity* of the carrier. To render the carrier responsible, it is not sufficient that the fault or privity is the fault or privity of somebody who is merely a servant or agent for whom the company is liable.

Under common law none of the common law exceptions, other than that of jettison,[502] apply where the carrier is negligent.[503] The common law exceptions were construed as subject to an implicit proviso 'unless the carrier has been negligent'.[504] The proviso in the fire exception seems to have been added just to make it extra clear that the carrier will only be responsible for fire caused by *his* actual fault or privity, but not for the actual fault or privity of his agents.[505] It leads to the result that the carrier will not easily be found responsible for damage caused by fire. This ties in with the intention of the English and American legislators to protect the interests of their carriers for commercial reasons. Because the carriers no longer had to take the risk of liability for damage to cargo in account the freight rates could be lower thus allowing for a competitive position into the shipping industry for English (and later) American ships.[506] It seems to have been the intention of the legislator to make the fire defence an almost unbeatable defence. For that reason the proviso 'unless caused by the actual fault or privity of the carrier' was added.

5.3.5 What is meant by 'fire' in the fire exception?

Dutch law: Fire

335. According to Royer the linguistic meaning of the word should prevail. That means that 'fire' means flames, glowing and singing. Heat that does not have the aforementioned characteristics, like the self heating of hay or heat caused by steam, is not 'fire' in the sense of the exception.[507] Cargo damage caused by chemicals or by explosion not causing flames is not damage covered by the fire exception.[508] Royer is of the opinion that linguistic interpretation of the exception leads to the conclusion that damage caused indirectly by fire, such as damage by smoke, heating or water used to extinguish the fire, is damage which will be covered by the exception.[509]

---

501. See supra § 3.5.2.
502. According to Carver 2005, p. 498.
503. Carver 2005, p. 498.
504. The Torenia, [1983] Lloyd's Rep. 210, 217, citing The Glendarroch, [1894] P. 226, 231. See also Travaux Préparatoires, p. 398 where, during the Diplomatic Conference of 1923, Lord Philimore said: 'Of course, if the owner causes it willfully he is responsible; no exception in the world would take away his responsibility.'
505. Travaux Préparatoires, p. 398.
506. See § 5.3.2.2.
507. Royer 1959, p. 521.
508. Royer 1959, p. 522.
509. Royer 1959, p. 523.

On the other hand other Dutch authors are of the opinion that scorching and smouldering is not damage in the sense of the fire exception and that visible flames are required to bring the damage under the fire exception.[510]

336. In the *Hua Fang* case cargo was partly on fire and partly heated to such an extent that fire could start at any moment. The District Court of Rotterdam held that:

> '..., if, as in this case, the self-heating of the cargo eventually develops such an intense heat to cause the cargo to burst into flames, the damage caused by self-heating which existed before the actual fire, is also covered by the fire exception.'[511]

337. This decision also illustrates that the District Court of Rotterdam requires actual flames for the damage to be covered by the fire exception. The same view was held by the courts in several older decisions.[512] The above shows that the opinion under Dutch law is that actual flames are required and that mere heating is not sufficient to allow the carrier to successfully invoke the exception.

English law: Fire

338. The modern well-known English reference books do not define the word 'fire'. Tetley does however discuss the definition.[513] Cooke e.a. presume that explosion caused by fire will be covered by the exception but explosions caused by something else than fire will not. [514] Damage caused by acts necessary to put out the fire will be covered by the exception.[515]

339. In *Tempus Shipping Co. v. Louis Dreyfus Co.*, Wright J. said:

> 'It is clear that fire due to spontaneous combustion constitutes a case of fire within the bill of lading exception of fire or an insurance against fire (if questions of inherent vice are excluded) or of fire within s. 502 of the Merchant Shipping Act: Greenshields, Cowie & Co. v. Stephens & Sons, Ltd.[516] In Knight of St. Michael[517] a loss of freight through heating of cargo was held to be a loss, not indeed by fire, but within the general words of the policy as ejusdem generis. *Mere heating, which has not arrived at the stage of incandescence or ignition, is not within the specific words "fire".*
> Thus in The Diamond[518] *damage due to smoke and water used to quench fire was held to be within the section as damage caused by reason of fire. I do not think the damage need*

---

510. Cleveringa 1961, p. 492 and Boonk 1993, p. 176.
511. Hua Fang, District Court of Rotterdam 30 December 1999, S&S 2001, 25.
512. See also the cases Kyrarini, District Court of Rotterdam 18 June 1982, S&S 1982, 112 and World Japonica District Court of Rotterdam 9 March 1962, S&S 1962, 39. Hua Fang, District Court of Rotterdam 30 December 1999, S&S 2001, 25.
513. Tetley 4th edition, chapter 17.
514. Cooke e.a. 2007, p. 1026. The Inchamaree (1887) 12 App. Cas. 484.
515. The Diamond (1906) P. 282. See also Cooke e.a. 2007, p. 1026.
516. Greenshields, Cowie & Co. v. Stephens & Sons, Ltd., [1908] A.C. 431.
517. Knight of St. Michael, [1898] P. 30.
518. The Diamond, [1906] P. 282.

> *be consummated on board the ship, since the words "on board" are to be construed with the word "fire" and not with "loss and damage." In the earlier statutes the words were "fire happening on board," and I do not think that the omission of the word "happening" was intended to change the effect of the section.* In the present case I think the damage and loss of the maize in the lighter was the direct and necessary consequence of the coal on board being on fire, and I, therefore, think that so far the statute applies.'[519] (emphasis added, NJM)

340. It can be deduced from the quoted passage that heating which has reached the state of incandescence is within the meaning of the word 'fire'.

341. It can indeed be argued that incandescence without flames should also be covered by the fire exception. The reason is that the carrier who discovers that cargo is glowing, should stop all ventilation and cool the boundaries of the glowing cargo. If he then succeeds in restoring the cargo to an acceptable temperature he will not be able to invoke the fire exception. However, if the carrier opened all the hatches, thus allowing air to enter and flames to erupt, he would not be liable because the damage was caused by fire. It would be unfair if the carrier who acts correctly in the case of a fire threat cannot invoke the fire defences to cover the loss of the smouldering cargo because he acted in the correct manner i.e. cooled the boundaries and starved the glowing cargo of oxygen thus preventing flames.

> *American law: 'Fire'*

342. Under American law there seems to be no discussion about the meaning of the word 'fire' in the exception. See e.g. the *Buckeye State* case.[520] It was held in that case that more than mere heating is required for the fire exception to apply.

5.3.6 What is meant by 'actual fault or privity'?

> *Dutch law: 'Actual fault or privity'*

343. The Dutch codification of the expression 'actual fault or privity' in art. 469 of the Dutch Commercial Code was first 'intent or fault of the carrier'[521] and later in art. 383 of Book 8 of the Civil Code 'the fault of the carrier personally'.[522] Fault is used in the sense of *culpa*.[523] The newer version in the Civil Code clarifies that the fault must be a personal fault of the carrier. In the older, Commercial Code version 'intent' or 'fault' of the carrier was the phrase. As both expressions are based on the Hague Rules these subtle differences are academic.

In 1961 Cleveringa wrote that the origins of the expression lead to the conclusion that the American interpretation should be followed.[524] Cleveringa does not, however at-

---

519. Tempus Shipping Co., Ltd v. Louis Dreyfus and Co., [1930] 1 K.B. 699; [1930] 36 Ll.L.L.Rep. 159.
520. Buckeye State, 39 F. Supp. 344, 1941 AMC 1238.
521. In Dutch: 'Opzet of schuld van de vervoerder'.
522. In Dutch: 'Veroorzaakt door de persoonlijke schuld van de vervoerder'.
523. A term of civil law, meaning fault, neglect, or negligence.
524. Cleveringa 1961, p. 494.

tempt to define the expression. Neither does Boonk, another well-known Dutch author of more recent date.[525]

Royer on the other hand discusses the question extensively.[526] According to Royer the word 'actual' in the expression 'actual fault or privity' has no significance.[527] Royer is of the opinion that 'actual fault or privity' is identical to the expression 'fault or neglect' used in the q-exception and that expressions should be construed in the same way that they are in the Dutch Civil Code. This solution makes sense because there is no international concept of 'fault' or misconduct.[528]

I have not been able to find any clear examples of 'actual fault or privity' in decisions of the lower Dutch courts. Also the Supreme Court of the Netherlands has not rendered a decision giving an example or definition of 'actual fault or privity'.

English and American law: 'Actual fault or privity'

344. English and American authors do not attempt to define the expression. Examples can however be derived from English and especially from American decisions. The American courts give the same meaning to the expression 'design or neglect' from the American Fire Statute as to the words 'actual fault or privity' which is used in the fire exception. The American courts construe the expressions as being negligence that either started the fire or prevented the fire to be extinguished.[529]

'Neglect' in the Fire Statute means the same as 'fault' in the fire exception.[530] 'Design' is construed as 'a causative act or omission, done or suffered wilfully or knowingly by the ship owner'.[531] It has been said that 'privity' therefore means the same.[532]

345. In *Asbestos Corp v. Compagnie de Navigation Fraissinet et Cyprien Fabre* the 2nd Circuit held that:

> 'an inexcusable condition of unseaworthiness of a vessel, which in fact causes the damage – either by starting a fire or by preventing its extinguishment– will exclude the ship-owners from the exemption of the Fire Statute and COGSA.'[533]

346. The 2nd Circuit agreed with the opinion given by Judge Levet in the District Court (SDNY).[534] Levet J. recognised that unseaworthiness does not prevent the application of the Fire Statute and that once the defendant has sustained the burden of proving that it comes within the exemption of COGSA § 1304(2) (b) or the Fire Statute the burden

---

525. Boonk 1993, p. 176-181.
526. Royer 1959, p. 546-559.
527. Royer 1959, p. 551.
528. For this reason art. 29(1) of the Convention on the contract for the International Carriage of Good by Road (CMR) provides: The carrier shall not be entitled to avail himself of the provisions of this chapter which exclude or limit his liability or which shift the burden of proof if the damage was caused by his wilful misconduct or by such default on his part as, in accordance with the law of the court or tribunal seised of the case, is considered as equivalent to wilful misconduct.
529. See infra.
530. Ta Chi Navigation, 677 F.2d 228.
531. The Strathdon, 89 F. 374, 378 (E.D.N.Y. 1898).
532. O'Conner & O'Reilly 2002, p. 116.
533. Asbestos Corp v. Compagnie de Navigation Fraissinet et Cyprien Fabre, 480 F.2d 669.
534. 345 F.supp. 814.

then shifts to the shipper to prove that the fire was caused by the 'design or neglect' or 'actual fault or privity' of the carrier. Levet J. said:

347. 'It is indeed unfortunate that all equipment aboard the *Marquette* available for fighting engine room fires was located in or controlled from the engine room. It was this "putting all the eggs in one basket" which led to the deplorable situation to which the chief engineer testified: "the ship was condemned as we had no further possibility of fighting the fire."
(...) It is incumbent upon every ship-owner to provide a seaworthy vessel, equipped with adequate means of fighting fire on board. The standard is whether it is reasonable for a ship-owner to provide certain apparatus to meet the contingency of fire (...) What is reasonable is what is required in light of all the circumstances. This court has no interest in imposing an unreasonable or higher standard than required upon the ship-owner. Minimal foresight, however, dictates that the engine room is highly volatile compartment of a ship and the possibility of fire breaking out is ever present. A ship-owner must anticipate and provide for the contingency that a fire may break out in the engine room disabling all fire fighting equipment located in the engine room. The owners of the Marquette through their "design or neglect" and "privity or knowledge" were negligent in placing all fire fighting equipment inside the engine room and failing to provide an emergency pump or fire system located or controlled from outside the engine room. This negligence on the part of the ship-owners displays a total disregard for minimal protection of cargo and rendered the Marquette unseaworthy. Under the circumstances this court concludes that the defendant-ship-owners are not exempt from liability under COGSA § 1304(2) (b) or the Fire Statute.'[535]

348. In *Sunkist Growers, Inc. v. Adelaide Shipping Lines* it was held that: 'The "design or neglect" being the failure to provide a proper compression or flange joint and to properly man and equip a trained crew prior to the commencement of the voyage.'[536]

Conclusion

349. The conclusion from these cases is that failure to fulfil the non-delegable duty to use due diligence to furnish a seaworthy ship does not render the carrier responsible. However if the ship is unseaworthy due to lack of due diligence and that unseaworthiness was due to 'design or neglect' and 'privity or knowledge' of the carrier, the carrier is therefore not exempt from liability under the fire exception or the Fire Statute.

5.3.7 Which persons are meant by 'the carrier'?

350. This paragraph does not concern the problems of the *identity* of the carrier. It assumes that it is known which entity is the carrier. The question is: whose actions can be attributed to the carrier?

---

535. Asbestos Corp v. Compagnie de Navigation Fraissinet et Cyprien Fabre, 345 F.supp. 814.
536. Sunkist Growers, Inc. v. Adelaide Shipping Lines, 603 F.2d 1327.

Dutch law: 'the carrier'

351. The acts of the owner of a sole proprietorship, the active partners of general partnership, the bookkeeper of a shipping company and the directors of a private company with limited liability can be attributed to the carrier. Within a legal person the acts of other persons than the directors can be attributed to 'the carrier'. Decisions on this point from other fields of law are also relevant to determine which people can be identified with the carrier.[537] In the *Portalon* case the court of appeal held the acts of those who are in actual control of the corporation are to be attributed to the carrier. The acts of the captain of a ship cannot be attributed to the carrier.[538] Under Dutch law acts of the governing bodies of a legal person are attributed to the legal person. Also acts of those whose conduct is, according to societal opinion, to be attributed to the legal person are considered acts of the legal person.[539] Considering their societal position, the conduct of the captain and chief engineer is not considered as conduct of the legal person.[540]

English law: 'the carrier'

352. The phrase 'actual fault or privity' also appeared in the English Fire Statute of the Merchant Shipping Act 1894.[541] Under that statute it was clear that this phrase did not merely denote the fault of someone for whom the carrier was responsible, but required personal fault in the carrier, or where as is usual the carrier is a corporation, its *alter ego* or 'directing mind and will'.[542] 'More recent authority in a different context has made it clear that this may however require a further discrimination as to "whose act (or knowledge or state of mind) was *for this purpose* intended to count as the act etc. of the company?"'[543] In the *Meridian Global Funds Management Asia Ltd. v. Securities Commission* case Lord Hoffman in delivering the judgement of the Privy Council said:

> 'One possibility is that the court may come to the conclusion that the rule was not intended to apply to companies at all; for example, a law which created an offence for which the only penalty was community service. Another possibility is that the court might interpret the law as meaning that it could apply to a company only on the basis of its primary rules of attribution, i.e. if the act giving rise to liability was specifically authorised by a resolution of the board or an unanimous agreement of the shareholders. But there will be many cases in which neither of these solutions is satisfactory; in which the court considers that the law was intended to apply to companies and that, although it excludes ordinary vicarious liability, insistence on the primary rules of attribution would in practice defeat that intention. In such a case, the court must fashion a special rule of attribution for the particular substantive rule. This is always a

---

537. Boonk 1993, p. 180.
538. Portalon, Court of Appeal The Hague 30 December 1966, S&S 1967, 28.
539. Supreme Court of The Netherlands, 6 April 1979, NJ 1980, 34.
540. Prins Maurits, Supreme Court of The Netherlands 4 October 1991, S&S 1992, 92, NJ 1992, 410.
541. See supra.
542. Lennard's Carrying Co. Ltd v. Asiatic Petroleum Co. Ltd (The Edward Dawson), [1915] A.C. 705, 713-714. See also Carver 2005, p. 608.
543. Meridian Global Funds Management Asia Ltd v. Securities Commission [1995] 2 A.C. 500, 507 and Carver 2005, p. 608.

matter of interpretation: given that it was intended to apply to a company, how was it intended to apply? Whose act (or knowledge, or state of mind) was *for this purpose* intended to count as the act etc. of the company? One finds the answer to this question by applying the usual canons of interpretation, taking into account the language of the rule (if it is a statute) and its content and policy.'[544]

353. In de *Apostolis* the court held that the fault or privity of the 'general manager' of the vessel's managers counted as actual fault or privity of the owners.[545]

American law: 'the carrier'

354. Under American law the answer to the question which people are to be identified with the carrier is complicated because the Fire Statute and fire exception often both apply in the same case. The question of who is 'owner' under the American Fire Statute and 'carrier' under COGSA is not considered separately in American decisions. This creates the impression that 'owner' and 'carrier' are the same entities which, strictly speaking, is incorrect. The proviso of the American Fire Statute reads: '..., unless such fire is caused by the design or neglect of such *owner*' (emphasis added, NJM). 'Owner' is the (legal) person who owns the ship. The Limitation Act (of which the Fire Statute is part of) also provides that:

> '[t]he charterer of any vessel, in case he shall man, victual, and navigate such vessel at his own expense, or by his own procurement, shall be deemed the owner of such vessel within the meaning of the provisions of title 48 of the Revised Statutes relating to the limitation of the liability of the owners of vessels; and such vessel, when so chartered, shall be liable in the same manner as if navigated by the owner thereof.'[546]

355. The proviso of COGSA reads 'unless caused by the actual fault or privity of *the carrier*.' COGSA defines 'carrier' in art 1 sub a COGSA as: 'the *owner* or the *charterer* who enters into a contract of carriage with a shipper.' (emphasis added, NJM).

356. In *Westinghouse Electric*, referring to the *Ta Chi Navigation* case, the court held:

> 'It has long been held that the COGSA fire exemption and the Fire Statute exemption are the same (...) except that COGSA extends to the "carrier", not just the "owner" as in the Fire Statute.'[547]

357. I shall not go into the different scopes of application of the fire exception and Fire Statute and restrict myself to some considerations from American cases.

358. In *Asbestos Corp v. Compagnie de Navigation Fraissinet et Cyprien Fabre* the district court held that:

---

544. [1995] 2 A.C. 500, 507.
545. The Apostolis, [1996] 1 Lloyd's Rep. 475.
546. 46 U.S.C. §182.
547. Ta Chi Navigation, 677 F.2d 225.

5.3 THE FIRE EXCEPTION

'Negligence on the part of the master, any crew member or agent is not imputed to the owner. However, courts have found that fault of managing agents to whom the corporation delegates the task of inspection, decisions on precautions, and the like is the fault of the owner, ...'.[548]

359. In the *Tecomar S.A* the words 'managing officer' were said to mean 'anyone whom the corporation has delegated general management of general superintendence of the whole or a particular part of the business.'[549]

360. In *Westinghouse Electric*, reference was made to a decision of the US Supreme Court in *Consumers Import* concerning the application of the fire defences. The US Supreme Court held that:

'..., the negligence was, (...), by shore-based persons who were delegated the task of designating and planning the stowage. Because the delegees were not managerial agents with a broad range or responsibility in the corporation and because they were "qualified by experience to perform the work," such negligence was not the "design or neglect" of the owner.'[550]

361. In *Union Oil Co. v. Point Diver* the 5th Cir. held that:

'[a] finding of neglect of owner means personal negligence, or in the case of a corporate owner, negligence of managing officers and agents as distinguished from that of the Master or his subordinates.'[551]

362. In *Sunkist* the 9th Circuit held:

'In Albina Engine & Machine Workers v. Hershey Chocolate Corp., 295 F.2d 619 (CA9 1961), we held that:

"neglect of the owner" under the Fire Statute refers to "the neglect of managing officers and agents as distinguished from that of the master or other members of the crew or subordinate employees."'[552]

363. It can be concluded that under the Fire Statute and under the COGSA fire exception the personal negligence of the owner or carrier will beat a fire defence. In a corporation the negligence should be negligence of corporate managers and agents, who are acting within the scope of their authority for that negligence to be imputed to the owner/carrier. Negligence of the captain and crew can not to be imputed to the owner or the carrier.

---

548. Asbestos Corp v. Compagnie de Navigation Fraissinet et Cyprien Fabre, (1973) A.M.C. 1683 (2nd Cir. 1973).
549. Tecomar S.A, 465 F.Supp. 1150.
550. Westinghouse Electric, 734 F.2d 199.
551. Union Oil Co. v. Point Diver, 756 F.2d 1223 (5Cir. 1985).
552. Sunkist, F.2d 1327, 1336.

5.3.8 The relationship between the duties of the carrier and the fire exception

American law

364. Under the law of the 2nd, 5th and 11th Circuits the mere breach of a duty causing damage by fire is not sufficient to overcome the fire exception. A breach of a duty entailing actual fault or privity of the carrier personally is required. In the 9th Cir. however, if the claimant proves that unseaworthiness caused the fire, the carrier can only rely on a fire defence if he proves his personal due diligence to make the ship seaworthy. The duty to exercise due diligence to make the ship seaworthy is an overriding obligation under the law of the 9th Circuit.[553]
Below the situation under Dutch and English law is discussed.

Dutch law

365. Cleveringa is of the opinion that the duties contained in art. IIII(1) and (2) H(V)R are not affected by the proviso of the fire exception and that the proviso does not have much significance.[554] Royer follows the American point of view that the carrier is only responsible for damage caused by his personal fault and that the fire exception prevails above the duty contained in art. III(1) H(V)R if the actual fault or privity of the carrier was not the cause of the fire.[555] According to Boonk justice is done to the words 'Subject to the provisions of Article IV, ...' in art. III(2) and the proviso in the fire exception if the duty contained in art. III(1) is considered a more fundamental duty than the duty contained in art. III(2). This means that fire due to a lack of due diligence to provide a seaworthy ship which is not equal to actual fault or privity of the carrier *will* render the carrier responsible. However fire caused by a breach of art. III(2) which is not equal to actual fault or privity of the carrier, *will not* cause the fire exception defence to fail.[556]

366. In the *Portalon* the court of appeal held that the carrier could not avail himself of the fire exception if lack of due diligence to make the ship seaworthy caused the fire. The court of appeal also held that the cargo interest could not beat the fire exception by proving the carrier was in breach of one of his duties contained in art. III(1) or (2). The court of appeal held that:

> 'the [Travaux Préparatoires] of the Hague Rules do not show with certainty that (...) contrary to what is the case with the other exceptions, it was the intention to allow the exoneration for damage by fire (...) even if the carrier did not fulfil his primary duty to exercise due diligence to make the ship seaworthy and to properly and carefully care for the cargo.'[557]

367. The court of appeal clarified its opinion when discussing the third complaint of the cargo interests which was aimed against the decision of the district court that neg-

---

553. The Maurienne, [1959] 2 Lloyd's Rep. 105.
554. Royer 1959, p. 494.
555. Royer 1959, p. 540 and p. 542.
556. Boonk 1993, p. 179.
557. Court of Appeal of The Hague 30 December 1966, S&S 1967, 28.

ligent treatment of the cargo does not beat the fire exception. The court of appeal allowed this point of appeal and thus held that the duty to properly and carefully care for the cargo is an overriding duty.

368. In the *Hua Fang* however, the District Court of Rotterdam held:

> 'A carrier can not avail himself of the fire exception if the fire was caused by his actual fault or privity as stated in art. 4(2)b H(V)R or by unseaworthiness which was a result of lack of due diligence which the carrier must exercise ex art. 3(1) H(V)R before and at the beginning of the voyage. Because of the system of the H(V)R the cargo interests must state, and if necessary prove that the fire is a result of these factors which will overcome the fire exception. A possible breach of the duty contained art. 3(2) H(V)R to exercise due diligence [sic] for the care of the cargo, however, is not significant if that breach caused the fire, because a breach of that duty does not set aside the application of the fire exception, unless the fire was caused by actual fault or privity of the carrier.'[558]

369. In the *Boschkerk* the district court and the appeal court held that the fire exception will exonerate the carrier if the damage was caused by servants of the carrier but not if the fire was caused by a lack of due diligence to make the ship seaworthy.[559]

370. The above shows that the opinion of Dutch authors and courts are divided regarding the question if the duty to care for the cargo properly and carefully is an overriding obligation. In other words the question: Will the fire exception apply if the fire was caused by (or could not be controlled due to) negligence in the care of the cargo where the negligence was not due to the actual fault or privity of the carrier? However, there is no doubt that the duty to exercise due diligence to make the ship seaworthy is an overriding obligation under Dutch law.

371. I doubt if the *Portalon* decision of The Hague Court of Appeal on 30 December 1966 would still be followed by Dutch courts because the decision that a breach of the duty contained in art. III(2) will cause the fire exception to fail is so evidentially contrary to the construction of the Rules by English and American courts.

English law

372. In *Maxine Footwear Co. Ltd. v Canadian Government Merchant Marine Ltd. (The Maurienne)*[560] a ship caught fire while still in port and after loading had begun. The fire had been caused by work negligently performed with an acetylene torch. Although the case was a decision of the Privy Council (Canada) under the Canadian Water Carriage of Goods Act, 1936 it seems to be the leading case in English law.[561] 'If the fire creates unseaworthiness during the period over which the ship must be seaworthy under the

---

558. District Court of Rotterdam 30 December 1999, S&S 2001, 25.
559. District Court of Rotterdam 30 June 1964, S&S 1965, 54, confirmed by the Court of Appeal of The Hague 19 June 1966, S&S 1966, 87.
560. Maxine Footwear Co. Ltd v. Canadian Government Merchant Marine Ltd (The Maurienne), [1959] 2 Lloyd's Rep. 105.
561. See Carver 2005, p. 608 and Scrutton 1996, p. 444 Cooke e.a. 2007, p. 1026.

Rules, [the fire exception] does not apply, for the loss is caused by unseaworthiness which is not an excepted peril'.[562]

373. In *Apostolis* the court of appeal held:

> 'To show breach of art. III r. 1 AMJ must show that the carriers failed to make the ship seaworthy and that their loss or damage was caused by the breach, or in other words was caused by unseaworthiness.'[563]

374. This decision makes clear that causal connection between the lack of due diligence and the damage by fire is required to overcome the fire exception. This also is clear from *Maxine Footwear* where Lord Somervell of Harrow said:

> 'Art. III, Rule 1, is an overriding obligation. If it is not fulfilled *and the non-fulfilment causes the damage*, the immunities of Art. IV cannot be relied on. This is the natural construction apart from the opening words of Art. IV, Rule 2. The fact that that Rule is made subject to the provision of Art. IV and Rule 1 is not so conditioned makes the point clear beyond argument.'[564] (emphasis added, NJM)

375. Art. III(2) H(V)R and of the English COGSA start with the words 'Subject to the provisions of article IV,...'. As was said above these words have been referred to as being an indication that art. III(1) is an overriding obligation.[565] In the *Apostolis* the meaning of the opening words of art. III(2) in relation to the proviso of the fire exception was discussed. Tuckey J. of the Queen's Bench Division said:

> 'Article III, r. 2, which would otherwise impose liability on owners on the basis of my findings of fact, *is expressed to be subject to the provisions of art. IV*. Article IV, r. 2 says no liability for fire "unless" caused by actual fault or privity. (...) The fault and privity provision is an exception to an express exemption and therefore, following general principles of construction, it is for the party alleging that the exception applies to establish it.' (emphasis added, NJM)

376. On appeal the court of appeal held:

> '..., the allegation of privity against the owners must fail, and the defence under art. IV, r. 2 succeeds. In this context it is therefore of less importance whether the owners *would otherwise been liable under art. III, r. 2.*'[566] (emphasis added, NJM)

377. The above shows that if the fire is due to lack of due diligence to make the ship seaworthy the carrier will be responsible. If, however, the fire is due to failure to fulfil

---

562. Carver 2005, p. 608 referring to Maxine Footwear (see supra). See also Scrutton 1996, p. 444.
563. A. Meredith Jones v. Vangemar Shipping Co. (The Apostolis), [1997] 2 Lloyd's Rep. 241.
564. Maxine Footwear Co. Ltd v. Canadian Government Merchant Marine Ltd (The Maurienne),[1959] 2 Lloyd's Rep. 105, 113.
565. Ibid.
566. The Apostolis, [1997] 2 Lloyd's Rep. 241, 248 (Court of Appeal).

the duty of art. III(2) the carrier can rely on the fire exception unless the fire was caused by his actual fault or privity.

Conclusion

378. Under English and Canadian law and the law of the 9th Circuit the duty to exercise due diligence to make the ship seaworthy is an overriding obligation and the duty ex art. III(2) H(V)R regarding the care for the cargo is not. This follows from the words 'subject to the provisions of art. IV' in art. III(2). It has also been said that it follows from art. IV(1) which provides that if the damage was caused by unseaworthiness the carrier has to prove that he used due diligence. The fact that the carrier gets the burden to prove his due diligence would show that art. III(1) is an overriding obligation.[567] The last argument is less convincing than the argument that the meaning of art. IV(1) is to show that the law of the Harter Act is changed in the sense that the proof of due diligence is not a precondition to the application of one of the exception.[568]

379. So under English and Canadian law III(1) H(V)R is an overriding obligation and III(2) is not. Why is this so? At common law, as would be expected, the duty make the ship seaworthy is an absolute duty. That duty and the duty to care for the cargo properly and carefully are both overriding obligations.[569]

380. Under the Hague Rules the duty to make the ship seaworthy was reduced to a duty to exercise due diligence to make the ship seaworthy. The question of why the Hague Rules changed the common law rule that both duties of the carrier (regarding seaworthiness of the ship and care for the cargo) are both overriding obligations to the rule that only the duty to exercise due diligence to make the ship seaworthy is an overriding obligation is discussed in § 4.7. The new rule is to the advantage of carriers. This is contrary to the compromise character of the Rules. The actual result of the overriding obligation rule and in my opinion the reason that it exists, is for the sake of the fire exception. The fire exception could only exist in the same form as the fire statute if the overriding obligation rule was introduced.

5.3.9 The burden of proof

Dutch law: the burden of proof

381. The cargo interests first have to prove damage to the cargo which occurred after loading. The carrier will then prove that the damage was caused by fire and invoke the fire exception. If the cause of the fire remains unknown the carrier can rely on the fire exception.[570] The cargo interests can either prove that the fire was due to unseaworthiness or due to the actual fault or privity of the carrier.[571] In the former instance the

---

567. Clarke 1976, p. 161.
568. See the Damodar Tanabe, 903 F.22 675, 684-685. See also § 5.1.
569. Paterson SS Ltd v. Canadian Co-operative Wheat Producers Ltd., 49 Ll.L.L.R. 42. See supra § 4.2. See also Carver 2005, p. 499.
570. Corrientes II, Court of Appeal The Hague 20 april 1993, S&S 1995, 11 and Karimata, District Court of Amsterdam 25 June 1975, S&S 1976, 6.
571. Cleveringa 1961, p. 493.

carrier will have to prove that he used due diligence to make the ship seaworthy (art. IV lid 1 H(V)R). In the latter instance the carrier will be responsible. This is the system according to the H(V)R. However in the *Hua Fang* the District Court of Rotterdam held that:

> 'A carrier can not rely on the fire exception if the fire was caused by the carrier's actual fault or privity as stated in art. IV(2)b, or by unseaworthiness due to lack of due diligence before and at the beginning of the voyage ex art. III(1). It follows from the system of the H(V)R that the cargo interests have to (...)[572] prove that the fire was caused by these causes which will successfully deprive the carrier of the fire defence.'[573]

382. In my opinion the court misstated the system of the H(V)R. Art. IV(1) clearly provides that if the loss or damage was caused by unseaworthiness the carrier has to prove that he exercised due diligence to make the ship seaworthy. The cargo interests only have to prove that the loss or damage caused by unseaworthiness. They do not have to prove the carrier's failure to exercise due diligence.

383. According to Schadee failure to fulfil the duty contained in art. III(2) H(V)R will also overcome the fire exception. The cargo interest have the burden of proving the failure to fulfil the duty contained in art. III(2).[574]
As is seen above this was also the view held by the court of appeal in the *Portalon* case. The opinion of Schadee was written over fifty years ago and I do not think it will be followed by courts in the Netherlands today because it is evidentially contrary to the construction of the fire exception by English and American courts.

English law: the burden of proof

384. The cargo interests first have to prove damage to the cargo which occurred after loading. If the cargo interests can prove that the ship was unseaworthy at the beginning of the voyage and that unseaworthiness caused the fire then the carrier will have the burden of proving that due diligence was exercised to make the ship seaworthy (art. IV(1) H(V)R).[575] If the ship became unseaworthy because of the fire and the carrier can not prove due diligence before and at the beginning of the voyage then he can not rely on the exception.[576] The cargo interests have the burden of proving actual fault or privity.[577]

American law: the burden of proof

385. As was discussed above the 9th Cir. has held that the carrier can not assert the fire exception unless he proves that he exercised due diligence to make the ship seawor-

---

572. The omitted words state the system of Dutch law that something alleged only has to be proven if the other party sufficiently disputes the allegations.
573. Rotterdam District Court 30 December 1999, S&S 2001, 25.
574. Schadee 1954, p. 766-767.
575. See also Cooke e.a. 2007, p. 1017.
576. Maxine Footwear, (1959) 2 Lloyd's Rep. 105. See also Baughen 2001, p. 120.
577. The Apostolis (1996) 1 Lloyd's Rep. 475 op p. 501. Carver 2005, p. 608.

thy.[578] The 2nd, 5th and 11th Circuits do not require this proof of the carrier. The shipper can prove that the carrier caused the damage either by proving that a negligent act of the carrier caused the fire or that such an act prevented the fire's extinguishment.[579] In the 2nd, 5th and 11th Circuits fire caused by merely a lack of due diligence will not be sufficient to rebut the fire exception.[580]

5.3.10 The intended construction of the fire exception

386. What is meant by the words 'the carrier's actual fault'? Objective construction does not help. The French text uses the expressions 'le fait ou la faute du transporteur'. To discover what the framer meant I shall resort to subjective construction, i.e. what did the framers mean? The Travaux Préparatoires do not give a definite explanation. Bearing the common law roots in mind it is permissible to study common law. Mr. Justice Jocobucci of the Canada Supreme Court explained the meaning as follows:

> 'The leading Anglo-Canadian case setting out the meaning of the words "actual fault or privity" and its application to a corporate shipowner is Lennard's Carrying Co. v. Asiatic Petroleum Co., [1915] A.C. 705 (H.L.), affirming [1914] 1 K.B. 419 (C.A.). The words "actual fault or privity" were found to denote something personal and blameworthy to a shipowner as opposed to a constructive fault arising under the doctrine of respondeat superior. In the oft quoted words of Viscount Haldane L.C. at p. 713-714:
> It must be upon the true construction of that section in such a case as the present one that the fault or privity is the fault or privity of somebody who is not merely a servant or agent for whom the company is liable upon the footing respondeat superior, but somebody for whom the company is liable because his action is the very action of the company itself. It is not enough that the fault should be the fault of a servant in order to exonerate the owner, the fault must also be one which is not the fault of the owner, or a fault to which the owner is privy; and I take the view that when anybody sets up that section to excuse himself from the normal consequences of the maxim respondeat superior the burden lies upon him to do so.'[581]

387. The intention of the framers was that the carrier can not rely on the fire exception if the fire was caused by the fault or privity of someone whose action is the very action of the company itself as opposed to fault or privity of somebody who is merely a servant or agent for whom the company is liable.
Reading the Rules as a whole it can be deduced that the carrier can not invoke the exceptions of art. IV if the cause of the fire is non-fulfilment of art. III(1). The carrier can invoke the fire exception if the cause was non-fulfilment of art. III(2) (because that art. applies subject to the provisions of art IV) unless the cause can be qualified as actual fault or privity. Still reading the Rules as a whole it can also be deduced that art. VIII of the Rules will leave carriers the benefit of the Fire Statutes. If the Fire Statutes were the same as the fire exception there would be no reason to specifically refer to the applica-

---

578. See supra (The Sunkist case).
579. Asbestos Corp. Ltd., supra, 480 F.2d at 672.
580. See supra.
581. 'The Rhone' and 'Peter A.B. Widener', [1993] 1 Lloyd's Rep. 600.

bility of the Fire Statutes. This indicates that the Fire Statutes were thought to be a stronger defence than the fire exception.

388. The object of the fire exception in combination with art. VIII is that carriers will not be responsible for damage by fire unless:

(i) it was caused by the actual fault or privity of the carrier (as opposed to constructive fault or privity) or
(ii) by non-fulfilment of art. III(1) unless a Fire Statute applies.

5.3.11 Conclusion

389. The English and American Fire Statutes are very important defences for the sea carrier under English and American law. The defence will only fail if the fire was caused by the actual fault or privity of the owner. Even if the fire was caused by unseaworthiness at the beginning of the voyage the fire defence can be relied upon. The defence will only fail if it can be proven that the unseaworthiness was caused by the actual fault or privity of the carrier.[582] The fire exception is also a very strong defence (although less so than the Fire Statutes). The fire exception will fail if the fire was caused by lack of due diligence to make the ship seaworthy. Under English law this is the result of the concept of the overriding obligation to exercise due diligence to make the ship seaworthy. The reason for such a wide ranging exemption for damage caused by fire is rarely stated in English decisions. In American decisions it however becomes clear that the reason for such a strong defence is to make sure that the carrier will, in principle, not be responsible for damage caused by fire. This allowed the carrier to reduce the freight rates. The conclusion is that the fire defences were intended to be practically unbeatable.

It can be wondered whether such reasoning is still valid in the modern era. Other carriers (i.e. road, rail and air carriers) do not have a similar defence against liability for damage by fire. Is the risk of fire at sea greater than in other forms of transport and if so, is it still justified to have legislation which protects the sea carrier to such a great extent as the maritime fire defences? It is beyond the scope of this book to discuss these questions. Risk analysis would have to show if the risk of fire at sea is greater and the consequences more severe than in other modes of carriage and economic research would have to show what the economical consequences would be of removing the defence. However, although there is considerable opposition to the retention of the fire exception (as well as the nautical fault exception)[583] the fire exception has been retained in the UNCITRAL Draft Instrument on Carriage of Goods by Sea but in a different form.

390. In the draft instrument the fire exception is worded under art. 18:

1. The carrier is liable for loss of or damage to the goods, as well as for delay in delivery, if the claimant proves that the loss, damage, or delay, or the event or circumstance

---
582. See infra.
583. UNCITRAL WG III document WP.101.

that caused or contributed to it took place during the period of the carrier's responsibility as defined in chapter 4.

2. The carrier is relieved of all or part of its liability pursuant to paragraph 1 of this article if it proves that the cause or one of the causes of the loss, damage, or delay is not attributable to its fault or to the fault of any person referred to in article 19.

3. The carrier is also relieved of all or part of its liability pursuant to paragraph 1 of this article if, alternatively to proving the absence of fault as provided in paragraph 2 of this article, it proves that one or more of the following events or circumstances caused or contributed to the loss, damage, or delay:

(...)
(f) fire on the ship
(...)

Art. 19 provides that the carrier is liable for the breach of its obligations under this Convention caused by the acts or omissions of:
(a) any performing party;
(b) the master or crew of the ship;
(c) employees or agents of the carrier or a performing party; or
(d) any other person that performs or undertakes to perform any of the carrier's obligations under the contract of carriage, to the extent that the person acts, either directly or indirectly, at the carrier's request or under the carrier's supervision or control.

391. It is clear that this fire exception is not nearly as far reaching as the fire exception of the Hague Rules. The carrier bears the burden of proving either the exception or the absence of fault. If he chooses to prove fire he will have to prove fire on the ship. Furthermore the reference to article 19 in article 18(2) makes it clear that if the fire is caused by the fault of one of the carrier's employees the carrier will also be liable. This certainly will make it easier for cargo interests to defeat the fire exception in the new instrument than under the Hague (Visby) Rules.

5.4 Perils of the sea

5.4.1 Introduction

392. The 'perils of the sea exception' has been an important and strong defence of carriers from earliest times.[584] The exception is contained in art. IV(2)c H(V)R and reads:

> 'neither the carrier nor the ship shall be responsible for loss or damage arising or resulting from:
> (...)
> (c) Perils, dangers and accidents of the sea or other navigable waters.'

393. The expression 'Perils of the Sea' is construed differently in different legal systems. The applicable law will be of influence on the carrier's chance to successfully invoke the exception or not. The *Bunga Seroja* case of the High Court of Australia is a well

---

[584] Bunga Seroja, High Court of Australia, 22 October 1998, ETL 1999, p. 459 and [1999] 1 Lloyd's Rep. 512. See also Tetley 4th ed., chapter 18, p. 4.

researched case regarding the perils of the sea exception.[585] After extensive historical and comparative law study the judges in that case reached a decision which has been criticised by Tetley.[586] Regardless of Tetley's criticism the case is, in my opinion, one of the best researched judgements written on the application of the perils of the sea exception and for that reason the case is referred to relatively often in this paragraph. In the *Bunga Seroja* case a comparison is made between the application of the exception in the UK, the USA, Canada and Australia. The case shows that there are two schools of thought. Under American and Canadian law the event which caused the damage has to be unforeseeable for the exception to succeed. This requirement does not however exist under English and Canadian law. Below the application of the exception under English, American, Canadian and Australian law is researched. Then the application of the exception under Dutch law is researched. First however, the exception will be discussed in general whereby the historical background of the exception also plays a role. I will conclude that the application of the exception in the Netherlands is similar to the application of the exception under Australian law. I will also conclude that the nature of the exception leads to the conclusion that the carrier can not rely on it if the loss or damage was caused by lack of due diligence to provide a seaworthy ship or to care for the cargo properly and carefully. The carrier can only rely on the exception if he fulfilled the duties contained in art. III(1) and (2). The carrier has to prove that the cause of the loss or damage was unavoidable to be able to rely on the exception.

5.4.2 Elements that may constitute a peril of the sea

394. In *Bunga Seroja* Judge Kirby derived a number of factual considerations from existing cases which can help to decide whether a particular event at sea amounts to a peril of the sea. Regarding these Kirby said:

> 'These [factual considerations] might include the construction of the vessel, the size and capacity of the vessel, whether the vessel was suitably constructed, normally equipped and properly maintained, whether the event giving rise to the damage or loss was a freak occurrence, the intensity and predictability of any weather or other hazard encountered and whether it could have been guarded against by the ordinary exertions of a carrier's skill and prudence. Yet none of these circumstances is decisive. They are no more than factual indicia.'[587]

395. Another element often considered relevant in court rulings on the question whether a perils of the sea defence should be accepted is the question whether the incident could have been foreseen, which is often regarded as a controversial issue. It largely depends on the applicable law whether a perils of the sea defence will be accepted if the event could have been foreseen. Foreseeability therefore often plays a decisive part. In this section I will take a closer look at the element of foreseeability.

---

585. Bunga Seroja, [1999] 1 Lloyd's Rep. 512 and ETL 1999, p. 459.
586. Tetley 4th ed., chapter 18, p. 7.
587. Bunga Seroja, [1999] 1 Lloyd's Rep. 512 sub 147.

5.4.3 The construction of the exception under various legal systems

5.4.3.1 *English law*

396. In *Thames and Mersey Marine Ins. Co. v. Hamilton, Fraser & Co.* Lord Macnaghten pointed out that a rigid definition of the expression 'perils of the sea' should be avoided. He said:

> 'I think that each case must be considered with reference to its own circumstances, and that the circumstances of each case must be looked at in a broad commonsense view.'[588]

397. In the 1988 edition of Marine Cargo Claims Tetley also notes that in England courts have been careful not to formulate rigid definitions of the exception.[589] Despite the fact that a precise definition cannot be formulated, under English law certain elements are often important in deciding the question whether an incident may be considered to be a Peril of the Sea. The two most controversial elements are foreseeability and the question whether an incident must be of an extraordinary nature to qualify as a peril. These two elements will be discussed below.

The requirement that the event was unforeseeable

398. According to Tetley English courts continue to reject the 'perils of the sea defence' in cases where the bad weather was foreseeable, and require that it be, if not exceptional, at least unanticipated. Tetley cites four English cases to prove his point.[590] After reading the decisions cited by Tetley it becomes clear that the 'foreseeable' aspect is merely a point of view and is not an element which will decide the case.

399. In *The Coral* the exception was not allowed because the cause of the damage was negligent stowing of the cargo.[591]

400. In *The Tilia Gorthon* Mr. Justice Sheen did indeed say:

> 'It seems highly probable that none of the deck cargo would have been lost but for the violence of the storm. But the evidence as to the weather has not satisfied me that the conditions encountered were such as could not and should not have been contemplated by the ship-owners. Fortunately for mariners, winds of 48-55 knots (Beaufort force 10) are encountered infrequently. But they are by no means so exceptional in the North Atlantic in the autumn and winter that the possibility of encountering them can be ignored. A ship embarking

---

588. Thames and Mersey Marine Ins. Co. v. Hamilton, Fraser & Co. (1887) 12 A.C. 484.
589. Tetley 1988, p. 437-438. Tetley refers to three pre Hague Rules decisions: Thames and Mersey Marine Insurance Co. v. Hamilton, Fraser & Co., (1887) 12 App. Cas. 484, The Xantho (1887) 12 App. Cas. 503 and Hamilton Fraser & Co. v. Pandorf & Co., (1887) 12 App. Cas. 518.
590. Tetley refers to The Friso [1980] 1 Lloyd's Rep. 469, 472; The Torenia [1983] 2 Lloyd's Rep. 210 at p. 214-215; The Tilia Gorthon [1985] 1 Lloyd's Rep. 552 at p. 555; The Coral [1992] 2 Lloyd's Rep. 158 at p. 162.
591. The Coral [1992] 2 Lloyd's Rep. 158.

on a voyage across the Atlantic Ocean at that time of year ought to be in a condition to weather such a storm.'[592]

401. Sheen went on to consider that:

> 'It is not possible for me to say precisely what force ultimately broke the tensioner. But, even if the tensioner had less than its designed strength, the evidence supports the view that any defect was latent. It could not have been discovered by any reasonable inspection of the tensioner. Mr. Holm looked at each tensioner before it was secured to the eye plate. It would be unreasonable to expect any ship-owner or his crew to do more than that. In those circumstances, the loss did not result from any failure to exercise due diligence to make the ship seaworthy. There must be judgement for the defendants.'[593]

402. This decision shows that foreseeability is a *point of view* and not the decisive factor. A requirement of unforeseeability can also not be derived from the The Torenia[594] and The Friso.[595]
In *The Torenia* the loss was caused by unseaworthiness which was discoverable by the use of due diligence and in *The Friso* Mr. Justice Sheen held that the ship was not seaworthy on sailing.

403. In *The Xantho,* Lord Herschell gave the following point of view regarding the exception:

> 'I think it clear that the term "perils of the sea" does not cover every accident or casualty which may happen to the subject-matter of the insurance on the sea. It must be a peril "of" the sea. Again, it is well settled that it is not every loss or damage of which the sea is the immediate cause that is covered by these words. They do not protect, for example, against that natural and inevitable action of the winds and waves, which results in what may be described as wear and tear. *There must be some casualty, something which could not be foreseen as one of the necessary incidents of the adventure. The purpose of the policy is to secure an indemnity against accidents which may happen, not against events which must happen.* It was contended that those losses only were losses by perils of the sea, which were occasioned by extraordinary violence of the winds or waves. I think this is too narrow a construction of the words, and it is certainly not supported by the authorities, or by common understanding. It is beyond question, that if a vessel strikes upon a sunken rock in fair weather and sinks, this is a loss by perils of the sea. And a loss by foundering, owing to a vessel coming into collision with another vessel, even when the collision results from the negligence of that other vessel, falls within the same category. Indeed, I am aware of only one case which throws a doubt upon the proposition that every loss by incursion of the sea, due to vessel coming accidentally (using that word in its popular sense) into contact with a foreign body, which penetrates it and causes a leak, is a loss

---
592. The Tila Gorthon, [1985] 1 Lloyd's Rep. 552, 555.
593. The Tila Gorthon, [1985] 1 Lloyd's Rep. 552, 556.
594. The Torenia [1983] 2 Lloyd's Rep. 210.
595. The Friso [1980] 1 Lloyd's Rep. 469.

by a peril of the sea. I refer to the case of *Cullen v. Butler*, where a ship having been sunk by another ship firing upon her in mistake for an enemy, the Court inclined to the opinion that this was not a loss by perils of the sea. I think, however, this expression of opinion stands alone, and has not been sanctioned by subsequent cases.'[596]

404. The Dutch author Royer is of the opinion that it is doubtful whether it can be concluded from *The Xantho* that unforeseeability is required because an extremely narrow concept of unforeseeability is observed in this particular case, from which it follows that unforeseeability is only required for those incidents which necessarily have to occur during the voyage, such as '*wear and tear*'. Royer says that the concept of unforeseeability is therefore only applicable to damage-causing incidents which will always happen, like the normal wear and tear.[597]

405. Royer quotes a passage from the case *Nichols v. Marland*[598] (1876) in where it was said that:

> 'It could not reasonably have been anticipated, though if it had been anticipated the effect might have been prevented.'

which, according to Royer, once more shows that unforeseeability is not a separate requirement in addition to inevitability.[599]

406. Another case in which the court held that unforeseeability is not a requirement is *Hamilton, Fraser and Co. v. Pandorf and Co.*[600] In this case rats had made a hole in a pipe through which seawater could enter the cargo and cause damage. Lord Fitzgerald said:

> 'The accident was fortuitous, unforeseen, and actually unknown until the ship reached her destination and commenced unloading. *I do not however, mean to suggest that to constitute a peril of the sea the accident or calamity should have been of an unforeseen character.*'[601] (emphasis added, NJM)

The emphasised passage makes it clear that the event need not to have been unforeseeable to constitute a peril of the sea.

407. Regarding the expressions 'events which could not be foreseen and guarded against' and 'events which could not be foreseen or guarded against', Carver writes:

> 'Even abnormal weather conditions can be foreseen: the test really seems to be how practicable it would have been to guard against them. A sure way to guard against maritime adventure is not to go to sea at all, but it is rare that a carrier will be regarded as wrong in setting out [see the *Bunga Seroja* case which is dis-

---

596. The Xantho, (1887) L.R. 12 App. Cas. 503, 509.
597. Royer 1959, p. 581-582.
598. The case is not available on Westlaw but the following citation was found for it: (1876) L.R. 2 Ex.D. 1.
599. Royer 1959, p. 581 footnote 41.
600. (1887) 12 A.C. 518; the quotation is from Hodges 1999, p. 368.
601. Hamilton Fraser & Co. v. Pandorf & Co., (1887) 12 App. Cas. 518, 528.

cussed in this paragraph, NJM]. It seems therefore that the emphasis should really be on the phrase "guarded against" rather than on foreseen'.[602]

408. The *Bunga Seroja* case contains a good study of the question whether unforeseeability is required for a successful peril of the sea defence under English law. In that case a distinction was made between Anglo-Australian law on the one hand and American-Canadian law on the other. It was made clear that Canadian and American law do require that the event was unforeseeable. This requirement does not exist in Australian and English law. In the *Bunga Seroja* case McHugh J. said:

> 'Under the Anglo-Australian approach, *the critical question is not whether the peril can be foreseen* or guarded against but whether the harm causing event was of the sea and fortuitous, accidental or unexpected. If it was, a further question arises as to whether that event was the effective cause of the loss. This approach restricts the immunity of the carrier for the loss or damage by reference to the carrier's negligence rather than by reference to the foreseeability or severity of the peril.'[603] (emphasis added, NJM)

409. An example may help to answer that question. If a ship sets out to sea and the forecast weather is bad then it is foreseeable that rough weather may be encountered. However, if that rough weather also causes damage to the cargo, even though all the necessary care was taken and due diligence was used, then that cargo damage may be unexpected. If a carrier were to send a ship on a voyage *knowing* that cargo damage was imminent then he will not be able to rely on the perils of the sea exception.

410. It can be concluded that under English law there is no requirement that the event that caused the damage was unforeseeable. The occurrence of the damage should, however, be unexpected. Undeniably there are English decisions in which the word 'unforeseeable' is used. Unforeseeability is, however, merely one of the aspects which can play a role.

Extraordinary nature of the damage causing event

411. Under English law there is no requirement that the event that caused the damage is extreme or extraordinary.[604] E.g. rough seas are common incidents of a voyage but, under English law, often constitute a peril of the sea. Damage caused by a ship striking rocks is not an extraordinary or extreme event but will constitute a peril of the sea if the damage was not avoidable by due diligence and reasonable skill and care.[605]

---

602. Carver 2005, p. 609.
603. Bunga Seroja, High Court of Australia, 22 oktober 1998, [1999] 1 Lloyd's Rep. 512 sub 101 referring to : 'The Xantho, (1887) 12 App.Cas. 503 at p. 510; Hamilton Fraser, (1887) 12 App.Cas. 518 at p. 525; Gosse Millerd Ltd. v. Canadian Government Marine Ltd., [1929] A.C. 223 at p. 230; Silver v. Ocean Steamship Co., [1930] 1 K.B. 416 at p. 435; Paterson Steamships, [1934] A.C. 538 at p. 548'.
604. See Carver 2005, p. 213 and Carver 1982, p. 166.
605. See The Xantho (1887) 12 A.C. 503, 509 per Lord Herschell and Hamilton v. Pandorf (1887) 12 A.C. 518, 527 per Lord Bramwell. See in the same sense Scrutton 1996, Art. 110 and Tetley 4th ed. ch. 18, p. 5.

Tetley also remarks that 'English admiralty law defines peril in terms of the foreseeability and possibility of averting the danger, rather than in terms of its irresistibility or extraordinary character.'[606]

5.4.3.2 *American law*

412. It will be hard for a perils of the sea defence to succeed under American law. American courts require that an event was unforeseeable and of extraordinary nature to constitute a peril of the sea. In the words of Carver '[t]he law in the United States has often been stated in a way requiring more extreme situations than those which would give rise to the defence in England.'[607]
American law was strongly influenced by a definition of 'perils of the sea' by Judge Hough in the *Rosalia*. Hough defined such a peril as:

> 'something so catastrophic as to triumph over those safeguards by which skilful and vigilant seamen usually bring ship and cargo to port in safety.'[608]

413. This definition was later elaborated by Judge Hand in the *Naples Maru* case. Hand said:

> 'The phrase "Perils of the Sea", has at times been treated as though its meaning were esoteric; Judge Hough' s vivid language in the "Rosalia" has perhaps given currency to the notion. That meant nothing more, however, than that the weather encountered must be too much for a well found vessel to withstand.'[609]

414. Both of these definitions emphasise the requirement that the event is extraordinary or extreme ('catastrophic, too much (...) to withstand'). Besides those requirements American courts also require that the event was unforeseeable.

The requirement that the event was unforeseeable

415. Tetley has derived the following definition from a number of American decisions:

> 'A peril of the sea may be defined as some catastrophic force or event that would not be expected in the area of the voyage, at that time of the year and that could not be reasonably guarded against.'[610]

416. American courts do indeed require that the event that caused the damage was unforeseeable for it to constitute a peril of the sea. One of the first decisions of the U.S. Su-

---

606. Tetley 4th ed. ch. 18, p. 5.
607. Carver 2005, p. 610.
608. Rosalia (1920) 264 F. 285, 288. See also Tetley 1988, p. 431.
609. Naples Maru (1939) 264 F.2d 32, 34. See also Tetley 1988, p. 432.
610. Tetley 1988, p. 432. Tetley derived this definition from: Rosalia, 264 F. 285 at p. 288 (2 Cir. 1920) and the Naples Maru, 106 F.2d 32 at p. 34, 1939 A.M.C. 1087 at p. 1090 (2 Cir. 1939) and the Shickshinny, 45 F. Supp. 813 at p. 817-819, 1942 A.M.C. 910 at p. 916-917 (S.D. Ga. 1942). The definition is repeated in the 4th edition of Marine Cargo Claims (ch. 18, p. 14).

preme Court concerning the application of the perils of the sea defence was the *Edwin I Morrison* case. In that case the Supreme Court held:

> 'Perils of the sea were excepted by the charter party, but the burden of proof was on the respondents to show that the vessel was in good condition, and suitable for the voyage, at its inception, and the exception did not exonerate them from liability for loss or damage from one of those perils to which their negligence, or that of their servants, contributed (...) It was for them to show affirmatively the safety of the cap and plate, and that they were carried away *by extraordinary contingencies, not reasonably to have been anticipated*. We do not understand from the findings that *the severity of the weather encountered by the Morrison was anything more than was to be expected upon a voyage such as this down that coast and in the winter season*, or that she was subjected to any greater danger than a vessel so heavily loaded, and, with a hard cargo, might have anticipated under the circumstances.'[611] (emphasis added, NJM)

417. The consideration that '[t]he weather was to be expected' indicates that an aspect of unforeseeability does play a role. In the later case *Johnson v. S.S. Schickshinny*, unforeseeability was also required. The District Court held:

> 'The damage was done and found on March 30th, before the hurricane force of the wind arrived. Unquestionably, rough weather and heavy seas were encountered, but where a vessel is subjected to no greater risk or damage than reasonably might have been anticipated on the voyage, peril of the sea furnishes no immunity. (...) If the severe weather should be regarded as so unusual, unexpected, and "catastrophic as to triumph over those safeguards by which skilful and vigilant seamen usually bring ship and cargo to port in safety" (...) , or if we substitute the words "of such a character" for "catastrophic" (...) the ship is still liable if its negligence contributed to the loss.'[612]

418. According to Royer American law does not require unforeseeability if the event is such that the damage could not be guarded against.[613] In Royer's opinion this follows from the definition in the *Giulia* case where the requirement was that the event be of 'of extraordinary nature'. Although this implies unforeseeability (if an event is of 'extraordinary nature it is usually unforeseeable) the definition in *Giulia* contains the word 'or':

> 'Perils of the seas are understood to mean those perils which are peculiar to the sea, and which are of an extraordinary nature *or* arise from irresistible force or overwhelming power, and which cannot be guarded against by the ordinary exertions of human skill and prudence.'[614] (emphasis added, NJM)

---

611. Bradley Fertilizer Co. v. Lavender (The Edwin I. Morrison) (1894) 153 U.S. 199, 211.
612. Johnson v. S.S. Schickshinny (1942) 45 F.Supp. 813.
613. Royer 1959, p. 584.
614. The Giulia, 218 F. 744, 746.

419. According to Royer this definition shows that an event causing damage which could not be guarded against, does not also have to be unforeseeable.[615] In my opinion however, it is not possible to reach such a conclusion based on a selection from the numerous definitions. I agree with Judge Chase where he said in *The Makalla*:

> 'A multiplication of definitions will result only in a multiplication of words without serving any useful purpose. The difficult task is not to define in general terms a peril of the sea, but to determine whether some established facts and circumstances, like those proved in this case, fall within a sound definition. There opinions may be at variance and give to close cases little value as precedents. Yet this situation obtains largely throughout the whole administration of justice because it is impossible to do away entirely with the human element in applying the law to the facts.'[616]

420. The cases discussed above make it clear that, regardless of certain definitions which seem to indicate otherwise, under American law unforeseeability is required for a peril of the sea defence to succeed. As most things are foreseeable a perils of the sea defence will not easily succeed under American law. There is a great amount of American authority to prove this.[617] It is also the opinion of most authors. As far as I know, Royer is the only author who concludes that, under American law, unforeseeability is not required for an event to constitute a peril of the sea. Sturley and Tetley emphasise that American courts will not decide that a foreseeable event can constitute a peril of the sea. American courts tend to decide that a seaworthy ship should be able to cope with conditions which could reasonably be expected. On the other hand English and commonwealth courts will decide that foreseeable risks can fall within the exception.[618] In the *Bunga Seroja* case[619] The High Court of Australia also distinguishes between American/Canadian law and Anglo/Australian law.[620]

Extraordinary nature of the event

421. In *Bunga Seroja* the judges Gaudron, Gummow en Hayne established that the Anglo-Australian construction of the perils of the sea exception differs from the American-Canadian construction. Under American and Canadian law 'losses to goods on board which are peculiar to the sea and 'are of an extraordinary nature or arise from irresistible force or overwhelming power,...' will constitute a peril of the sea. On the other hand under English and Australian law it is not required that the event that causes the damage is extraordinary in nature.[621] The peril par excellence under U.S. case-law is, however, invariably one linked with 'rough weather'. 'Mere bad weather at sea is, of course, not enough to create a presumption of peril. The prevailing weather condi-

---

615. Royer 1959, p. 584.
616. The Makalla, 40 F.2d 418.
617. See the Bunga Seroja case for a discussion of that authority.
618. Sturley 1997, p. 311. Sturley refers to inter alia to Great China Metal Indus. Co. v. Malaysian International Shipping Corp., [1994] 1 Lloyd's Rep. 455, 470.
619. Bunga Seroja, [1999] 1 Lloyd's Rep. 512.
620. See infra (Australian law).
621. See infra.

tions must at least be of such force to overcome the strength of a well-found ship and the usual precautions of good seamanship.'[622]

422. In *The Rosalia*, Judge Hough said that a peril of the sea 'means something so catastrophic as to triumph over those safeguards by which skilful and vigilant seaman usually bring ship and cargo to port safely.'[623] In the *Giula* the definition was '..., those perils which are peculiar to the sea, and which are of an *extraordinary nature* or which arise from *irresistible force or overwhelming power*, and which cannot be guarded against by the ordinary exertions of human skill and prudence.'[624] (emphasis added, NJM)

423. Although, as was mentioned above, one should be careful of drawing general conclusions from specific cases, it can safely be said that under American law, when the event that causes damage is rough weather, mere rough weather is not sufficient. The weather must be extraordinarily rough. Also the event must be unforeseeable for the perils of the sea defence to succeed under American law.[625] The result is that under American law the perils of the sea defence will rarely succeed.
In the *Bunga Seroja* case the judges concluded that the American construction of the perils of the sea exception is also followed in Canada. Below I shall make clear why I do not entirely agree with that finding in *Bunga Seroja*.

424. The American construction deprives the carrier of an important exception. It is unfair towards the carrier because the carrier may be responsible for damage which he could not prevent by using due diligence and proper care and for which event the Rules provide a defence. That defence is however, rendered practically useless under American law.

5.4.3.3 *Canadian law*

425. Although this book mainly concerns a comparison of English, American and Dutch law I shall also discuss Canadian and Australia law in this paragraph. The main reason is that a lot of the research for this paragraph is based on the *Bunga Seroja* judgement[626] in which the High Court of Australia also compared Canadian law to English and American law. Under Canadian law, as under American law, the damage causing event has to be unforeseeable to constitute a peril of the sea. However, under Canadian law it is not required that the event is extraordinary in nature.

The requirement that the event was unforeseeable

426. Tetley writes: '[t]he unforeseeability and the inevitability of the bad weather have frequently been reiterated as the major elements of the peril exception in Canadian

---

622. Tetley, 4th ed., ch. 18, p. 19. Tetley refers to Chiswick Products, Ltd. v. S.S. Stolt Avance 257 F. Supp. 91, p. 95, affirmed 387 F.2d 645 (5 Cir. 1968).
623. The Rosalia, 264 F. 285.
624. Tetley 2005, p. 2 referring to: 'The Giulia 218 F, 744 at p. 746 (2 cir. 1914)' and six other decisions where the same was said.
625. See also Schoenbaum 2003, p. 624. See also the Bunga Seroja case.
626. Bunga Seroja, [1999] 1 Lloyd's Rep. 512 and ETL 1999, p. 459.

maritime law'.[627] And cites *Canadian National Steamships Ltd. v. Bayliss*[628] as authority. A passage from that judgement from which a definition of the perils of the sea exception can be derived has been repeated a number of times by the Canada Supreme Court.

427. In *Falconbridge Nickel Mines etc* the Canada Supreme Court held:

> 'The meaning of the phrase "perils of the sea" in this context has been discussed in a number of cases and from time to time has given rise to what appears to be some conflict of judicial opinion which was in my view attributable to the slightly different approach taken in marine insurance cases to that taken where the sole question at issue relates to the interpretation of the bill of lading, but the cases of Parrish and Heinbecker Ltd. et Al v. Burke Towing and Sabotage Co. Ltd., [1943] S.C.R. 179, Goodfellow Lumber Sales v. Verreault, [1971] S.C.R. 522; [1971] 1 Lloyd's Rep. 185, and N. M. Paterson & Sons Ltd. v. Mannix, [1966] S.C.R. 180; [1966] 1 Lloyd's Rep. 139, appear to me to make it plain that this Court has approved and adopted at least for bill of lading cases the test laid down by Sir Lyman Duff in Canadian National Steamships v. Bayliss, [1937] S.C.R. 261, where he said of the defence of "perils of the sea":
> *The issue raised by this defence was of course an issue of fact and it was incumbent upon the appellants to acquit themselves of the onus of showing that the weather encountered was the cause of the damage it was of such a nature that the danger of damage to the cargo arising from it could not have been foreseen or guarded against as one of the probable incidents of the voyage.* [The italics are my own.]'[629]

428. The emphasised passage does not show that the rough weather was not to be foreseen. It shows that the damage to the cargo arising from the rough weather was not to be foreseen. However in *Kruger Inc. v. Baltic Shipping Co.* the Federal Court of Appeal held:

> 'With respect to the exception for perils of the sea, *counsel for Baltic argued that the test was not whether the weather was foreseeable but rather whether the consequences of the weather, viz. the loss of the ventilators, could have been reasonably foreseen and guarded against.* We do not think this statement of the test is correct. It is not the loss of ventilators that is a peril of the sea although the loss of ventilators was found to be the instrumentality or means which gave rise to the loss of ship and cargo.
> The phrase "perils, danger, and accidents of the sea" in Article IV, paragraph 2(c) of the Hague Rules has been interpreted to mean perils which could not have been foreseen or guarded against as probable incidents of the intended voyage.[630] The trial judge was correct, based on the authorities,[631] when he concluded on the basis of the evidence that the weather encountered by the ship:

---

627. Tetley, 4th ed, ch. 18, p. 3.
628. Canadian National Steamships Ltd. v. Bayliss (1937) S.C.R. 261, 263.
629. Falconbridge Nickel Mines etc, [1973] 2 Lloyd's Rep. 469, 473.
630. In particular, Charles Goodfellow Lumber Sales Ltd. v. Verreault, supra; Canadian National Steamships v. Bayliss. [1937] 1 D.L.R. 545 (S.C.C.).
631. Ibid. See also Blackwood Hodge Ltd. v Ellerman & Bucknall S.S. Co., [1963] 1 Lloyd's L.R. 454 (Q.B.).

... while unquestionably severe, which is well recognized by the Plaintiffs, was in fact foreseen and could even have been guarded against. At the very least, it is abundantly clear that the weather could and should have been foreseen and that it could have been guarded against.'[632]

429. Also in the *Bunga Seroja* case the judges of the High Court of Australia reached the conclusion that both American and Canadian law require the damage causing event (that is the weather, and not the damage caused) to be unforeseeable.[633]

430. It can be concluded that for a successful perils of the sea defence under Canadian law the carrier must prove that the damage causing event was unforeseeable and that the damage could not be guarded against. In this sense the Canadian construction is similar to the American construction which also requires the damage causing event to be unforeseeable.

Extraordinary nature of the event

431. Referring to the *Bunga Seroja*,[634] *Keystone Transports v. Dominion Steel and Coal Corp*[635] and *Goodfellow Lumber Sales Ltd. v. Verrault*[636] Carver remarks that the English, Canadian and Australian view enables the defence to be triggered off somewhat more easily than in the United States, thus pushing back the burden of raising negligence in respect of seaworthiness or care of cargo on to the claimant with consequent problems of proof.[637]
In *Keystone Transports Ltd. v. Dominion Steel & Coal Corp. Ltd.*, goods were damaged by seawater. The wind during the voyage was described as 'fresh' and 'strong' which can not be called extreme. The Supreme Court of Canada held: '..., *it is clear that to constitute a peril of the sea the accident need not be of an extraordinary nature or arise from irresistible force. It is sufficient that it be the cause of damage to goods at sea by the violent action of wind and waves, when such damage cannot be attributed to someone's negligence.*[638] (emphasis added, NJM)

432. In *Kruger Inc. v. Baltic Shipping Co.* Pinard J. of the Federal Court of Canada held: 'Therefore, it is not so much the severity of the storm that must be considered here as the fact that it could have been foreseen or guarded against as a probable incident of the intended voyage in the North Atlantic, at that time of the year.'[639]

433. A good example of an event causing damage that can not be called 'extraordinary' is the event which caused damage in *Consolidated Mining & Smelting Co. v. Straits Towing Ltd.*[640] In that case two barges containing cargo was left at a mooring. There was a 10 to 15 knot wind which is called a gentle to moderate breeze on the Beaufort scale. At the

---

632. Kruger Inc. v. Baltic Shipping Co., [1989] C.L.D. 790.
633. See infra.
634. Bunga Seroja, [1999] 1 Lloyd's Rep. 512
635. Keystone Transports v. Dominion Steel and Coal Corp., [1943] AMC 371.
636. Goodfellow Lumber Sales Ltd v. Verrault, [1971] 1 Lloyd's Rep. 185.
637. Carver 2005, p. 610.
638. Keystone Transports v. Dominion Steel and Coal Corp., [1943] AMC 371.
639. Kruger Inc. v. Baltic Shipping Co., 11 F.T.R. 80.
640. Consolidated Mining & Smelting Co. v. Straits Towing Ltd., [1972] 2 Lloyd's Rep. 497.

time of mooring the water was at the highest level of the year. It was accepted that the barges were holed by underwater obstructions in the form of pilings causing the barges to take water and sink which caused the loss of or damage to the cargo. Mr. Justice Cattanach of the Canada British Columbia Admiralty District said:

> 'It follows from the foregoing authorities that in order to be a peril of the sea within the exemption from liability under art. IV of the Rules there must be something which could not be foreseen as one of the necessary incidents of the adventure. Therefore the question that follows is whether the defendant should have foreseen that the barges would swing at their moorings at the booming ground in Port McNeill, sheer off a piling, become impaled upon that piling and sink. In my opinion there was nothing which should have alerted the defendant to the possibility of the pilings to which the barges were moored would give way.'[641]

The perils of the sea defence was allowed. Also in this judgement no reference was made to the requirement of an event which should be extraordinary.

5.4.3.4 *Australian law*

434. Although this book mainly concerns a comparison of English, American and Dutch law I shall also discuss Australian law at this point. The main reason is that a lot of the research for this paragraph is based on the *Bunga Seroja* judgement[642] of the High Court of Australia. The *Bunga Seroja* judgement is the leading case concerning the construction of the perils of the sea exception. The judgement is based on historical analysis of the Rules and on a comparative law study of the application of the Rules. In the *Bunga Seroja* decision the Australia High Court allowed a perils of the sea defence for damage caused by very rough weather in the Great Australian Bight (which is renowned for severe weather). The weather forecast had warned for gales, rough to very rough seas and a moderate to heavy swell. The weather was actually much rougher. Winds of force 10 to 11 Beaufort and wave heights of 10-11.5 m were encountered.[643] In the *Bunga Seroja* decision the court relied on its previous decision in *Gamlen*.[644] Also in that decision the High Court concluded that there is a difference between the Canadian/American and Anglo/Australian construction of the perils of the sea defence.

435. In *Gamlen*, Mason and Wilson, JJ. said that:

> '[t]here is a difference between the Anglo-Australian conception of "perils of the sea" and the United States-Canadian conception. According to the latter, "perils of the sea" include losses to goods on board which are peculiar to the sea and "are of an extraordinary nature or arise from irresistible force or overwhelming power, and which cannot be guarded against by the ordinary exertions of human skill and prudence": The Giulia (...) adopting Story on Bail-

---

641. Consolidated Mining & Smelting Co. v. Straits Towing Ltd., [1972] 2 Lloyd's Rep. 497, 505-505.
642. Bunga Seroja, [1999] 1 Lloyd's Rep. 512 and ETL 1999, p. 459.
643. Great China Metal Industries Co. Ltd v. Malaysian International Shipping Corporation Berhad (The Bunga Seroja), [1999] 1 Lloyd's Rep. 512.
644. Gamlen, [1980] 142 C.L.R. 142.

ments, s. 512(a). In the United Kingdom and Australia it is not necessary that the losses or the cause of the losses should be "extraordinary" (Carver Carriage by Sea, vol. 1, 12th ed. (1971), s. 161; Skandia Insurance Co. Ltd. v. Skoljarev). Consequently sea and weather conditions which may reasonably be foreseen and guarded against may constitute a peril of the sea.'[645]

436. In *Bunga Seroja* all six of the judges[646] decided that the *Gamlen* decision is correct.[647] The conclusion is that under Australian law unforeseeability of the damage causing event is not required for that event to constitute a peril of the sea. It is also not required that the event that caused the damage must be of an extraordinary nature to constitute a peril of the sea.

The requirement that the event was unforeseeable

437. In *Bunga Seroja* Gaudron, Gummow and Hayne said:

> 'In Gamlen Mason and Wilson JJ said that "sea and weather conditions *which may reasonably be foreseen and guarded against may constitute a peril of the sea.*" The fact that the sea and weather conditions that were encountered could reasonably be foreseen, or were actually forecast, may be important in deciding issues like an issue of alleged want of seaworthiness of the vessel, an alleged default of the master in navigation or management, or an alleged want of proper stowage. Similarly, the fact that the conditions encountered could have been guarded against may be very important, if not decisive, in considering those issues. (Their decision may then make it unnecessary to consider the perils of the sea exception). But if it is necessary to consider the perils of the sea exception, *the fact that the conditions that were encountered could reasonably be expected or were forecast should not be taken to conclude that question. To that extent we agree with what was said by Mason and Wilson JJ in Gamlen*. Such an approach, even if it is different from the American and Canadian approach, better reflects the history of the rules, their international origins and is the better construction of the rules as a whole.'[648] (emphasis added, NJM)

438. The other judges in *Bunga Seroja* expressed the same view.[649]

439. Regarding the foreseeability Callinan said that:

> 'although there is authority for, and much to commend, the proposition that the expression "perils of the sea" should be confirmed to unforeseen or exceptional events, or overwhelming force of the sea: in short, events that could not be reasonably guarded against. The fact that advances in shipbuilding technology, communications, and navigational aids provide the means of significantly reducing exposure to the perils of the sea however defined, make such a propo-

---
645. Bunga Seroja, [1999] 1 Lloyd's Rep. 512 sub 39.
646. Gaudron, McHugh, Gummow, Kirby, Hayne and Callinan.
647. See Bunga Seroja points 51, 72, 96, 102, 217, 224 and 226.
648. Bunga Seroja, [1999] 1 Lloyd's Rep. 512 sub 51.
649. Bunga Seroja, [1999] 1 Lloyd's Rep. 512 sub 217.

sition in modern times more attractive still. Similarly, more reliable methods of assessing the force of the elements are now becoming available (...) However the thrust of the relevant rules taken as a whole is, in my opinion clear. They are designed principally to exonerate shippers and more particularly, carriers who have not been guilty of want of due diligence or fault. Accordingly, in cases in which the carrier has acted as expressly required by the rules, and is not guilty of negligence, and, events at sea can be shown to be the cause of the loss and damage, the carrier should be entitled to immunity'.[650]

440. The above makes clear that under Australian law all aspects of the case play a role and the aspect that an event was foreseeable is only one aspect that plays a role but is certainly not decisive. Conditions for a successful perils of the sea defence is that the carrier used due diligence to provide a seaworthy ship and treated the cargo properly and carefully.

Extraordinary nature of the event

441. In *Bunga Seroja* Gaudron, Gummow and Hayne said:

> 'there is a difference between the Anglo-Australian conception of "perils of the sea" and the United States-Canadian conception. *According to the latter, "perils of the sea" include losses to goods on board which are peculiar to the sea and "are of an extraordinary nature* or arise from irresistible force or overwhelming power, and which cannot be guarded against by the ordinary exertions of human skill and prudence": The Giulia adopting Story on Bailments, s 512(a). *In the United Kingdom and Australia it is not necessary that the losses or the cause of the losses should be "extraordinary"* (Carver, Carriage by Sea, vol 1, 12th ed (1971), s 161; Skandia Insurance Co. Ltd. v. Skoljarev). Consequently sea and weather conditions which may reasonably be foreseen and guarded against may constitute a peril of the sea.'[651] (emphasis added, NJM)

442. I disagree with the quoted consideration. Above I discussed that in my opinion under Canadian law it is not required that the event is of an extraordinary nature for it to constitute a peril of the sea.

443. Kirby remarks that the intensity (and predictability) of the weather are circumstances which play a role in deciding weather a perils of the sea defence should succeed but that none of the circumstances is decisive.[652] This shows that an ordinary event (e.g. rough weather) can also constitute a peril of the sea.

444. The conclusion from *Bunga Seroja* is that an ordinary event can also constitute a peril of the sea.

---

650. Bunga Seroja, [1999] 1 Lloyd's Rep. 512 sub 221-222.
651. Bunga Seroja, [1999] 1 Lloyd's Rep. 512 sub 39.
652. Bunga Seroja, sub 147.

Bunga Seroja: comments

445. The *Bunga Seroja* decision makes it clear that unforeseeability and 'extraordinary nature' are aspects which are to be taken into consideration. They are however not decisive. All aspects of the case should be considered when judging if the peril of the sea defence can succeed or should fail. The carrier must however have fulfilled the duties imposed on him by art. III(1) and III(2). The exception will fail if the carrier's negligence in fulfilling these duties was the cause of the damage.

446. The decision has been criticised by Tetley who is of the opinion that the distinction made in the decision between the Canadian/American construction on the one hand and the Anglo/Australian construction on the other, contrary to what the Australia High Court says, does not exist. Tetley is of the opinion that English and Canadian authorities require unforeseeability as one the necessary elements of the defence (the other element is inevitability, but that is disputed by nobody).[653] As I have discussed in this paragraph unforeseeability is not required under English and Canadian law and Tetley's arguments are unconvincing. Tetley writes: '[t]he conclusion of the High Court in The Bunga Seroja is therefore that the carrier need only prove due diligence and proper care of the cargo in order to exculpate himself from liability for a claim resulting from damage done during a storm at sea, *however severe and however expected or expectable the storm may have been.*[654] (emphasis added, NJM)

447. I disagree with Tetley's conclusion on *Bunga Seroja*. In *Bunga Seroja* the planned voyage was in the Great Australian Bight which is renowned for severe weather. The weather forecast warned for gales, rough to very rough seas and a moderate to heavy swell. The decision to leave was based on the received weather reports. The weather encountered was however, worse than the weather predicted. Regarding weather Kirby J. said:

> 'None of the Judges below treated the intensity of the weather conditions, or the fact that gales had been forecast, as irrelevant. Neither did they treat them as determinative in the way that GCM urged. Instead, they adopted the correct course of examining all of the facts and circumstances. They concentrated attention upon whether the hazards encountered were such as could, and should, have been prevented by the carrier properly and carefully conducting itself with this particular vessel in this place and these circumstances. They asked whether the loss or damage shown arose, or resulted from, the sea hazard or from a want of proper and careful conduct on the part of the carrier. Not only was the approach taken by their Honours clearly open to them. In my view, it was correct. The conclusion reached was inevitable.'[655]

448. I agree with Kirby's remarks on the decision to sail. Kirby said:

> 'The extremes of weather encountered by *Bunga Seroja* went beyond the gale conditions forecast. They were so extreme that structural damage was done to

---
653. Tetley, 4th ed., ch. 18, p. 7-9.
654. Tetley, 4th ed., ch. 18, p. 9.
655. Bunga Seroya, [1999] 1 Lloyd's Rep. 512 sub 148.

the ship. This is a factual consideration often regarded as relevant in these cases. The various alternatives propounded to avoid the loss of or damage to cargo were convincingly rejected. The only one which remained for this Court (not having been seriously propounded below) was that the ship should not have ventured forth from Burnie. Assuming, contrary to my inclination, that such an argument was available at such a late stage of the litigation, it could not succeed. If every ship of the size, structure and functions of *Bunga Seroja* were obliged to remain in, or return to, harbour upon receipt of weather forecasts predicting gales in the Great Australian Bight or like stretches of ocean, serious inefficiencies would be introduced into the sea carriage of goods. The consequent costs of ships standing by would be wholly disproportionate to the marginal utility of such precautions.'[656]

Obviously, in the unlikely event that a captain decides to sail into a typhoon with the knowledge that the ship will sink and/or the cargo will be lost or damaged, there will not be a peril of the sea because the ship should have avoided the typhoon, either by staying in port or by deviating from its course. In other words, the damage was avoidable. This is one example whereby the ship should not sail if she is in port.

5.4.3.5 *Dutch law*

449. There are decisions in The Netherlands that show that ordinary rough weather can also constitute a peril of the sea.[657] There is no consensus in the Dutch courts about the question if the damage causing event has to have been unforeseeable for it to constitute a peril of the sea.

The requirement that the event was unforeseeable

450. Schadee defines a peril of the sea as 'an event of the sea[658] causing unavoidable damage.'[659] Schadee concludes from a decision of the Supreme Court of The Netherlands[660] and the absence of information proving otherwise in the legislative history of the enactment of the Hague Rules in The Netherlands that under Dutch law the event causing the damage does not have to be unforeseeable to constitute a peril of the sea.[661] In Schadee's opinion an ordinary storm can constitute a peril of the sea.[662] As is clear from Schadee's definition the damage must be unavoidable. Schadee writes that '[t]his means that a competent carrier would not reasonably have been able to prevent the damage caused by the event'.[663]

---

656. Bunga Seroja, [1999] 1 Lloyd's Rep. 512 sub 149.
657. See e.g. Amsterdam Court of Appeal, 13 December 1990, S&S 1991, 87 (Bickersgracht). In that case the wind force during the entire voyage was 5-7. Because of spray blowing over the cargo could not be ventilated causing damage to the cargo.
658. The Dutch word 'zee-evenement' is used which literally means 'sea-event'.
659. Schadee 1955, p. 690.
660. Schadee 1955, p. 690. Schadee refers to RvdW 1954, 108 but meant 1954, 29 (also published in NJ 1960, 462).
661. Schadee 1955, p. 690.
662. Schadee 1955, p. 690.
663. Boonk 1993, p. 183. See also Amsterdam Court of Appeal 6 mei 1966, S&S 1967/17 (Helena). In that case the perils of the sea defense was allowed even though the stowage could have been better. The Court of Appeal found it sufficient that reasonable care had been taken.

451. Royer writes that the degree of foreseeability is an important factor determining how unavoidable the damage will be. If an event is foreseeable then it will be easier to avoid damage caused by that event. This does not however mean that a carrier does not have to guard against the possible consequences of an unforeseen event. 'A vessel must have that degree of fitness which an ordinary careful and prudent owner would require his vessel to have at the commencement of her voyage having regard to all the probable circumstances of it.'[664] Also the cargo must be stowed in such a way that it can survive a voyage undamaged even if, e.g., rougher weather was encountered than was foreseen.

An unforeseeable event causing damage to the cargo will therefore not constitute a peril of the sea if the carrier could have avoided the damage by using due diligence to make the ship seaworthy and by handling and stowing the cargo properly and carefully.

Royer notes that in common law an event causing unavoidable damage does not necessarily have to have been unforeseeable for it to constitute a peril of the sea. The framers of the Hague Rules (who were for a significant part English) did not intend to introduce the additional requirement of unforeseeability for an event to constitute a peril of the sea.[665] Cleveringa and Boonk are also of the opinion that unforeseeability of the event is not required for a successful perils of the sea defence.[666] There is no consensus in the lower Dutch courts on the question of the requirement of unforeseeability.[667]

Quo Vadis

452. In the 1993 *Quo Vadis*[668] case the Supreme Court of The Netherlands rendered a judgement that corresponds with the point of view taken by the Dutch authors Boonk, Schadee, Royer and Cleveringa. The *Quo Vadis* was sailing from Northern Spain to Antwerp (Belgium) in the last days of December. The wind was SW 8-9 gusting to 10 Beaufort.[669] Seawater entering the engine room through open ventilation ports caused engine failure. The tug *Abeille Flandre* came to *Quo Vadis'* assistance and towed her to Brest. The owner of the *Quo Vadis* (Kroezen, who was also the captain of *Quo Vadis*) declared general average.

One of the defences of the owner against the claim for salvage payment was the perils of the sea exception. The owner stated that the seawater entered through open ventilation ports when the ship was entering the shallow waters of the continental shelf and suddenly encountered very rough ground seas.

453. The court of appeal held that Kroezen should have been prepared for the sudden rough shallow water waves in that area and in that season. According to the court of

---

664. McFadden v. Blue Star Line, [1905] 1 K.B. 697, 703 and Carver 2005, p. 500.
665. Royer 1959, p. 584.
666. Cleveringa 1961, p. 501. Boonk 1993, p. 182-183.
667. Unforeseeability was not required in the following decisions: District Court Rotterdam 2 September 1994, S&S 1994/113 (Act 7) and District Court Rotterdam 17 April 1956, NJ 1956/614 (Black Condor). In the following decisions the district courts did require that the event was unforeseeable: District Court Dordrecht 1 February1995, S&S 1996/89 (LEON), District Court Amsterdam 24 April 1974, S&S 1976/37 (Baarn), District Court Rotterdam 26 October 1971 en S&S 1972/5 (Leuve LLoyd).
668. SCN 11 June 1993, NJ 1995/235, S&S 1993/123.
669. A South Westerly wind in that area is one of the worst directions because the wind is blowing straight out of the Atlantic with no land mass in its way.

appeal Kroezen could have taken measures to avoid the damage in time. For this reason his perils of the sea defence failed. Kroezen appealed against the decision of the court of appeal.

At the Supreme Court Kroezen stated that unforeseeability is not required for a perils of the sea defence. According to Kroezen the real question was, if, when entering shallower water, the captain should always close ventilation ports because of the possibility of sudden ground seas causing water to be shipped on deck.

The Supreme Court did not agree and held that the decision of the court of appeal was correct. The Supreme Court held:

> '..., considering the time of the beginning of the voyage was 24 December and the voyage was from Northern Spain to Antwerp, the events stated by Kroezen can not be deemed to have been unexpected, meaning that measures could not have been taken in time, so that the sudden confrontation with rough beam seas can also not be considered to have been unexpected. The court of appeal obviously held that Kroezen could not rely on the perils of the sea defence *because it can not be said that Kroezen should not have been prepared for such ground seas*, so that he should be deemed to have been in a position to be capable of preventing the seawater from entering the engine room via the ventilation port.' (emphasis added, NJM)

454. So, in *Quo Vadis* engine failure caused by foreseeable rough seas and by open ventilation allowing seawater to enter the ship can not be a peril of the sea because the damage was avoidable. By taking the mere precaution of closing the ventilation ports the damage could have been avoided. The cause of the damage is lack of due diligence to make the ship seaworthy and not a peril of the sea. In the words of Royer 'the expression "perils of the sea" is limited to the point where the negligence of the carrier or his servants begins'.[670]

455. The *Quo Vadis* judgement demonstrates the importance of causality. If the cause of the damage was failure to fulfil the obligations regarding cargo and due diligence the carrier can not rely on the perils of the sea defence.

Extraordinary nature of the event

456. Cleveringa is of the opinion that a peril of the sea is a 'freak event which is violent and overwhelming'.[671] Thus Cleveringa follows the American view that a peril of the sea must be an extraordinary event. Schadee on the other hand does not think that the event should be of an extraordinary nature. He writes that unforeseeability is not required and that an 'ordinary storm' can also constitute a peril of the sea.[672] The reference to an 'ordinary storm' is an indication that Schadee is of the opinion that an extraordinary nature of the event is not required. Boonk attempts to deduce from decisions of the Dutch courts which wind force is required for a peril of the sea, and concludes that a minimum of force 9 or 10 is required. Boonk correctly writes that in the discussed cases the courts spent too little attention to the specific facts of the cases. He

---
670. Royer 1959, p. 573-574 see also Cleveringa 1961, p. 502.
671. Cleveringa 1961, p. 500.
672. Schadee 1955, p. 690.

correctly states that in certain situations less rough weather than a force 10-11 storm can constitute a peril of the sea, such as combinations of wind, sea, currents, sudden ground seas and duration of the rough weather.[673] The criterion is, according to Boonk, if the carrier could, under the given circumstances, have prevented or guarded against the damage caused by the rough weather.[674] Boonk is therefore also of the opinion that an event does not need to be extraordinary to constitute a peril of the sea. Hijmans van den Bergh[675] points out the the Hague Rules are based on English law and that under that law it is not required that the event needs to consist of 'causes which are uncommon'.

457. It can be concluded from the above that the prevailing opinion under Dutch law is that an ordinary event can also constitute a peril of the sea. There is however no consensus in the decisions of the Dutch courts.[676]

5.4.3.6 *The intended construction of the perils of the sea exception*

458. An objective construction of the expression will not lead to an intended construction. The subjective construction has to be used. What did the framers mean when they included the exception? From the Travaux Préparatoires it can be derived that the English attached great importance to the list of exceptions.[677] The exception was included in the list without explanation or comment. Sir Leslie Scott compared the list of exceptions to Moses and the table of stone on which the ten Commandments were written.[678] Sir Norman Hill, who was appointed by the shipowners to act for them, took a leading part in the original drafting of the Rules in 1921.[679] It was obvious that if Britain would not become party to the Rules, then there would be great uncertainty that they would be adopted by any other foreign power.[680] When some of the continental states opposed to the list of exceptions in art. IV(2) it was explained by Sir Norman Hill that the Rules could only be accepted by the British shipowners on unless 'we had in detail such exemptions as are agreed to be fair and proper'.[681] And Lord Phillimore explained that '[w]e have always been accustomed to have our bill of lading enumerate the excepted perils. It is perhaps not so scientific as the French form; on the other hand, it is safer because it leaves less to what is called the appreciation of the judge.'[682]

459. Sir Norman Hill, representative of British shipowners, took a prominent position in drafting the Rules and talked of 'such exemptions as are agreed to be fair and prop-

---

673. Boonk 1993, p. 184-185.
674. Boonk refers to the case note of Hijmans van den Bergh in NJ 1960/464.
675. Case note published in NJ 1960/464.
676. In the decision of the District Court Haarlem of 14 November 1972, S&S 1974/88 (Sealord Challenger) and Amsterdam Court of Appeal of 15 April 1955, NJ 1955/492 (PERICLES II) an event of extraordinary nature was not required. An event of extraordinary nature was however required in the following cases: District Court Arnhem 22 August 1992, S&S 1994/30 (Herm Kiepe), District Court Amsterdam 7 December 1988, S&S 1990/113 (Bickersgracht) and District Court Rotterdam 13 November 1987, S&S 1988/96 (Duke of Holland).
677. Travaux Préparatoires, p. 50.
678. Travaux Préparatoires, p. 378.
679. Report from the Joint Committee 1923, p. 24.
680. Report from the Joint Committee 1923, p. 17.
681. Travaux Préparatoires, p. 372-373.
682. Travaux Préparatoires, p. 373.

er. The Dutch author Blussé described the way the English drafters enforced there will with regard to art. IV (2) as 'something that looks like abuse of power'.[683]

460. I conclude that, although the English and American construction of the 'perils of the sea' exception was not uniform at the time when the Rules were drafted, a subjective construction of the Rules, using the Travaux Préparatoires and legislative history as aids, leads to the conclusion that the framers of the Rules intended the 'perils of the sea' exception to be construed according to English common law.

5.5 The catch all exception

5.5.1 Introduction

461. The q-exception provides:

> 'Neither the carrier nor the ship shall be responsible for loss or damage arising or resulting from:
> (...)
> q. Any other cause arising without the actual *fault or privity* of the carrier, *or* without the *fault or neglect* of the agents or servants of the carrier, but the burden of proof shall be on the person claiming the benefit of the exception to show that neither the actual fault or privity of the carrier nor the fault or neglect of the agents or servants of the carrier contributed to the loss or damage.' (emphasis added, NJM)

462. This residual exception is known as the 'catch all' exception or 'q-clause'. It is invoked where other exceptions do not apply. E.g. in *Goodwin, Ferreira & Co. Ltd., and others v. Lamport & Holt, Ltd.* the damage was caused to cotton which had been loaded into a lighter. The cause of the damage was a machine dropping out of its box when it was being loaded into the same lighter. The box that the machine was packed in was probably not strong enough. The n-exception (insufficiency of packing) did not apply because that exception has reference to the packing of the particular goods in respect of which or to which loss or damage arises.[684]

463. Below the following issues will be discussed:

(1) Which events are covered by the words 'any other cause'?
(2) How do the words 'actual fault or privity' relate to the words 'fault or neglect'?
(3) Which persons are meant with 'agents or servants of the carrier'?
(4) How is the burden of proof divided?
(5) What is the meaning of the word 'or' in the exception?

---

683. Blussé van Oud Alblas 1929, p. 53. Travaux Préparatoires, p. 378.
684. Goodwin, Ferreira & Co. Ltd., and others v. Lamport & Holt, Ltd., 34 Ll.L.L.Rep. 192.

5.5.2 Which events are covered by the words 'any other cause'?

464. It has been said that although the phrase 'other cause' is not accompanied by a word such as 'whatsoever', and hence appears to refer back to the enumerated perils, there is nothing in them from which the *eiusdem generis*[685] can be derived, with the result that the phrase must have wide application.[686] In *The Chyebassa* Lord Sellers said:

> '"Any other cause" would clearly include theft or malicious damage to the ship, ...'[687]

465. In that case plaintiffs' goods were shipped from Calcutta to Rotterdam on defendants' motor vessel the *Chyebassa* under bills of lading incorporating the Hague Rules. Goods were delivered damaged by sea-water owing to shipowners' stevedores stealing a storm valve cover plate during unloading and loading of other cargo at Port Sudan.

466. Lord Justice Sellers said:

> 'It is beyond question, I think, *that the appellants could not have escaped liability if the stevedores' men in the performance of the work in hand had damaged or stolen the cargo they had to handle*. But the men involved did not damage the cargo which they were handling and did not steal any of it. They took the opportunity to remove a very small part of the ship itself in order to steal it and in so doing so damaged the ship that sea water could enter.
> The removal was not ship's work. It was not in the ship's interest and did not purport to be. It was in no way incidental to or a hazard of the process of discharge and loading. If a complete stranger had entered the hold unobserved and removed the plate, par. (q) would I think apply if the shipowner could prove that it was a stranger who removed the cover and reasonable care had been taken to prevent strangers getting on board the ship and due diligence generally had been exercised. In the present case the act of the thief ought I think to be regarded as the act of a stranger. The thief in interfering with the ship and making her, as a consequence, unseaworthy, was performing no duty for the shipowners at all, neither negligently nor deliberately nor dishonestly. He was not in fact their servant and no question therefore strictly arises of his acting outside the scope of his employment. The appellants were only liable for his acts when he, as a servant of the stevedores, was acting on behalf of the appellants in the fulfilment of the work for which the stevedores had been engaged. Without that the appellants were in no relationship at all with the thief.

---

685. 'This term is chiefly used in cases where general words have a meaning attributed to them less comprehensive than they would otherwise bear, by reason of particular words preceding them: e.g., the Sunday Observance Act, 1677 (29 Car. 2, c.7), enacts that no tradesman, artificer, workman, labourer, or other person whatsoever, shall follow his ordinary calling on Sunday; here (...) the word "person" is confined to those of callings of the same kind as those specified by the preceding words, so as not to include a farmer.' (Wharton's Law Lexicon, Fourteenth Edition, Third Impression, London: Steven's and Sons, Sweet and Maxwell: 1949.)
686. Carver 2005, p. 617 citing A.E. Potts & Co. v. Union SS Co. of New Zeeland, [1946] N.Z.L.R. 276.
687. Leesh River Tea Co. Ltd v British India S.N. Co. Ltd (The Chyebassa), [1966] 2 Lloyd's Rep. 193.

Hourani v. T. & J. Harrison; Brown & Co. v. Same, (1927) 28 Ll.L.Rep. 120; (1927) 32 Com. Cas. 305, established that although stevedores appointed, as here, are independent contractors, the men employed by them to discharge the cargo must be regarded as servants of the shipowner for that purpose within the meaning of par. (q).'[688] (emphasis added, NJM)

467. And Lord Justice Danckwerts added:

'The theft could not have been prevented by any reasonable diligence of the shipowners through the officers and crew of the ship.
Accordingly, in my view, the shipowners are not liable for the damage to the tea which resulted from sea water entering the hold through the absence of the plate.'[689]

468. And Lord Justice Salmon:

'The stevedoring company was engaged by the defendants to handle the cargo and their servants became the defendants' agents for that purpose. *Accordingly, if they handled the cargo negligently and thereby damaged it or some other cargo, either directly or indirectly, the defendants would be responsible for their negligence.* If, for example, the stevedores had so negligently handled the cargo at Port Sudan that they knocked off the cover plate, there could have been no answer to this claim. *Moreover, if the stevedores handled the cargo dishonestly, for example if they stole it, the defendants would be liable to its owners for the stevedores' dishonest acts.* It seems to me however that the theft in this case had nothing to do with the handling of the cargo. The stevedore's employment merely afforded him the opportunity of stealing the plate. No doubt the defendants owed the plaintiffs a duty to take care that no one stole any part of the ship if the theft of such part might render the ship unseaworthy and damage the cargo. There was however no breach of that duty. The fact that the thief was a stevedore was quite fortuitous as the theft had nothing to do with the work upon which he was engaged. The fact that his employment on board presented him with the opportunity to steal does not, in my judgement, suffice to make the defendants liable: see Morris v. C. W. Martin & Sons, Ltd., [1965] 2 Lloyd's Rep. 63 (...), where all the relevant authorities on this branch of the law are elaborately discussed.'[690]

469. To summarise: If a stevedore steals a part of the ship, thus causing damage to the cargo, the carrier can rely on the q-clause because the stevedore was acting outside the scope of his duties. If, however, the stevedore were to have stolen the cargo that he was employed to load and stow, the carrier could not rely on the q-clause.

---

688. Leesh River Tea Co. Ltd v British India S.N. Co. (The Chyebassa), [1966] 2 Lloyd's Rep. 193.
689. Ibid.
690. Ibid.

5.5.3 How do the words 'actual fault or privity' relate to the words 'fault or neglect'?

470. The expressions 'actual fault or privity' and 'fault or neglect' have the same meaning. It has been said that the words 'actual fault or privity' come from the Fire Statute (s. 502 of the Merchant Shipping Act 1894).[691] A distinction between the expressions 'fault or neglect' and 'actual fault or privity' was probably made because under English law the latter expression can only mean the carrier or shipowner himself. For this reason it is necessary to have regard to the directing mind of the carrier.[692] The expression 'actual fault or privity' could therefore not be used to indicate a fault of servants or agents of the carrier. In the official French text no such distinction was made. The French text of the Hague Rules only uses the expression 'du fait ou de la faute'.[693]

5.5.4 Which persons are meant with 'agents or servants of the carrier'?

471. In *Heyn v. Ocean Steamship Co.* Justice Mackinnon said:

> 'It is therefore one of the duties of the carrier to discharge the goods (...) and if he employs an independent stevedore contractor to carry out that part of his duty, namely the duty of discharging the cargo, I think *the workmen of that independent stevedore contractor are within the meaning of this provision the agents or servants of the carrier.*'[694] (emphasis added, NJM)

472. See, however, the *Chyebassa* case which is also discussed below. In that case one of the stevedore's men stole a part of the ship and this was the cause of cargo damage. The court ruled that under those circumstances the carrier could rely on the q-clause. 'Servants' must mean, according to Carver, 'employees' acting in the course of their employment.[695]

Agents

473. What the word 'agent' means is less clear but it seems to refer to a person performing work for which the carrier is responsible such as loading or unloading by a stevedore and his employees.[696]

474. In *Hourani v. T. & J. Harrison* cargo, or portions of the cargo, had been stolen by the men employed by the stevedores in the discharge of the goods, and the shipowners contended that under the terms of the bill of lading they were exempt from liability. Regarding the question of which persons could be considered 'agents' of the carrier Lord Justice Bankes said:

---

691. Carver 2005, p. 617 and Cooke et.al 2007, p. 1046. See also supra § 5.3.
692. See also § 5.3 and Carver 2005, p. 617.
693. '..., du fait ou de la faute du transporteur ou du fait ou de la faute des agents, ...'
694. Heyn v. Ocean Steamship Co., (1927) 27 Ll.L.L.Rep. 334, 337.
695. Carver 2005, p. 617.
696. Hourani v. T. & J. Harrison (1927) 28 Ll.L.L.Rep. 120.

'..., [in] the case of Machu v. London & South Western Railway, (1848), 2 Exch. 415, a very similar case, (...) the Court held that for the purpose of construing an Act of Parliament in somewhat similar terms to this statute, the servants of the independent contractor would be the agents of the railway company for the purposes of the construction of the statute; and so here it seems to me impossible to put any reasonable construction upon this statute except by regarding the servants of the persons who are employed by the shipowner in order to fulfil his statutory obligation to discharge the vessel, as being his agents for that purpose.'[697]

475. In the same case Lord Justice Atkin said:

'The other question is the question as to whether or not the servants of the master stevedore at Vera Cruz can be said to be, within the meaning of the clause, the agents or servants of the ship. Mr. Clement Davies did not dispute that the master stevedore himself was to be considered an agent of the ship, and I think he was quite right in so holding. There was a statutory obligation on the ship to discharge, and they performed that duty by entering into a contract with the master stevedore, who for that purpose was their agent in performing their statutory duty; and, to my mind, that in itself would be sufficient to support the matter, because it is plain that the master stevedore, according to our law, would be responsible for the tortuous acts of his servants done in the scope of their employment; but quite apart from that I think that the servants of the stevedore for this purpose are also the agents of the ship, and I think it is made plain by the reasoning of the Court in the case that my Lord has referred to, of Machu v. London & South Western Railway , *sup.*, where the Court had to deal with words which were narrower in their meaning; where they had to deal with the word "servants", and where the Court held that the servants of the sub-contractor of the carrier were, within the meaning of the Carriers Act, servants of the carrier; and I think that that is sound and applies to this case.'[698]

The Chyebassa

476. In this case a storm valve cover plate was stolen from the ship by a stevedore who was employed to load cargo.[699] The court of appeal held that, under these circumstances, the stevedore was not to be considered a servant or agent of the shipowner and allowed the carrier's appeal.

5.5.5 How is the burden of proof divided?

477. The q-clause provides the following division of the burden of proof:

'..., but the burden of proof shall be on the person claiming the benefit of this exception to show that neither the actual fault or privity of the carrier nor the

---
697. Ibid.
698. Ibid.
699. Leesh River Tea Co. Ltd v. British India S.N. Co. (The Chyebassa), [1966] 2 Lloyd's Rep. 193. See § 5.5.2.

fault or neglect of the agents or servants of the carrier contributed to the loss or damage.'

478. The division of the burden of proof as provided by the q-clause is an exception to the usual division.[700] To rely on the q-clause the carrier has to prove the cause of the damage and that this cause or these causes were not a result of his actual fault or privity nor of the fault or neglect of his agents or servants. This proof will usually be difficult and that is the reason a carrier will primarily try to rely on another exception if possible.

479. Under American law and English law and also in the views of Tetley and Von Ziegler the carrier will not be able to rely on the q-clause if the cause of the loss or damage is not known. The carrier must not only prove his fault did not cause the damage but also what other cause was responsible.[701] Carver however says:

> 'It is not in principle necessary that the carrier prove how the event occurred: it may sometimes be possible simply to prove that all care was taken. This will however be rare.'[702]

480. Carver cites *Pendle & Rivet v. Ellerman Lines Ltd.*[703] and *The City of Baroda.*[704] In the latter case Mr. Justice Roche did indeed say that it may be possible that the carrier need not prove how the event occurred:

> 'In many cases it would be sufficient I think to prove general care that was exercised with regard to the management of a ship and cargo, but in this case it has become, on my view of the facts, material for the defendants also to say that, besides general care in arranging for watching, the watching was vigilantly and properly carried out. The same view of the method in which a bailee, and a shipowner is after all a bailee of goods, may discharge the onus of proof is illustrated and explained both in the judgement of Walton, J., and of the Court of Appeal, in the case of Bullen v. Swan Electric Engraving Co., 22 T.L.R. 275, 23 T.L.R. 258. Sir Gorell Barnes, giving the judgement of the Court of Appeal, said this (at p. 259):
> "They were left, therefore, to the consideration of well-known principles of law. One of these was that a gratuitous bailee must show that the loss occurred through no want of reasonable care on his part – that was to say, as much care as a prudent man would use in keeping his own property. The plaintiffs' contention (now this is the passage bearing on this case) was that the defendants must show that the loss happened in some way which they could account for, and that in relation to that particular matter and at that particular moment of time proper care was taken. No authority had been cited for such a proposition as that. It was enhancing the burden of proof upon a defendant to an absurd

---

700. Von Ziegler 2002, p. 444. Zie ook Royer 1959, p. 284.
701. See Von Ziegler 2002, p. 445, Tetley, 4th ed., chapter 23, p. 4-6, Schoenbaum 2004, p. 709. Pendle & Rivet, Ltd v. Ellerman Lines, Ltd., 29 Ll.L.L.Rep. 133, 136 and Quaker Oats v. M/V Torvanger, 734 F.2d 238.
702. Carver 2005, p. 618.
703. Pendle & Rivet Ltd. v. Ellerman Lines Ltd. 29 Ll.L.L.Rep. 133.
704. The City of Baroda, 25 Ll.L.L.Rep. 437.

extent if he had to prove not only that he had taken every reasonable care but also that he knew how the loss happened."

That good general principle, which I should adhere to and apply wherever possible, does not, I think, for the reasons I have given, extend far enough to protect the defendants in this case. They have proved to my satisfaction that there was a theft; in proving it they have proved that the watchmen were concerned, and it has not been proved, but on the contrary I think, that those watchmen watched vigilantly. In those circumstances I give judgement for the plaintiffs with costs.'[705]

481. Although the possibility exists that the carrier will not be liable for loss or damage by unknown causes I do not know of any decisions where the carrier could rely on the q-clause for damage or loss by unknown causes.
In order to be able to rely on the q-clause it seems to me that the carrier should also prove the cause of the loss. How else will he be able to prove that the cause of the damage is not attributable to his fault? This is also the point of view taken by the UNCITRAL Working Group III.[706] Art. 18(1) of the UNCITRAL draft convention reads:

> 'The carrier is liable for loss of or damage to the goods, as well as for delay in delivery, if the claimant proves that *the loss, damage, or delay,* or the event or circumstance that caused or contributed to it *took place during the period of the carrier's responsibility,* ....' (emphasis added, NJM)

The emphasised section shows that the carrier will be responsible for unexplained losses which occurred during the period of the carrier's responsibility.

482. The burden of proof for the q-clause is not a shifting burden of proof as it is for the other exceptions.[707] In *Quaker Oats Co. v. M/V Torvanger,* regarding the burden of proof in the q-clause, the 5th Circuit (citing Gilmore and Black) held that:

> 'The carrier's burden of establishing "his own freedom from contributing fault ... is no mere burden of going forward with evidence, but a real burden of persuasion, with the attendant risk of nonpersuasion." Gilmore and Black, The Law of Admiralty § 3-37 at p. 168; § 3-43 (2nd ed. 1975). *Consequently, the burden of proof does not return to the plaintiff, but rather judgement must hinge upon the adequacy of the carrier's proof* that he was free from any fault whatsoever contributing to the damage of the goods entrusted to his carriage, ...' .[708] (emphasis added, NJM)

483. In the same case it was held, that to rebut the presumption of fault when relying upon its own reasonable care, the carrier must further prove that the damage was caused by something other than its own negligence. The 5th Circuit also held that

---
705. The City of Baroda, 25 Ll.L.L.Rep. 437, 442.
706. See document A/CN.9/544, paragraph 97: The Working Group's consensus is that the carrier should be held responsible for unexplained losses.
707. See Boonk 1993, p. 223.
708. Quaker Oats Co. v. M/V Torvanger, 734 F.2d 238.

once the shipper establishes a prima facie case, under the policy of the law the carrier must explain what took place or suffer the consequences.'[709]

5.5.6 What is the meaning of the word 'or' in the exception?

484. The second 'or' in the text: '..., any other cause arising without the actual fault or privity of the carrier *or* without the fault or neglect of the agents or servants of the carrier', should be read as 'and'.[710] This means that the carrier does not only have to prove the absence of his own fault or privity but also the absence of the fault or neglect of his servants or agents.

485. In *Hourani Harrison* Lord Justice Atkins said:

> 'Again, I disagree with the learned Judge in his view that the word "or" can never have a conjunctive sense; I think it quite commonly and grammatically can have a conjunctive sense. It is generally disjunctive, but it may be plain from the collocation of the words that it is meant in a conjunctive sense, and certainly where the use of the word as a disjunctive leads to repugnance or absurdity, it is quite within the ordinary principles of construction adopted by the Courts to give the word a conjunctive use. Here it is quite plain that the word leads to an absurdity, because the contention put forward by the shipowners in this matter amounts to this, as my Lord said, that if a shipowner himself breaks open a case and steals the contents of it, he is exempted from liability under this section if none of his servants stole the part of the case or broke it open. That seems to me to be a plain absurdity. In addition to that, there is a repugnancy because it is plainly repugnant to the second part of the section. Therefore, I say no more about that.'[711]

5.5.7 Dutch law

Royer's system

486. Royer is the author of the most important Dutch book on the liability of the carrier under the Hague Rules. In Royer's theory the q-clause contains the general rule as to the carrier's liability and the general rule for the division of the burden of proof.[712] He distinguishes that 'general rule' provided by IV(2)q from the specific Rule IV(1) and the specific exceptions a, b and c-p. The division of the exceptions into four groups makes sense. The list of exceptions does contain the different types as specified in the four groups. IV(1), a, b and q are types of their own. The exceptions c-p can indeed be grouped together as specific exceptions based on the absence of the carrier's fault.[713]

---

709. Quaker Oats Co. v. M/V Torvanger 734 F.2d 238, 243.
710. Hourani v. Harrison, [1927] 28 Ll.L.L.Rep. 120.
711. Ibid.
712. Royer 1959, p. 183.
713. Schoenbaum makes a further distinction within the c-p group. The distinction is made between 'overwhelming natural forces: perils of the sea and act of God' and 'Overwhelming human forces: act of war, act of public enemies, restraint of princes, quarantine, strikes, riots and civil commotions' (Schoenbaum 2004).

The q-exception is a general exception based on the absence of the carrier's fault and furthermore it contains its own burden of proof.

487. In Royer's view the 'general rule' consists of three principles. These are (i) The basis of liability is that the carrier is only liable for damage caused outside his fault and outside the fault of his employees and agents; (ii) if the damage was caused by more than one cause and one of those causes was a fault of the carrier or his employees or agents then the fault should be deemed to be the relevant cause of the damage; (iii) the carrier has to prove that neither his fault nor the fault of his employees or agents caused the damage.[714]

488. Royer compares the four specific 'groups' to the general rule contained in the q-exception to find out if the three principles of the general rule apply to those four specific groups. He summarises the conclusion in the table shown below. A plus means that the principle applies, a minus that it does not apply and +/- that the principle partially applies.[715]

	(i) basis of liability	(ii) cause	(iii) burden of proof
IV(1)	+	+	–
IV(2)a	+/–	+	–
IV(2)b	+	+/–	–
IV(2)c-p	+	+	–

489. If I have understood Royer's system correctly it would mean that according to the table above the first principle also applies to the fire exception. I find this hard to understand because the fire exception can also be invoked if the fire was caused by the fault of the carrier's employees.[716] Another point which is not very clear is Royer's conclusion that the carrier is not required to prove the absence of a fault in the c-p group. This conclusion is debatable for the perils of the sea exception (art. IV(2)c). To rely on that exception the carrier does have to prove that the damage was unavoidable and this may require proving that due diligence was exercised and that the cargo was stowed properly and carefully.[717] On the other hand it could be said that the proof of the cause will include the proof of absence of fault so that the Royer's point of view that the carrier does not have to prove the absence of his fault is correct.

490. I think Royer has over analysed the q-exception and tried to create a system around it which was not intended by the framers. Also I doubt whether the framers of the Rules meant the q-clause to be the general rule. It seems more likely that the q-clause is a typical residual clause. Indeed at the Diplomatic Conference of October 1923[718] Mr. Sohr pointed out that:

> '..., the scope of item (q) was not to promulgate a general principle of which the preceding items were an illustration. The text, first of all, sanctioned those ex-

---

714. Royer 1959, chapter V.
715. Royer 1959, p. 303.
716. See § 5.3.
717. See § 5.4.
718. Meeting of the Sous-Commission Second Plenary Session on 6 October 1923.

ceptions commonly accepted in bills of lading and which, from now on, would offer a means of release for shipowners. Furthermore, it appeared to be a broad provision, but it was not the principle underlying the whole article.'[719]

491. Published cases concerning a successful invocation of the q-exception are rare. In the *Gooiland* case bales of tobacco were damaged due to sweat. During the voyage the hatches could not be opened to ventilate due to heavy weather. The mechanic ventilation system was not sufficient to prevent the sweat. The carrier successfully invoked the q-exception.[720]

492. In the *Boknis* steel rolls were negligently stowed in a container by the shipper. During heavy weather the container of steel rolls started shifting and caused damage to other cargo. The Rotterdam District Court held that a carrier can not rely on the q-clause for damage caused to other cargo by negligent stowing of a container by the shipper of that container. The carrier is responsible because the damage caused by the shifting container containing the negligently stowed rolls of steel was also caused by negligent stowing of that container.[721]

493. In the *Bernd Gunda* bags of sugar dried and caked due to a change of humidity. The drying and caking decreased the volumes of the bags giving the bags space to shift against the ships side and tear open. The drying and caking of the sugar is not something that the carrier can control. The carrier quoted the following passage from Lloyd's Survey Handbook:

> 'Sugar. Special care should be exercised in ascribing the cause of damage to this commodity, particularly in the case of alleged water or moisture damage. If not dry to the point at which it is in equilibrium with the relative humidity of the atmosphere, sugar may continue to lose moisture in storage, stowage etc., dry and tend to cake. Similarly, if the sugar is too dry it will absorb moisture from the atmosphere until it attains equilibrium and if atmospheric conditions change and it dries again it will tend to cake. If the sugar is excessively dried it may suffer in lustre and from dust formation. Sugar dried to equilibrium by the manufacturer will, if exposed to atmosphere of high humidity, i.e. in damp localities or during the voyage, inevitably re-absorb moisture to the higher level of the surrounding atmosphere.
> The absorption or loss of moisture after leaving the manufacturers' premises will not be apparent until there is a further change in the relative humidity of the atmosphere. For instance, sugar which has been packed in a relative humidity of, say 65%, may well await shipment in a relative humidity of 85% and will come to equilibrium with the atmosphere and, to all intents and purposes, sugar will appear to be unaffected. After loading into the vessel, however, the relative humidity to the atmosphere may fall to 65% and under these circumstances the sugar will lose moisture. During this process it will dry and cake.'

---

719. Travaux Préparatoires, p. 427.
720. Amsterdam District Court 16 June 1971, S&S 1972, 6 (Gooiland).
721. Rotterdam District Court 1 July 1983, S&S 1983, 117 (Boknis).

494. The holds of the ship had been inspected before loading and were found to be dry the court held that the carrier could not be held responsible for the loss of the sugar.[722]

495. In the *Rio Parana* a cargo of maize was damaged by self heating. The maize would have been delivered in good condition if the voyage could have been completed in the ordinary time. Due to circumstances outside the fault of the carrier the voyage took 11 weeks instead of 6 weeks. The court held that the carrier could rely on the q-clause to escape liability.[723]

496. In 1959 (before the *Chyebassa* decision was rendered[724]) Royer concluded that the carrier is responsible for damage or loss caused by the people in his service, regardless if they are working within the scope of their duties. The carrier is also responsible for all other persons if he uses their services for the fulfilment of the contract of carriage.[725] It is unlikely that this view will be followed after the *Chyebassa* decision.

5.5.8 The intended construction

497. From the above it follows that the q-clause is a residual exception and was not meant as a general rule.

5.5.9 Conclusion

498. Published decisions in which the carrier successfully relied on the q-clause are rare. It is rare for the q-clause to be invoked successfully where none of the other exceptions apply.[726] To escape liability the carrier must prove the cause of the damage and the absence of his fault.

---

722. Rotterdam District Court 15 October 1982, S&S 1983. 104 (Bernd Gunda). See for a similar case Rotterdam District Court 7 January 1980, S&S 1980, 74 (Almut Bornhofen).
723. Rotterdam District Court 4 May 1981, S&S 1981, 111 (Rio Parana).
724. See supra § 5.5.4.
725. Royer 1959, p. 318.
726. See also Aiken et al 2006, p. 285.

Chapter 6
Division of the burden of proof under the H(V)R[727]

6.1 Introduction

499. The H(V)R do not provide a general rule for the division of the burden of proof.[728] That is not surprising because as the official name[729] shows, the Hague Rules were not intended to govern all aspects of law relating to carriage of goods by sea under a bill of lading.[730] The Rules do however contain some specific provisions. Art. IV(1) provides a rule for the division of the burden of proof in case of loss or damage caused by unseaworthiness. In that case art. IV(1) specifically provides that the carrier has to prove that he complied with art. III(1). This rule relieves the cargo interest of the hard task of having to prove that the carrier did not exercise use due diligence to provide a seaworthy ship. He can suffice with the proof of loss or damage caused by unseaworthiness and thus place the burden of proving due diligence on the carrier. The other specific allocation of the burden of proof is provided by the 'catch all' exception art. IV (2) q. That exception provides that the carrier wishing to avail himself of that exception has the burden of proving that he exercised due diligence to provide a seaworthy ship and that there was no negligence regarding treatment of the cargo.

500. This chapter will start with the allocation of the burden of proof in general and thereafter will deal with the division of the burden of proof for the specific exceptions of art. IV(1) and (2). The various views on the division of the burden of proof in case of a cargo claim will be discussed below.

6.2 In general

The Popi M

501. Before discussing the division of the burden of proof in general under the Rules, I should like to point out that national law of civil procedure can be of influence. The main question is: when is a matter proven? Should there be absolute certainty or is a reasonable amount of probability sufficient? The answer to this question and other questions of proof and evidence should be found in the applicable national law as the

---

727. See for an earlier version of this chapter Hendrikse & Margetson 2006.
728. The UNCITRAL draft convention does provide a division of the burden of proof in article 18. See document A/CN.9/WG.III/WP.101 on <www.uncitral.org> under Working Group III.
729. The International Convention for the Unification of Certain Rules of Law Relating to Bills of Lading of 25 August 1924.
730. Von Ziegler 2002, p. 385.

matter is not dealt with by the Hague Rules.[731] E.g. in *The Kapitan Sakharov*[732], a case concerning loss of life and cargo damage due to the explosion of a container of dangerous cargo, reference was made to the decision of the House of Lords in *The Popi M*.[733] The *Kapitan Sakharov* case was governed by the Hague Rules. The *Popi M* concerned a ship which sank due to unclear circumstances. The owners claimed that the loss was a peril of the sea and claimed under the hull insurance policy. The defendants denied that the loss was caused by a peril of the sea. They attributed the loss due to unseaworthiness of the vessel.

502. In first instance Bingham J. said:

> '(1) on the evidence the submission by the defendants that the loss was caused by wear and tear would be rejected;
> (2) although the submission by the plaintiffs that the cause of water entering the vessel was contact by the vessel with a moving submerged object, i.e., a submarine, was inherently improbable, on the balance of probabilities that explanation would be accepted and since such a collision with a submarine fell within the policy cover against perils of the sea, the plaintiffs succeeded against each defendant for his proportionate share of the insured value of the vessel.'[734]

503. The case before the House of Lords mainly dealt with the question of what is meant by proof of a case on a balance of probabilities.[735] Although the *Popi M* is a case concerning hull insurance and not a cargo claim under the H(V)R it is still interesting as an illustration of the views regarding the question of when something is proven or not.

504. Lord Brandon of Oakbrook said in his well-known speech:

> 'My Lords, the late Sir Arthur Conan Doyle in his book "The Sign of Four", describes his hero, Mr. Sherlock Holmes, as saying to the latter's friend, Dr. Watson: "how often have I said to you that, when you have eliminated the impossible, whatever remains, however improbable, must be the truth?" It is, no doubt, on the basis of this well-known but unjudicial dictum that Mr. Justice Bingham decided to accept the shipowners' submarine theory, even though he regarded it, for seven cogent reasons, as extremely improbable.
> In my view there are three reasons why it is inappropriate to apply the dictum of Mr. Sherlock Holmes, to which I have just referred, to the process of fact-finding which a Judge of first instance has to perform at the conclusion of a case of the kind here concerned.

---

731. See for example Cooke et al 2007, p. 978 where the authors refer to the example of the maxim res ipsa loquitur as applied in common law. Another example is the rule under Dutch law that under specific conditions the division of the burden of proof is reversed (the reversal rule or in Dutch 'omkeringsregel').
732. The Kapitan Sakharov, [2002] 2 Lloyd's Rep. 225.
733. The Popi M, [1985] 2 Lloyd's Rep. 1. This is a case concerning the proof of a 'peril of the sea' in the marine insurance sense.
734. The Popi M, [1985] 2 Lloyd's Rep. 1, 1.
735. The Popi M, [1985] 2 Lloyd's Rep. 1, 2.

The first reason is one which I have already sought to emphasize as being of great importance, namely, that the Judge is not bound always to make a finding one way or the other with regard to the facts averred by the parties. He has open to him the third alternative of saying that the party on whom the burden of proof lies in relation to any averment made by him has failed to discharge that burden. No Judge likes to decide cases on burden of proof if he can legitimately avoid having to do so. There are cases, however, in which, owing to the unsatisfactory state of the evidence or otherwise, deciding on the burden of proof is the only just course for him to take.

The second reason is that the dictum can only apply when all relevant facts are known, so that all possible explanations, except a single extremely improbable one, can properly be eliminated. That state of affairs does not exist in the present case: to take but one example, the ship sank in such deep water that a diver's examination of the nature of the aperture, which might well have thrown light on its cause, could not be carried out.

The third reason is that the legal concept of proof of a case on a balance of probabilities must be applied with common sense. It requires a Judge of first instance, before he finds that a particular event occurred, to be satisfied on the evidence that it is more likely to have occurred than not. If such a Judge concludes, on a whole series of cogent grounds, that the occurrence of an event is extremely improbable, a finding by him that it is nevertheless more likely to have occurred than not, does not accord with common sense. This is especially so when it is open to the Judge to say simply that the evidence leaves him in doubt whether the event occurred or not, and that the party on whom the burden of proving that the event occurred lies has therefore failed to discharge such burden.

In my opinion Mr. Justice Bingham adopted an erroneous approach to this case by regarding himself as compelled to choose between two theories, both of which he regarded as extremely improbable, or one of which he regarded as extremely improbable and the other of which he regarded as virtually impossible. He should have borne in mind, and considered carefully in his judgement, the third alternative which was open to him, namely, that the evidence left him in doubt as to the cause of the aperture in the ship's hull, and that, in these circumstances, the shipowners had failed to discharge the burden of proof which was on them.'[736]

505. In *Popi M* Lord Brandon of Oakbrook concluded:

'In my opinion the only inference which could justifiably be drawn from the primary facts found by Mr. Justice Bingham was that the true reason of the ship's loss was in doubt, and it follows that I consider that neither Mr. Justice Bingham nor the Court of Appeal were justified in drawing the inference that there had been a loss by perils of the sea, whether in the form of collision with a submerged submarine or any other form.'

---

736. Popi M, [1985] 2 Lloyd's Rep. 1, 6.

506. The question of when a statement is proven shall depend on national law and doctrine.

The burden of proof under the H(V)R in general

507. In general the view on the division of the burden of proof is:

1. the cargo interest proves a *prima facie* case by proving damage and e.g. showing a clean bill of lading;
2. the carrier proves that the damage was caused by one of the excepted perils provided by art. IV(2). The choice of exception will determine what the carrier must prove.[737] There are different points of view regarding what the carrier should prove at this point to escape liability.[738]
The carrier could also rely on the exemption for unseaworthiness provided by art. IV(1). In that case he will have to prove that he used due diligence to provide a seaworthy ship.[739]
Instead of proving the above it is said that the carrier can rebut the prima facie case against him by proving that he complied with his duties as contained in art. III(1) and III(2). Schoenbaum cites American cases in which it was decided that the carrier can escape by proving the damage was caused by an excepted peril *or* that he used due diligence to prevent the damage.[740] The option of proving compliance with art. III(1) is in my view the same as proving the exemption of art. IV(1) or art. IV(2)q.
3. Next the cargo interest will have to prove that the carriers' negligence[741] was at least a concurrent cause of the loss. If the cargo interest can prove that unseaworthiness caused the loss or damage the carrier will have to prove that he used due diligence to provide a seaworthy ship[742];
4. if the loss or damage was caused by concurrent causes one of which being non-fulfilment of the duties contained in art. III(1) and (2) the carrier has the burden of proving for which part he is not liable. If he fails in that proof he will be liable for the entire loss or damage.[743]

6.3 Common law

6.3.1 In general

508. There are two competing principles regarding the division of the burden of proof in claims on the contract of carriage under a bill of lading. At common law the divi-

---

737. See infra.
738. See infra.
739. Ex art. 4(I).
740. See Schoenbaum 2004, volume 1, p. 677. In my view the second option is the proof of the q- or 'catch all' exception. It is not clear why the possibility of proving the absence of fault is mentioned separately as if it were an additional way to escape liability besides the q-exception.
741. E.g. non-fulfilment of the duties of art. III(2) or in case of the fire exception actual fault or privity of the carrier. In The Amstelslot ([1963] 2 Lloyd's Rep. 223, 235) it was said that lack of due diligence is negligence.
742. Ex art. IV(I).
743. The Canadian Highlander, [1928] 32 Ll.L.L.Rep. 91 and The Torenia, [1983] 2 Lloyd's Rep. 210.

sion of the burden of proof is based on *The Glendarroch*[744] case.[745] In that case Lord Esher held that the carrier only needs to assert and prove that the damage was caused by an excepted peril. The cargo interest has the burden of proving the carrier's negligence.[746] The second view is based on the assumption that a contract for the carriage of goods is a contract of bailment, in which case the division of the burden of proof resulting from that bailment will be observed.[747] This implies that the carrier must prove the absence of negligence as well as the fact that the damage is a result of an excepted peril.[748] There is no binding House of Lords decision as to which of the two views should apply under the Hague (Visby) Rules.[749] Below the different views will be discussed in detail followed by my own point of view.

6.3.2 The Glendarroch

509. *The Glendarroch* case has been an important judgement in respect of the division of the burden of proof in cases concerning claims based on a contract of carriage of goods under a bill of lading. In *The Glendarroch* case the bill of lading contained the usual common law exceptions including the perils of the sea exception, but it did not contain the exemption from negligence. The cargo interests held the carrier liable for non-delivery. The carrier invoked the perils of the sea exception. The judge in first instance, Sir F.H. Jeune, ruled that the carrier had the burden of providing evidence that the damage was caused by an excepted peril and that it was caused by something other than its own negligence.[750] On appeal, however, the court of appeal decided that if the incident causing the damage was one of the excepted perils, the cargo interest should prove the carrier's negligence by showing that the carrier was not entitled to invoke the exception in question. Referring to Roman law[751], Lord Justice Lopes repeated the general rule that the burden of proof lies on the person who affirms a particular thing:

> 'If, however, the excepted cause by itself is sufficient to account for the loss, it appears to me that the burden of shewing that there is something else which deprives the party of the power of relying on the excepted cause lies on the person who sets up that contention.'[752]

6.3.3 The Canadian Highlander[753]

510. *The Canadian Highlander* was carrying a cargo of sheets of tin under a bill of lading. Upon arrival it turned out that the sheets had rust damage caused by exposure to rainwater while the ship was in dry dock for repairs. The rainwater could enter the ship's

---

744. The Glendarroch, [1894] P. 226.
745. Carver 2005, p. 619.
746. The Glendarroch Rule will be discussed in more detail below.
747. Carver 2005, p. 618-619.
748. Gosse Millerd Ltd. v. Canadian Government Merchant Marine, [1927] 2 K.B. 432.
749. Carver 2005, p. 621.
750. Quoted in the appeal case of 1894, [1894] P. 226. The court of first instance considered: '...in order to excuse themselves from the damage to the goods it lay on the defendants [the carrier] to shew, not only a peril of the sea, but a peril of the sea not occasioned by their negligence'.
751. Digest, xxii. 3, 2. 'ei incumbit probation qui dicit, non qui negat.'
752. [1894] P. 226.
753. Gosse Millerd Ltd. v. Canadian Government Merchant Marine, (1927) 28 L1.L. L.Rep 88.

hold due to carelessness in moving and replacing the tarpaulins which were supposed to cover a hatch when work was being carried out in the hold. The case was governed by the Hague Rules. Judge Wright considered that the division of the burden of proof contained in the q-exception was implicitly applicable to all exceptions.[754] He thereupon held that the carrier is considered to be the bailee and that in case of cargo damage the carrier must therefore prove that he had exercised 'reasonable care' for the goods. He also said that:

> 'I do not think the terms of art. III put the preliminary onus on the goods-owner to give affirmative evidence that the carrier was negligent.'

511. Judge Wright based this conclusion on English authority pertaining to contracts of bailment:

> 'The carrier is a bailee and it is for him to show that he took reasonable care of the goods while in his custody (which includes the custody of his servants on his behalf) and bring himself, if there be loss or damage, within the specified immunities. It is, I think, the general rule applicable in English law to the position of bailee that the defendant (the bailee) is bound to restore the subject of the bailment in the same condition as that in which he received it, and it is for the defendant to explain or offer valid excuse for not having done so. It is for him to prove that reasonable care has been exercised.'[755]

512. Thus, in judge Wright's view the cargo interest only needs to prove loss or damage, whereupon the carrier has the burden of proving that the damage was caused by an excepted peril and that the damage was not a result of any negligence on his part.

513. A number of comments are in order: Firstly, regarding the conclusion that the division of the burden of proof under the q-exception is also applicable to all the other exceptions. I disagree. Like Von Ziegler I am of the opinion that the reason that the burden of proof is given specifically for the q-exception is because the division here differs from the traditional (i.e. as in *The Glendarroch* [756]) division of the burden of proof for the exceptions 4(2) (a-p).[757]
The second comment is the use of the words *reasonable care for the cargo*. In the Rules the obligation to care for the cargo is phrased as an absolute obligation to handle the cargo '*properly and carefully*'. Such an absolute obligation exceeds *reasonable care* which sounds more like an obligation to merely use due diligence. Finally Wright does not seem to recognise the necessity of uniform interpretation of an international convention. By declaring English law pertaining to the contract of bailment applicable to a convention that should be interpreted uniformly he did not assist the object of the convention: uniformity. Therefore I disagree with Wright's interpretation and agree

---

754. Art. IV(2)(q): Any other cause arising without the actual fault or privity of the carrier, or without the fault or neglect of the agents or servants of the carrier, but the burden of proof shall be on the person claiming the benefit of this exception to show that neither the actual fault or privity of the carrier nor the fault or neglect of the agents or servants of the carrier contributed to the loss or damage.
755. 28 Ll.L.L.Rep 88, 103.
756. See supra.
757. Von Ziegler 2002, p. 384 and Royer 1959, p. 283-284.

6.3.4 The Maltasian. Obiter dictum grounds[759]

Court of Session (Inner House)[760]

514. With respect to the division of the burden of proof Lord Clyde found that both the above discussed views can be found in court decisions. He thereupon said:

> '..., although in the latest edition of Scrutton on Charterparties [17th ed. (1964)], at p. 424 the view is expressed that the carrier will escape liability if the exception applies unless the goods owner in turn proves negligence.'

515. Lord Clyde's consideration shows that he is familiar with decisions that support both views, and he refers to Scrutton on Charterparties which advocates *The Glendarroch* rule. However Lord Clyde does not take up a position.

House of Lords[761]

516. The cargo interests cited *The Canadian Highlander*[762] as authority to assert that the carrier had not complied with the additional burden of proof that there had been no negligence on the part of the carrier. Lord Pearce (House of Lords) said:

> 'I have doubt whether Mr. Justice Wright was correct in saying (...) that such an additional onus lies on the defenders.'[763]

517. In the House of Lords, Lord Pearce is clear: in his obiter dictum opinion he shows to be an advocate of *The Glendarroch* rule.

6.3.5 The views of some authors

518. The authors of Carver believe that – in spite of the diverse case law – the prevailing doctrine seems to be that *The Glendarroch* rule still applies.[764] The authors observe that the majority of authority, including obiter dicta in the House of Lords favour the aforementioned view of Scrutton.
However the authors of Carver conclude that there is a strong case for applying the bailment rule, rather than the rule stemming from *The Glendarroch* because the latter rule creates considerable difficulties for cargo claimants in respect of matters peculiarly within the knowledge of the carrier.[765]

---

758. Carver 2005, p. 621 also notes that the prevailing opinion seems to have hardened into an assumption that the Glendarroch principles also apply under the Hague Rules.
759. [1965] 2 Lloyd's Rep. 37 and [1966] 2 Lloyd's Rep. 53.
760. The highest court in Scotland. Decision published in [1965] 2 Lloyd's Rep 37.
761. The Maltasian, [1966] 2 Lloyd's Rep 53.
762. See supra.
763. [1966] 2 Lloyd's Rep 53, 61.
764. Carver 2005, p. 621.
765. Carver 2005, p. 621.

Scrutton expresses the view that, except in cases where negligence or privity is expressly dealt with, as in the nautical fault and the fire exceptions, the carrier is protected against loss or damage if he can prove that the cases falls within the specific exception unless the goods-owner in his turn proves negligence.[766] Scrutton refers to a series of judgements which support his view, such as *The Glendarroch*, and thereupon lists a series of judgements which adhere to the other view i.e. that the carrier has the additional burden of proving that damage or loss was not due to his negligence. Scrutton notes that it can be doubted if the point has yet been fully argued in a case where it was material to the decision.[767] Scrutton correctly observes that the division of the burden of proof pertaining to the q-exception is provided by the q-exception itself. Other authors, too, believe that the cargo interest must proof unseaworthiness in accordance with *The Glendarroch*.[768] On the other hand, Cooke et al. take the view that in cases in which seaworthiness is not at issue Judge Wright's opinion in *The Gosse Millard* is to be preferred to *The Glendarroch Rule*.[769] They note that Judge Wright's view 'is more consistent with art. IV (2) sub q, which deals specifically with the carrier's fault or neglect and the burden of proof.'[770]

Clarke points out that '[a] significant feature of English common law is that, to establish a defence, generally the carrier does not have to prove that he was not negligent' and that in England, that perspective has been carried over to the Rules. Clarke notes that, although that is not the view in some civil law countries, it is the most widespread view.[771]

519. According to the Canadian author Tetley:

> 'Most more recent English decisions[772] and authors however, uphold the view that, in general, the carrier may rebut the claimant's prima facie case simply by proving that the loss was caused by an excepted peril. At that point, the onus switches to the cargo claimant to prove that the true cause of the loss was the carrier's negligence. That is also my position.'[773]

6.3.6 Common Law: conclusion

520. Opinions are divided among legal authors. In case law support is to be found for both views. I believe that in principle *The Glendarroch Rule* is the right one concerning this matter. This rule finds support in the aforementioned obiter dictum ground taken by the influential House of Lords in the *Maltasian* case.[774] It was the rule under common law and there is no reason to change that rule for the Hague Rules. However a hard and fast rule for every case can not be given as will be discussed below.

---

766. Scrutton 1996, p. 446.
767. Scrutton 1996, p. 446, footnote 28.
768. See Gaskell 2000, p. 274 and Wilson 2001, p. 269.
769. Cooke et al. 2007, p. 980.
770. Id.
771. Clarke 2000, p. 106.
772. Albacora S.R.L. v. Westcott & Laurence Line, Ltd. [1966] 2 Lloyd's Rep 53, 61 (H.L. per Lord Pearce) and at p. 64 (per Lord Pearson).
773. Tetley 4th ed, chapter 6, p. 10.
774. See also Carver 2005, p. 620.

6.4 Dutch Law

6.4.1 Authors

521. According to the leading Dutch authors the carrier only needs to prove a fact or circumstance as described in the invoked exception as cause of the damage. The carrier does not have an additional burden of proving that he complied with the obligations contained in article III (1) and (2).[775]

6.4.2 Dutch decisions

522. In the *Nordpol* case, the court held:

> 'The provisions under c to p do not release the carrier from liability for loss or damage caused by himself or his agents. They only pass the burden of proof concerning the carrier's fault to the cargo interest...'[776]

523. In the *Pericles II* case the court of appeal took the following position with respect to the burden of proof:

> 'In the main, the carrier is released by the causes mentioned [perils of the sea]; but the cargo interest may prove a special failure on the part of the carrier, which makes him liable because the loss or damage would not have occurred if the carrier had not failed imputably.
> This is not so for events covered by the q-exception. In that case the burden of proving the absence of negligence is expressly placed on the carrier.'[777]

524. In the *Hua Fang* case the Rotterdam District Court ruled that the cargo interests had to prove the carrier's failure to exercise due diligence to make the ship seaworthy.[778] According to the court this would be the system of the H(V)R. I do not agree. The system of the Hague Rules is that if the loss or damage was caused by unseaworthiness the *carrier* has to prove that he exercised due diligence to make the ship seaworthy (art. IV(1) H(V)R).[779]

525. In the *Corrientes II* case the cargo was damaged by fire. The court decided that in principle the cargo interest has the burden of proving that i) the cause of the fire was the carrier's failure to exercise due diligence to provide a seaworthy ship or ii) the cause of the fire was the actual fault or privity of the carrier.[780]

526. In the *Amilla* case, however, the court ruled contrary to the view of the authors cited above. In that case the carrier invoked the nautical fault exception. From the facts

---

775. Boonk 1993, p. 221, Schadee 1954, p. 766, Cleveringa 1961, p. 485, Korthals Altes & Wiarda 1980, p. 203, Royer 1959, p. 284, Loeff 1981, p. 156.
776. Nordpol, Rotterdam District Court 2 June 1959, S&S 1959, 43.
777. Pericles II, Amsterdam Court of Appeal 15 April 1955, NJ 1955, 492.
778. Rotterdam District Court 30 December 1999, S&S 2001, 25.
779. See supra § 5.3.9.
780. Corrientes II, Court of Appeal of The Hague 20 April 1993, S&S 1995, 11.

of the case the court decided that the ship was unseaworthy and that the carrier had not exercised due diligence to make the ship seaworthy. The court decided the carrier could only rely on the nautical fault exception after he disproved the court's assumption of unseaworthiness and lack of due diligence. According to the court a carrier can only rely on the nautical fault exception after he has successfully disproved the assumption of unseaworthiness, '... *because the carriers' duty contained in art IV [sic] par. 1 Hague Rules is weightier than his right to rely on an exception to escape liability.*'[781]

527. The first thing to wonder about in this decision is if the court meant the carriers' duty contained in art. IV(1) as it said or if the court was actually referring to the duty contained in art. III(1). The provision contained in art. IV(1) is not a really a duty but an allocation of the burden of proof in case of damage caused by unseaworthiness. Assuming the court actually meant the duty contained in art. III(1) (due diligence to provide a seaworthy ship) the court reached a correct decision on the wrong grounds. The reason given by the court was that the obligation is more important than the exception. Actually the court should have relied on the division given in art. IV(1). If the damage or loss was caused by unseaworthiness the carrier only has the burden of proving his *due diligence* and not (as the court required) proof of seaworthiness.
All in all this judgement is not a clear application of the system of the Hague Rules.

6.4.3 Dutch law: conclusion

528. The view expressed by Dutch authors and in Dutch cases is fairly clear. If the carrier can prove that the loss or damage was caused by an excepted peril he will not be responsible for the damage unless the cargo interests can disprove the excepted peril or prove that the loss or damage was due to a failure of the carrier to fulfil his duties regarding the cargo. If the cargo interests can prove loss or damage by unseaworthiness, art IV(1) provides that the carrier will be responsible unless he can prove due diligence was exercised to make the ship seaworthy.

6.5 Some other continental authors

529. The Belgian author Stevens is also of the opinion that the carrier only needs to invoke an exemption clause without having the additional burden of proving that he complied with the duties contained in art. III(1) and (2). Subsequently, the burden of proof shifts back to the cargo interest, who for his part may try to prove a failure on the part of the carrier.[782] The Swiss author Von Ziegler holds the same view.[783]

6.6 The author's opinion: the division of the burden of proof depends on the invoked exception

530. Which party should prove what and when should he prove it? It cannot be said which of the points of view described above is the correct point of view in general. The answer to the question shall depend on the facts of the case and the exception the carrier is relying on to escape liability. E.g., depending on the damage, proof of a peril of

---

781. Amilla, Amsterdam District Court 20 December 2000, S&S 2003, 99.
782. Stevens 2001, p. 215.
783. Von Ziegler 2002, p. 388-389.

the sea may involve the proof of due diligence or proof that the cargo was properly stowed because a peril of the sea is unavoidable damage caused by an event at sea.[784] I do not agree with Royer who wrote that the q-exception contains the general rule as to the liability of the carrier.[785] The exception contains the division of the burden of proof for the *q*-exception. It is not a general rule. A simple reading of the wording of the exception makes this clear:

> ',... but the burden of proof shall be on the person claiming the benefit of *this* exception,...' (emphasis added, NJM)

531. *A contrario* reasoning would suggest that the division of the burden of proof of negligence for the other exceptions is on the cargo interest.[786] Another indication is art. IV (1). If the loss or damage was caused by unseaworthiness the carrier has the burden of proving that he exercised due diligence to provide a seaworthy ship. The fact that the division of the burden of proof is expressly given for this exception implies that whenever loss or damage was caused by one of the other excepted perils contained in art. IV (2) the carrier only has the burden of proving that the excepted peril caused the damage.

According to the American author Schoenbaum: 'If the cargo interest *places in issue* the seaworthiness of the vessel or proper stowage, the carrier has the burden of proof of due diligence in these regards.'[787] The burden then returns to the cargo interest/shipper to show that the carrier's negligence was at least a concurrent cause of the loss.'[788] (emphasis added, NJM) It is unclear what is meant by '*places in issue*'. US COGSA requires that, for the carrier to be liable, there is proof that the unseaworthiness caused the loss. In other words there is causal connection between the unseaworthiness and the loss or damage.[789] The second phrase, however, is clear. It follows that the cargo interest must prove *negligence* (in conformity with *The Glendarroch* rule). Schoenbaum is however unclear. In the chapter on the burdens of proof he says the carrier can rebut the cargo interest's prima facie case by showing the damage was caused by one of the excepted causes or that it acted with due diligence to prevent the damage.[790] In the extensive footnote to this remark he goes on to say that 'under COGSA as well as the Harter Act, the duty of due diligence to care for the cargo [sic] and to make the vessel seaworthy are said to be conditions precedent to the enjoyment of any of the excepted causes.'[791] Schoenbaum cites two cases to support this view.[792] Both cases were governed by the Harter Act. Under the Harter act the duty of due diligence is indeed a condition precedent to the enjoyment of the exceptions, even if there is no causal relation-

---

784. See supra § 5.4.
785. Royer 1959, chapter V. See supra § 5.5.7 for a discussion of Royer's system.
786. See Von Ziegler 2001, p. 384.
787. Schoenbaum 2004, p. 678. The use of the expression 'due diligence' in connection with proper stowage is of course not correct. As mentioned above according to art. III(2) the cargo has to be stowed properly and carefully.
788. Schoenbaum 2004, p. 679.
789. Schoenbaum 2004, p. 682. Under the Harter Act the provision of a seaworthy vessel is a condition precedent for exemption (The Isis, 290 U.S. 333).
790. Schoenbaum 2004, p. 677.
791. Schoenbaum 2004, p. 678, footnote 16.
792. 685 F. Supp, 897 and 719 F.Supp. 479.

ship between the unseaworthiness and the damage.[793] In *The Isis* the US Supreme Court held:

> 'The maritime law abounds in illustrations of the forfeiture of a right or the loss of a contract by reason of the unseaworthiness of a vessel, though the unseaworthy feature is unrelated to the loss. The law reads into a voyage policy of insurance a warranty that the vessel shall be seaworthy for the purpose of the voyage. There are many cases to the effect that, irrespective of any relation of cause and effect, the breach of the warranty will vitiate the policy. What is implied is a condition, and not merely a covenant, just as here there is not a covenant, but a condition of exemption.'[794]

532. Schoenbaum is correct in his view that proof of due diligence to provide a seaworthy ship is a condition precedent to the enjoyment of the exceptions under the Harter Act. However, in the cases cited by Schoenbaum no mention is made of such a condition precedent under COGSA. It is unclear how Schoenbaum arrived at the opinion given in the aforementioned footnote.

533. In my view the burden of proof should be divided as follows:

1. The cargo interest makes a *prima facie* case by proving contract of carriage, showing a clean bill of lading and bringing evidence of the loss or damage.
2. The carrier proves the damage was caused by an excepted peril. What that proof should entail depends on the exception he is relying upon and the facts of the case.
a. E.g. damage caused by a nautical fault or by fire. The carrier can suffice with proof of the nautical fault or the fire and the causal connection between the exception and the damage. The cargo interest will then have the burden of (i) rebutting the existence of the peril or (ii) rebutting the causal connection between the peril and the damage or (iii) proving that the damage was (also) caused by the carriers' failure to fulfil his duties.[795] In case of the fire exception the cargo interest could attempt to prove the carriers' actual fault or privity caused the fire.
b. E.g. cargo is lost or damaged due to overwhelming human forces. The carrier could invoke one of the following exceptions: act of war, act of public enemies, restraint of princes, quarantine, strikes and riots and civil commotions. To benefit from one of these exceptions the carrier should prove that the excepted peril caused the loss or damage. Proof of the excepted peril also involves proof that the carrier could not avert the peril i.e. that he was not responsible for the cause of the quarantine or that he did not endeavour to avert a strike.[796] The cargo interest will then have to prove that the carrier did not take the correct measures in the face of the peril.[797] He can also try offering proof or rebut as discussed above under point a sub (i), (ii) and (iii).

---

793. 290 U.S. 333 (The Isis). Von Ziegler 2002, p. 379. Schoenbaum 2004, p. 682.
794. 290 U.S. 333, 352 (The Isis).
795. These duties are contained in art. III(1) and art. III(2). To use due diligence before and at the beginning of the voyage to make the ship seaworthy and to treat the cargo properly and carefully.
796. See in general Carver 2005, p. 498-499.
797. Id.

c. E.g. if cargo is damaged by overwhelming natural forces the carrier could rely on the exemptions for damage caused by perils of the sea or by an act of God. Damage caused by a peril of the sea is described as 'any damage to the goods carried caused by seawater, storms, collision, stranding, or other perils peculiar to the sea or to a ship at sea, which could not be foreseen *and guarded against* by the shipowner or his servants as necessary or probable incidents of the adventure'.[798] (emphasis added, NJM) This means that if e.g. seawater entered the hold via the hatches during rough weather, proof of damage due to a peril of the sea will include proof of due diligence to provide a seaworthy ship. If the carrier can not prove that he exercised due diligence to provide a seaworthy ship with respect to the hatches he will not be able to prove that the damage could not be guarded against. In the same sense: If rough weather caused damage to the cargo because the cargo was able to shift proof of damage due to a peril of the sea will include proof of compliance with the duty to load, stow and handle the cargo properly and carefully.

Once the carrier has established the proof of the cause of damage by one of these perils the cargo interest will have the burden of (i) disproving the existence of the peril or (ii) rebutting the causal connection between the peril and the damage or (iii) proving that the damage was (also) caused by the carrier's failure to fulfil his duties.

d. If the carrier wants to rely on the q-exception (any other cause arising without the actual fault or privity of the carrier etc) he will have to prove that the damage was not caused by his negligence. The cargo interest can counter with proof or rebuttal discussed under a.
e. The carrier can also invoke art. IV(I): damage caused by unseaworthiness which was not due to lack of due diligence to provide a seaworthy ship. He will have the burden of proving damage caused by unseaworthiness and the burden of proving the use of due diligence to provide a seaworthy ship.

3. If the carrier succeeds in the proof of damage caused by an excepted peril the cargo interest could also attempt to prove that the damage was caused (completely or partially) by unseaworthiness. The burden of proof will then shift back to the carrier to prove he used due diligence to provide a seaworthy ship.[799] The cargo can also try to prove damage due to non-compliance with art. III (2).

6.7 The intended division of the burden of proof

534. As was said above, the Rules do not contain a general rule for the division of the burden of proof. This indicates that the framers did not intend to create such a rule.

---

798. Carver 2005, p. 609. The requirement that the peril could not be foreseen does exist under U.S. law (see e.g Schoenbaum 2004, p. 697 and the authority cited there). It is however debatable how much importance should be given to the requirement that the peril could not be foreseen under English and Australian law. See Great China Metal Industries v. Malaysian International Shipping Corp. (The Bunga Seroja), [1999] 1 Lloyd's Rep. 512. See also § 5.4.
799. Art. 4(I) H(V)R.

6.8 Conclusion

535. The wording or nature/interpretation of the invoked exception will determine the content of the required proof and the division of the burden of proof. No general rule applies.

Chapter 7

Conclusions

536. In writing this dissertation I have reached a number of conclusions. The conclusions are presented below per chapter of the dissertation.

7.1 The intended construction of the H(V)R

537. If no uniform construction and application of a Rule exists the intended construction and application should be sought.[800] To find the intended construction three rules of construction are used: the textual or objective rule, the subjective rule and the teleological rule. Aids to construction are the following:[801]

The plain text of the convention should prevail if it is clear.
The Rules should be read as a whole.
The French text should prevail if another language is unclear.
If possible the Travaux Préparatoires can be used to find out what the framers meant by the words they used if the words are not clear.
The common law background should be taken into account when necessary.
The text of the convention can be interpreted so as to meet the object of the Rules.
The compromise character of the Rules should be borne in mind.

7.2 Duties of the carrier

538. An agreement wherein the duties to load and stow are given to the ~~carrier~~ shipper and is not contrary to the H(V)R.[802] At common law the duties 'to exercise care and skill in relation to the carriage of the goods and a special duty to furnish a ship that was fit for the adventure' are overriding obligations.[803]

7.3 Overriding obligation

539. At common law the expression 'overriding obligation' means that loss or damage (also) caused by a failure to fulfil the obligation means that the carrier will be responsible.[804]
The meaning under the English law governed by the H(V)R is that in the case of *competing* causes (i.e. the damage is a result of more than one cause and each of the causes

---

800. See supra § 2.6.
801. See supra § 2.6.
802. See supra § 3.9.5.
803. See supra § 4.7.
804. See supra § 4.7.

could have caused all of the damage) the culpable cause will be deemed to be the only relevant cause and the carrier will therefore be liable.[805]

The framers of the Hague Rules intended art. III(1) to be an overriding obligation and art. III(2) to be subject to the provisions of article IV. This means that if the damage is caused by lack of due diligence to make the ship seaworthy the carrier will not be allowed to invoke the exceptions of art. IV(2). He will however be able to escape liability if he can prove that the damage, or a part of the damage, was not caused by the non-fulfilment of art. III(1). In case of damage caused by non-fulfilment of the duty contained in art. III(2) the carrier can either prove that the damage or part of it was not caused by the non-fulfilment, or invoke an exception (a provision of article IV).[806]

7.4 Art. IV(1): loss or damage due to unseaworthiness

540. Art. IV(1) was not intended as an additional exception but as a division of the burden of proof.[807]

7.5 The 'nautical fault' exception

541. There seems to be consensus on the construction and application of art. IV(2)(a), i.e. there is no obvious lack of uniformity. Therefore there is no need to establish the intended construction and application of art. IV(2)(a).[808]

7.6 The fire exception

542. The object of the fire exception in combination with art. VIII is that carriers will not be responsible for damage by fire unless:

(i) it was caused by the actual fault or privity of the carrier (as opposed to constructive fault or privity) or
(ii) by non-fulfilment of art. III(1), unless a Fire Statute applies.[809]

543. The 9th Circuit construes the fire exception differently to the other American circuits. However, this does not lead to different results. The results of the 9th Circuit are the same as the other circuits only for different reasons. The 9th Circuit will deny the defence in cases of a breach of an overriding obligation by the carrier personally. In the other circuits the exception will also be denied, but in those circuits the reason would be that the fire was caused by the carrier's design or neglect. The difference in construction does not lead to a difference in application of the fire defences.[810]

---

805. See supra § 4.6.2.
806. See supra § 4.7.
807. See supra § 5.1.2.4.
808. See supra § 5.2.4.
809. See supra § 5.3.10.
810. See supra § 5.3.3.2.

7.7 Perils of the sea

544. The framers of the Rules intended the 'perils of the sea' exception to be construed according to English common law.[811]

7.8 The catch all exception

545. The q-clause is a typical residual clause. It was not intended as a general rule.[812]

7.9 Division of the burden of proof

546. The H(V)R do not provide a general rule for the division of the burden of proof. This indicates that the framers did not intend to create such a rule.[813]
The wording or nature/interpretation of the invoked exception will determine the content of the required proof and the division of the burden of proof. No general rule applies.[814]

---

811. See supra § 5.4.3.6.
812. See supra § 5.5.7.
813. See supra § 6.7.
814. See supra § 6.8.

Summary

1 Introduction

The research question is: If uniform construction of a Rule does not exist, how should the Rule be construed?
Per researched topic questions are formulated and these questions are answered under English, American and Dutch law. Incidentally Canadian and Australian law is also researched. The English language legal systems where chosen because of the Anglo/American roots of the Hague Rules and Dutch law was researched because I am qualified under Dutch law.

2 Construction of the Hague (Visby) Rules

To find the intended construction three rules of construction are used: the textual or objective rule, the subjective rule and the teleological rule. Aids to construction are the following:

The plain text of the convention should prevail if it is clear.
The Rules should be read as a whole.
The French text should prevail if another language is unclear.
If possible the Travaux Préparatoires can be used to find out what the framers meant by the words they used if the words are not clear.
The common law background should be taken into account when necessary.
The text of the convention can be interpreted so as to meet the object of the Rules.
The compromise character of the Rules should be borne in mind.

3 Duties of the carrier

Before and at the beginning of the voyage the carrier is required to exercise due diligence to make the ship seaworthy. The carrier is also required to treat the cargo properly and carefully. In principle these duties are non-delegable and the carrier will be responsible for errors of his servants and agents in the fulfilment of these duties.
The standards of the law regarding the due diligence to be exercised for seaworthiness are very high, demanding and uncompromising. Only in very exceptional circumstances does the law allow a defect to be overlooked and is liability avoided. The one concession relates to want of due diligence by the builder of a ship or a preceding owner from whom the new owner acquires possession. But even this exception is subject to the neutralising qualification that once the new owner acquires possession he will be liable for failure to detect defects making the ship unseaworthy which he ought to have discovered by the exercise of due diligence.

The duty to exercise due diligence to make the ship seaworthy is a non-delegable duty. There is no consensus regarding the question if the duty to properly and carefully load and stow the cargo can be delegated. Article III(8) provides that the requirement of proper care for the cargo cannot be delegated. However, this is not in keeping with existing practise. In the *Jordan II* case and in the earlier English decisions *Pyrene* and *Renton* existing commercial practise was recognised by the House of Lords and transfer of the responsibility for loading and stowing was deemed permissible. Therefore under English law, third party bill of lading holders may be harmed by the existence of a FIO(S)(T) clause between the shipper and the carrier of which they had no knowledge. In my view the Dutch Supreme Court takes a more reasonable view, which protects third party bill of lading holders who had no knowledge of a contractual delegation of the duty to load and stow properly and carefully. In the US there is a diversity of authority. The existing diversity is another obstacle to uniformity.

4 The relationship between the obligations of the carrier and the exceptions

Under English law the duty to exercise due diligence to make the ship seaworthy is an overriding obligation and the duty to handle the cargo in accordance with art. III(2) is not. Under American law this distinction is not made, save for the 9th Circuit in its application of the fire exception. Under Dutch law the duty to exercise due diligence to make the ship seaworthy is overriding but in a different sense than under English law. Under Dutch law the carrier will be responsible for the entire loss in case of damage caused by a coincidence of damage caused by unseaworthiness and by another, non culpable cause. There is no consensus regarding the question if the duty contained in art. III(2) is overriding under Dutch law.

The effect of the 'overriding obligation' rule is noticeable in cases concerning the fire exception. E.g. under English law it is possible that the carrier will not be responsible for damage by fire, even though his employees were negligent in the fulfilment of art. III(2) and that negligence caused the fire. However, if the fire was caused by a breach of the overriding obligation contained in art. III(1) the carrier will not be allowed to rely on the fire exception.

5 Some of the exceptions provided by art. IV H(V)R

5.1 Art IV(1): loss or damage due to unseaworthiness

Under Dutch law art IV(1) exempts the carrier from responsibility for damage caused by unseaworthiness if he can prove that he exercised due diligence to make the ship seaworthy. Under English law art. IV(1) is not treated as an exemption but as a division of the burden of proof. The Leesh River case clearly illustrates that under English law the exception provided by art. IV(1) only applies to circumstances that could not be discovered by exercising due diligence before and at the beginning of the voyage. The exception does not apply to unseaworthiness arising after the voyage commenced.

Art. IV(1) was actually added as a division of the burden of proof. This was necessary because under the Harter Act the carrier had to prove that he exercised due diligence to make the ship seaworthy before he could rely on a defence. This was even so if there was no causal connection between unseaworthiness and the damage. My conclusion is that art. IV(1) was not intended as an additional exception but as a division of the burden of proof.

5.2 The 'nautical fault' exception

There is little doubt about the meaning of the word 'navigation' in the nautical fault exception. The meaning of the word 'navigation' in the exception is the same as the meaning of the word in everyday speech. 'Navigation' means the art to sail a ship safely from a known position to the required position along a predetermined route.
The nautical fault exception also contains the expression 'management of the ship'. 'Management of the ship' should be distinguished from management of the cargo. The carrier is responsible for damage caused by mismanagement of the cargo. The carrier can rely on exception IV(2)a to escape liability for damage caused by an act or omission concerning the management of the ship. It can sometimes be hard to qualify an act (or omission) as management of the ship or as care of the cargo.
It is clear that the interpretation of the expression 'management of the ship' is not the problem. The problem is qualifying the act that caused damage. Was it an act primarily for the sake of the ship or was it an act primarily for the sake of the cargo? If the act causing cargo damage can be qualified as an act that could be said to have been done equally well for the sake of the ship as for the sake of the cargo then the exception should be interpreted strictly. It is a strong defence and if the scope of it's application were not restricted the exception would render the obligation contained in art. III(2) of no value.

5.3 The fire exception

The English and American Fire Statutes are very important defences for the sea carrier under English and American law. The defence will only fail if the fire was caused by the actual fault or privity of the owner. Even if the fire was caused by unseaworthiness at the beginning of the voyage the fire defence can be relied upon. The defence will only fail if it can be proven that the unseaworthiness was caused by the actual fault or privity of the carrier. The fire exception is also a very strong defence (although less so than the Fire Statutes). Under English law the fire exception will fail if the fire was caused by lack of due diligence to make the ship seaworthy. Under American law the defence will only fail if the carrier personally failed to exercise due diligence and that failure caused the fire. Failure of the carrier's employees or agents to exercise due diligence is not imputed to the carrier.
The reason for such a wide-ranging exemption for damage caused by fire is rarely stated in English decisions. In American decisions it however becomes clear that the reason for such a strong defence is to make sure that the carrier will, in principle, not be responsible for damage caused by fire. This allows the carrier to reduce the freight rates. The conclusion is that the fire defences were intended to be practically unbeatable.

5.4 Perils of the sea

Many authors are of the opinion that, because the exception originates from the common law, the English construction should be followed. Still there are clear differences in the application of the exception in different countries. Under American and Canadian law the requirement exists that the event causing the damage was unforeseeable. Under English and Australian law this requirement does not exist. It will be very hard under American and Canadian law for a carrier to escape responsibility by relying on the perils of the sea defence. Under American law the carrier will have to prove that he exercised his duties (ex art. III(1) and (2)), that the damage causing event was unforeseeable and that the damage causing event was extraordinary of nature.

Under Dutch law it was made clear in the *Quo Vadis* case that unforeseeability of the event is not required for a successful perils of the sea defence. Of course the carrier must prove that the damage was unavoidable. This is so under all of the legal systems discussed above. The Dutch construction concurs with the English and Australian construction of the exception.

My conclusion is that the framers of the Rules intended the 'perils of the sea' exception to be construed according to English common law.

5.5 The catch all exception

This residual exception is known as the 'catch all' exception or 'q-clause'. It is often involved where other exceptions do not apply, and seems mainly to be successful in cases of pilferage.

The division of the burden of proof as provided by the q-clause is an exception to the usual division. To rely on the q-clause the carrier has to prove the cause of the damage and that this cause or these causes were not a result of his actual fault or privity or of the fault or neglect of his agents or servants. This proof will usually be difficult and that is the reason a carrier will primarily try to rely on another exception if possible. In case of damage caused by an unknown cause the carrier will not be able to successfully invoke the q-exception.

6 Division of the burden of proof under the Hague (Visby) Rules

The wording or nature/interpretation of the invoked exception will determine who has to prove what. No general rule applies.

Samenvatting

1 Inleiding

De onderzoeksvraag luidt: hoe dient een regel van de H(V)R te worden uitgelegd indien een uniforme uitleg van die regel ontbreekt?
Per onderwerp van onderzoek zijn vragen geformuleerd en deze vragen zijn beantwoord onder Engels, Amerikaans en Nederlands recht. Bij sommige onderwerpen zijn de vragen ook naar Canadees en Australisch recht beantwoord. De Engelstalige rechtssystemen zijn gekozen vanwege de Anglo/Amerikaanse geschiedenis van de Hague Rules en Nederlands recht is onderzocht omdat ik in het Nederlandse recht ben afgestudeerd.

2 Uitleg van de Hague (Visby) Rules

Om de bedoelde uitleg van de onderzochte regels te vinden worden drie regels van uitleg gebruikt: de tekstuele of objectieve regel, de subjectieve regel en de teleologische regel. De volgende hulpmiddelen worden gebruikt voor de uitleg van een regel:

Grammaticale uitleg van de tekst van het verdrag geldt als de juiste uitleg indien het duidelijk is.
Het verdrag dient als een geheel te worden gelezen.
De uitleg van de Franse tekst prevaleert indien een andere taal onduidelijk is.
Indien mogelijk, kunnen de Travaux Préparatoires worden geraadpleegd om te achterhalen wat de verdragsopstellers bedoelden met de woorden die zij gebruikten.
Daar waar nodig dient rekening te worden gehouden met de *common law* achtergrond van het verdrag.
De tekst van het verdrag dient zo te worden uitgelegd dat het tegemoet komt aan het doel van het verdrag.
Rekening dient te worden gehouden met het compromiskarakter van het verdrag.

3 Verplichtingen van de vervoerder

Vóór en bij aanvang van de reis dient de vervoerder redelijke zorg te betrachten om het schip zeewaardig te maken. De vervoerder is ook verplicht de vervoerde zaken behoorlijk en zorgvuldig te laden, te behandelen, te stuwen, te vervoeren, te bewaren, te verzorgen en te lossen. In principe zijn deze verplichtingen niet delegeerbaar en is de vervoerder aansprakelijk voor fouten van zijn hulppersonen of ondergeschikten.
De wettelijke maatstaf met betrekking tot de mate van redelijke zorg die dient te worden betracht voor de zeewaardigheid is zeer hoog, veeleisend en onwrikbaar. Het recht laat slechts onder zeer buitengewone omstandigheden toe dat een tekortkoming

de vervoerder niet wordt aangerekend. De enige concessie heeft betrekking op het gebrek aan redelijke zorg van de scheepsbouwer of de vorige eigenaar van het schip van wie de nieuwe eigenaar het schip overneemt. Maar zelfs deze uitzondering is onderhevig aan de neutraliserende kwalificatie dat de nieuwe eigenaar wel aansprakelijk is voor defecten die het schip onzeewaardig maken en die hij had kunnen of moeten ontdekken door het betrachten van redelijke zorg. De verplichting om redelijke zorg voor de zeewaardigheid te betrachten is een niet delegeerbare verplichting.

Er is geen heersende leer met betrekking tot de vraag of de verplichting om de lading goed en voorzichtig te laden en stuwen delegeerbaar is. Artikel III (8) brengt mee dat deze verplichting niet delegeerbaar is. Echter, dit is niet in overeenstemming met de praktijk. In *Jordan II* (House of Lords) en in daaraan voorafgaande Engelse zaken, *Pyrene* en *Renton*, werd rekening gehouden met de bestaande handelspraktijk en heeft de House of Lords geoordeeld dat de verplichting om goed en voorzichtig te laden en te stuwen delegeerbaar is. Dat brengt met zich dat onder Engels recht derde cognossementhouders mogelijk schade ondervinden wegens het bestaan van een FIO(S)(T) beding tussen de afzender en de vervoerder waarvan de derde cognossementhouder geen weet had. Naar mijn mening is het standpunt van de Hoge Raad redelijker. Dit standpunt beschermt derde cognossementhouders die geen weet hadden van een contractueel beding tussen de afzender en de vervoerder dat ertoe strekt dat de afzender aansprakelijk is voor laden en stuwen. In de Verenigde Staten is de rechtspraak verdeeld. Deze verdeeldheid hindert de gewenste uniformiteit.

4 De verhouding tussen de verplichtingen van de vervoerder en de ontheffingsgronden

Onder Engels recht is de verplichting om redelijke zorg te betrachten voor de zeewaardigheid van het schip een *overriding obligation* en de verplichting met betrekking tot de zorg voor de lading (artikel III (2)) niet. Onder Amerikaans recht wordt dit onderscheid niet gemaakt, behalve door de negende Circuit met betrekking tot de toepassing van de brandexceptie.

Onder Nederlands recht is de verplichting om redelijke zorg voor de zeewaardigheid te betrachten een *overriding obligation* maar in een andere zin dan onder Engels recht. Onder Nederlands recht zal de vervoerder aansprakelijk zijn voor het gehele verlies of de gehele schade veroorzaakt door een samenloop van een culpoze en een niet-culpoze schadeveroorzakende oorzaak. Er is geen heersende leer met betrekking tot de vraag of de verplichting uit artikel III (2) *overriding* is onder Nederlands recht.

Het effect van de *overriding obligation* regel doet zich kennen in zaken met betrekking tot de brandexceptie. Bijvoorbeeld, onder Engels recht is het mogelijk dat de vervoerder niet aansprakelijk is voor schade door brand, zelfs wanneer zijn ondergeschikten of hulppersonen tekort zijn geschoten in de verplichting uit artikel III (2) en dat tekortschieten de brand heeft veroorzaakt. Echter, als de brand veroorzaakt was door het schenden van de *overriding obligation* van artikel III (1) dan zal de vervoerder geen beroep kunnen doen op de brandexceptie.

5 Enige excepties uit artikel IV H(V)R

5.1 Artikel IV (1): schade of verlies door onzeewaardigheid

Onder Nederlands recht is de vervoerder op grond van artikel IV (1) niet aansprakelijk voor schade of verlies veroorzaakt door onzeewaardigheid indien hij kan bewijzen dat hij redelijke zorg had betracht om het schip zeewaardig te maken. Echter, onder Engels recht wordt artikel IV (1) niet gezien als een exceptie maar als een bewijslastverdeling. De *Leesh River* zaak laat duidelijk zien dat onder Engels recht de exceptie van artikel IV (1) alleen geldt met betrekking tot omstandigheden die niet ontdekt konden worden door gebruik van redelijke zorg vóór en bij aanvang van de reis. De exceptie heeft geen betrekking op onzeewaardigheid ontstaan na aanvang van de reis.
Artikel IV (1) is opgenomen als een bewijslastverdeling. Dit was nodig omdat onder de *Harter Act* de vervoerder eerst diende te bewijzen dat hij vóór en bij aanvang van de reis redelijke zorg voor de zeewaardigheid had betracht voordat hij een beroep kon doen op een exceptie. Zelfs indien er geen clausaal verband was tussen onzeewaardigheid en de schade. Daarom is mijn conclusie dat artikel IV (1) niet is opgenomen als een additionele exceptie maar als een bewijslastverdeling.

5.2 De nautische fout exceptie

Er is weinig twijfel over de betekenis van het woord 'navigatie' in de nautische fout exceptie. Het woord 'navigatie' in de exceptie is hetzelfde als de betekenis van het woord in het dagelijks spraakgebruik. 'Navigatie' betekent de kunst om van een bekende positie naar de gewenste positie te varen langs een vooraf bepaalde route.
De nautische fout exceptie bevat ook de uitdrukking 'behandeling van het schip'. 'Behandeling van het schip' dient te worden onderscheiden van behandeling van de lading. De vervoerder is aansprakelijk voor schade veroorzaakt door verkeerde behandeling van de lading. De vervoerder kan slechts op de nautische fout exceptie rekenen voor schade veroorzaakt door een handeling, onachtzaamheid of nalatigheid bij de behandeling van het schip. Het is soms moeilijk om een handeling of nalaten te kwalificeren als behandeling van het schip of behandeling van de lading. Het moge duidelijk zijn dat de uitleg van de uitdrukking 'behandeling van het schip' niet het probleem is. Het probleem is het kwalificeren van de handeling of het nalaten dat de schade veroorzaakte. Betrof het een handelen of nalaten primair de behandeling van het schip of primair voor de behandeling van de lading? Als een handeling of nalaten waaruit ladingschade voortvloeit zowel gekwalificeerd kan worden als behandeling van het schip als wel als behandeling van de lading, dan dient de nautische fout exceptie eng te worden uitgelegd in die zin dat de vervoerder er geen beroep op kan doen. Het is immers een zeer sterke exceptie en als haar reikwijdte niet wordt ingeperkt, dan is het mogelijk dat de verplichting van artikel III (2) wordt uitgehold.

5.3 De brandexceptie

De Engelse en Amerikaanse Fire Statutes zijn onder Amerikaans en Engels recht zeer belangrijke excepties. De exceptie zal alleen falen als de brand is veroorzaakt door persoonlijke schuld van de vervoerder. De vervoerder kan zelfs met succes rekenen op de Fire Statutes indien de brand veroorzaakt is door onzeewaardigheid voor de aanvang van de reis. De Fire Statutes zullen alleen falen indien bewezen wordt dat de onzeewaardigheid een gevolg was van de persoonlijk schuld van de vervoerder. Ook de brandexceptie van de H(V)R is een zeer sterke exceptie, zij het niet zo sterk als de Fire Statutes. Onder Engels recht zal de brandexceptie alleen falen indien de brand veroorzaakt is door gebrek aan redelijke zorg om het schip zeewaardig te maken. Onder Amerikaans recht zal de brandexceptie alleen falen indien de vervoerder persoonlijk geen redelijke zorg heeft betracht voor de zeewaardigheid van het schip en dat daardoor de brand ontstond. Het nalaten van ondergeschikten of hulppersonen van de vervoerder om redelijke zorg te betrachten wordt niet toegerekend aan de vervoerder.

De bestaansreden van zulke sterke ontheffingsgronden voor aansprakelijkheid voor schade als gevolg van brand wordt niet duidelijk uit Engelse rechtspraak. Uit Amerikaanse rechtspraak wordt echter duidelijk dat zo een sterke brandexceptie bestaat om er voor te zorgen dat de vervoerder in principe niet aansprakelijk zal zijn voor schade door brand. Hierdoor kan de vervoerder de prijs voor het vervoer (de vracht) verlagen en zodoende zijn concurrentiepositie verbeteren.

Mijn conclusie is dat het de bedoeling van de verdragsopstellers was dat de brandexcepties praktisch onverslaanbaar dienden te zijn.

5.4   Perils of the sea

Veel auteurs zijn van mening dat gezien de *common law* achtergrond van de exceptie de Engelse uitleg dient te worden gevolgd. Echter, er zijn duidelijke verschillen in de toepassing van de exceptie in verschillende rechtstelsels. Onder Amerikaans en Canadees recht bestaat het vereiste dat het schadeveroorzakende evenement onvoorzienbaar was. Onder Engels en Australisch recht is onvoorzienbaarheid van het evenement niet vereist. Onder Amerikaans en Canadees recht zal een vervoerder niet snel met succes een beroep kunnen doen op de 'perils of the sea' exceptie. Onder Amerikaans recht dient de vervoerder te bewijzen dat hij zijn verplichtingen uit artikel III (1) en (2) heeft nageleefd, dat het schadeveroorzakende evenement onvoorzienbaar was en dat het evenement buitengewoon van aard was.

Onder Nederlands recht is in HR *Quo Vadis* duidelijk gemaakt dat de onvoorzienbaarheid van het evenement niet vereist is voor een succesvol beroep op de 'perils of the sea' exceptie. Uiteraard dient de vervoerder wel te zorgen dat de schade onvermijdelijk was. Dit laatse is een vereiste onder alle rechtstelsels die ik onderzocht heb. De Nederlandse uitleg komt overeen met de Engelse en Australische uitleg van de exceptie.

Mijn conclusie is dat de verdragsopstellers beoogden dat de 'perils of the sea' exceptie diende te worden uitgelegd volgens het Engelse *common law*.

5.5   De q-exceptie

Dit is de zogenaamde vangnet-exceptie. Het wordt ingeroepen indien andere excepties niet van toepassing zijn en lijkt het meeste te slagen in zaken met betrekking tot diefstal van lading.

De bewijslastverdeling in de q-exceptie wijkt af van de gebruikelijke bewijslastverdeling. Om op de exceptie te kunnen rekenen dient de vervoerder te bewijzen wat het schade-evenement was en dat dit schade-evenement niet een gevolg was van schuld of nalatigheid van zijn ondergeschikte of hulppersonen. Dit is een moeilijke bewijsopdracht en het is ook de reden dat de vervoerder meestal primair zal proberen om een andere exceptie in te roepen. In geval van schade als gevolg van een onbekende oorzaak zal de vervoerder niet op de q-exceptie kunnen rekenen.

6 Bewijslastverdeling onder de H(V)R

De bewoording of aard/uitleg van de ingeroepen exceptie zal bepalen wie wat dient te bewijzen. Een algemene regel bestaat niet.

Appendix I Hague Visby Rules

Article I Definitions

In these Rules the following expressions have the meanings hereby assigned to them respectively, that is to say,
(a) 'carrier' includes the owner or the charterer who enters into a contract of carriage with a shipper;
(b) 'contract of carriage' applies only to contracts of carriage covered by a bill of lading or any similar document of title, in so far as such document relates to the carriage of goods by water, including any bill of lading or any similar document as aforesaid issued under or pursuant to a charter-party from the moment at which such bill of lading or similar document of title regulates the relations between a carrier and a holder of the same;
(c) 'goods' includes goods, wares, merchandise and articles of every kind whatsoever, except live animals and cargo which by the contract of carriage is stated as being carried on deck and is so carried;
(d) 'ship' means any vessel used for the carriage of goods by water;
(e) 'carriage of goods' covers the period from the time when the goods are loaded on to the time they are discharged from the ship.

Article II Risks

Subject to the provisions of Article VI, under every contract of carriage of goods by water the carrier, in relation to the loading, handling, stowage, carriage, custody, care and discharge of such goods, shall be subject to the responsibilities and liabilities and entitled to the rights and immunities hereinafter set forth.

Article III Responsibilities and Liabilities

1. The carrier shall be bound, before and at the beginning of the voyage, to exercise due diligence to
(a) make the ship seaworthy;
(b) properly man, equip and supply the ship;
(c) make the holds, refrigerating and cool chambers, and all other parts of the ship in which goods are carried, fit and safe for their reception, carriage and preservation.
2. Subject to the provisions of Article IV, the carrier shall properly and carefully load, handle, stow, carry, keep, care for and discharge the goods carried.
3. After receiving the goods into his charge, the carrier, or the master or agent of the carrier, shall, on demand of the shipper, issue to the shipper a bill of lading showing among other things

(a) the leading marks necessary for identification of the goods as the same are furnished in writing by the shipper before the loading of such goods starts, provided such marks are stamped or otherwise shown clearly upon the goods if uncovered, or on the cases or coverings in which such goods are contained, in such a manner as should ordinarily remain legible until the end of the voyage;
(b) either the number of packages or pieces, or the quantity, or weight, as the case may be, as furnished in writing by the shipper;
(c) the apparent order and condition of the goods:
Provided that no carrier, master or agent of the carrier shall be bound to state or show in the bill of lading any marks, number, quantity, or weight which he has reasonable ground for suspecting not accurately to represent the goods actually received or which he has had no reasonable means of checking.
4. Such a bill of lading shall be prima facie evidence of the receipt by the carrier of the goods as therein described in accordance with paragraphs 3(a), (b) and (c).
However, proof to the contrary shall not be admissible when the bill of lading has been transferred to a third party acting in good faith.
5. The shipper shall be deemed to have guaranteed to the carrier the accuracy at the time of shipment of the marks, number, quantity and weight, as furnished by him, and the shipper shall indemnify the carrier against all loss, damages and expenses arising or resulting from inaccuracies in such particulars. The right of the carrier to such indemnity shall in no way limit his responsibility and liability under the contract of carriage to any person other than the shipper.
6. Unless notice of loss or damage and the general nature of such loss or damage be given in writing to the carrier or his agent at the port of discharge before or at the time of the removal of the goods into the custody of the person entitled to delivery thereof under the contract of carriage, or, if the loss or damage be not apparent, within three days, such removal shall be prima facie evidence of the delivery by the carrier of the goods as described in the bill of lading.
The notice in writing need not be given if the state of the goods has at the time of their receipt been the subject of joint survey or inspection.
Subject to paragraph 6bis the carrier and the ship shall in any event be discharged from all liability whatsoever in respect of the goods, unless suit is brought within one year of their delivery or of the date when they should have been delivered. This period may, however, be extended if the parties so agree after the cause of action has arisen.
In the case of any actual or apprehended loss or damage the carrier and the receiver shall give all reasonable facilities to each other for inspecting and tallying the goods.
6bis. An action for indemnity against a third person may be brought even after the expiration of the year provided for in the preceding paragraph if brought within the time allowed by the law of the Court seized of the case. However, the time allowed shall be not less than three months, commencing from the day when the person bringing such action for indemnity has settled the claim or has been served with process in the action against himself.
7. After the goods are loaded the bill of lading to be issued by the carrier, master or agent of the carrier, to the shipper shall, if the shipper so demands, be a 'shipped' bill of lading, provided that if the shipper shall have previously taken up any document of title to such goods, he shall surrender the same as against the issue of the 'shipped' bill of lading, but at the option of the carrier such document of title may be noted at the port of shipment by the carrier, master, or agent with the name or names of the

ship or ships upon which the goods have been shipped and the date or dates of shipment, and when so noted the same shall for the purpose of this Article be deemed to constitute a 'shipped' bill of lading.

8. Any clause, covenant or agreement in a contract of carriage relieving the carrier or the ship from liability for loss or damage to or in connection with goods arising from negligence, fault or failure in the duties and obligations provided in this Article or lessening such liability otherwise than as provided in these Rules, shall be null and void and of no effect.

A benefit of insurance or similar clause shall be deemed to be a clause relieving the carrier from liability.

Article IV Rights and Immunities

1. Neither the carrier nor the ship shall be liable for loss or damage arising or resulting from unseaworthiness unless caused by want of due diligence on the part of the carrier to make the ship seaworthy, and to secure that the ship is properly manned, equipped and supplied, and to make the holds, refrigerating and cool chambers and all other parts of the ship in which goods are carried fit and safe for their reception, carriage and preservation in accordance with the provisions of paragraph 1 of Article III.

Whenever loss or damage has resulted from unseaworthiness, the burden of proving the exercise of due diligence shall be on the carrier or other person claiming exemption under this article.

2. Neither the carrier nor the ship shall be responsible for loss or damage arising or resulting from

(a) act, neglect, or default of the master, mariner, pilot or the servants of the carrier in the navigation or in the management of the ship;
(b) fire, unless caused by the actual fault or privity of the carrier;
(c) perils, dangers and accidents of the sea or other navigable waters;
(d) act of God;
(e) act of war;
(f) act of public enemies;
(g) arrest or restraint of princes, rulers or people, or seizure under legal process;
(h) quarantine restrictions;
(i) act or omission of the shipper or owner of the goods, his agent or representative;
(j) strikes or lock-outs or stoppage or restraint of labour from whatever cause, whether partial or general;
(k) riots and civil commotions;
(l) saving or attempting to save life or property at sea;
(m) wastage in bulk or weight or any other loss or damage arising from inherent defect, quality or vice of the goods;
(n) insufficiency of packing;
(o) insufficiency or inadequacy of marks;
(p) latent defects not discoverable by due diligence;
(q) any other cause arising without the actual fault and privity of the carrier, or without the fault or neglect of the agents or servants of the carrier, but the burden of proof shall be on the person claiming the benefit of this exception to show that neither the

actual fault or privity of the carrier nor the fault or neglect of the agents or servants of the carrier contributed to the loss or damage.

3. The shipper shall not be responsible for loss or damage sustained by the carrier or the ship arising or resulting from any cause without the act, fault or neglect of the shipper, his agents or his servants.

4. Any deviation in saving or attempting to save life or property at sea or any reasonable deviation shall not be deemed to be an infringement or breach of these Rules or of the contract of carriage, and the carrier shall not be liable for any loss or damage resulting therefrom.

5. (a) Unless the nature and value of such goods have been declared by the shipper before shipment and inserted in the bill of lading, neither the carrier nor the ship shall in any event be or become liable for any loss or damage to or in connection with the goods in an amount exceeding 666.67 units of account per package or unit or 2 units of account per kilogramme of gross weight of the goods lost or damaged, whichever is the higher.

(b) The total amount recoverable shall be calculated by reference to the value of such goods at the place and time at which the goods are discharged from the ship in accordance with the contract or should have been so discharged.

The value of the goods shall be fixed according to the commodity exchange price, or, if there be no such price, according to the current market price, or, if there be no commodity exchange price or current market price, by reference to the normal value of goods of the same kind and quality.

(c) Where a container, pallet or similar article of transport is used to consolidate goods, the number of packages or units enumerated in the bill of lading as packed in such article of transport shall be deemed the number of packages or units for the purpose of this paragraph as far as these packages or units are concerned. Except as aforesaid such article of transport shall be considered the package or unit.

(d) The unit of account mentioned in this Article is the Special Drawing Right as defined by the International Monetary Fund. The amounts mentioned in sub-paragraph (a) of this paragraph shall be converted into national currency on the basis of the value of that currency on the date to be determined by the law of the Court seized of the case. The value of the national currency, in terms of the Special Drawing Right, of a State which is a member of the International Monetary Fund, shall be calculated in accordance with the method of valuation applied by the International Monetary Fund in effect at the date in question for its operations and transactions. The value of the national currency, in terms of the Special Drawing Right, of a State which is not a member of the International Monetary Fund, shall be calculated in a manner determined by that State.

Nevertheless, a State which is not a member of the International Monetary Fund and whose law does not permit the application of the provisions of the preceding sentences may, at the time of ratification of the Protocol of 1979 or accession thereto or at any time thereafter, declare that the limits of liability provided for in this Convention to be applied in its territory shall be fixed as follows:

(i) in respect of the amount of 666.67 units of account mentioned in sub-paragraph (a) of paragraph 5 of this Article, 10,000 monetary units;

(ii) in respect of the amount of 2 units of account mentioned in sub-paragraph (a) of paragraph 5 of this Article, 30 monetary units.

The monetary unit referred to in the preceding sentence corresponds to 65.5 milligrammes of gold of millesimal fineness 900. The conversion of the amounts specified in that sentence into the national currency shall be made according to the law of the State concerned. The calculation and the conversion mentioned in the preceding sentences shall be made in such a manner as to express in the national currency of that State as far as possible the same real value for the amounts in sub-paragraph (a) of paragraph 5 of this Article as is expressed there in units of account.

States shall communicate to the depositary the manner of calculation or the result of the conversion as the case may be, when depositing an instrument of ratification of the Protocol of 1979 or of accession thereto and whenever there is a change in either.

(e) Neither the carrier nor the ship shall be entitled to the benefit of the limitation of liability provided for in this paragraph if it is proved that the damage resulted from an act or omission of the carrier done with intent to cause damage, or recklessly and with knowledge that damage would probably result.

(f) The declaration mentioned in sub-paragraph (a) of this paragraph, if embodied in the bill of lading, shall be prima facie evidence, but shall not be binding or conclusive on the carrier.

(g) By agreement between the carrier, master or agent of the carrier and the shipper other maximum amounts than those mentioned in sub-paragraph (a) of this paragraph may be fixed, provided that no maximum amount so fixed shall be less than the appropriate maximum mentioned in that sub-paragraph.

(h) Neither the carrier nor the ship shall be responsible in any event for loss or damage to, or in connection with, goods if the nature or value thereof has been knowingly misstated by the shipper in the bill of lading.

6. Goods of an inflammable, explosive or dangerous nature to the shipment whereof the carrier, master or agent of the carrier has not consented, with knowledge of their nature and character, may at any time before discharge be landed at any place or destroyed or rendered innocuous by the carrier without compensation, and the shipper of such goods shall be liable for all damages and expenses directly or indirectly arising out of or resulting from such shipment.

If any such goods shipped with such knowledge and consent shall become a danger to the ship or cargo, they may in like manner be landed at any place or destroyed or rendered innocuous by the carrier without liability on the part of the carrier except to general average, if any.

Article IVbis Application of Defences and Limits of Liability

1. The defences and limits of liability provided for in these Rules shall apply in any action against the carrier in respect of loss or damage to goods covered by a contract of carriage whether the action be founded in contract or in tort.

2. If such an action is brought against a servant or agent of the carrier (such servant or agent not being an independent contractor), such servant or agent shall be entitled to avail himself of the defences and limits of liability which the carrier is entitled to invoke under these Rules.

3. The aggregate of the amounts recoverable from the carrier, and such servants and agents, shall in no case exceed the limit provided for in these Rules.

4. Nevertheless, a servant or agent of the carrier shall not be entitled to avail himself of the provisions of this Article, if it is proved that the damage resulted from an act or

omission of the servant or agent done with intent to cause damage or recklessly and with knowledge that damage would probably result.

Article V Surrender of Rights and Immunities, and Increase of Responsibilities and Liabilities

A carrier shall be at liberty to surrender in whole or in part all or any of his rights and immunities or to increase any of his responsibilities and liabilities under the Rules contained in any of these Articles, provided such surrender or increase shall be embodied in the bill of lading issued to the shipper.
The provisions of these Rules shall not be applicable to charter-parties, but if bills of lading are issued in the case of a ship under a charter-party they shall comply with the terms of these Rules. Nothing in these Rules shall be held to prevent the insertion in a bill of lading of any lawful provision regarding general average.

Article VI Special Conditions

Notwithstanding the provisions of the preceding Articles, a carrier, master or agent of the carrier and a shipper shall in regard to any particular goods be at liberty to enter into any agreement in any terms as to the responsibility and liability of the carrier for such goods, and as to the rights and immunities of the carrier in respect of such goods, or his obligation as to seaworthiness, so far as this stipulation is not contrary to public policy, or the care or diligence of his servants or agents in regard to the loading, handling, stowage, carriage, custody, care and discharge of the goods carried by water, provided that in this case no bill of lading has been or shall be issued and that the terms agreed shall be embodied in a receipt which shall be a non-negotiable document and shall be marked as such.
Any agreement so entered into shall have full legal effect.
Provided that this Article shall not apply to ordinary commercial shipments made in the ordinary course of trade, but only to other shipments where the character or condition of the property to be carried or the circumstances, terms and conditions under which the carriage is to be performed are such as reasonably to justify a special agreement.

Article VII Limitations on the Application of the Rules

Nothing herein contained shall prevent a carrier or a shipper from entering into any agreement, stipulation, condition, reservation or exemption as to the responsibility and liability of the carrier or the ship for the loss or damage to, or in connection with the custody and care and handling of goods prior to the loading on and subsequent to the discharge from the ship on which the goods are carried by water.

Article VIII Limitation of Liability

The provisions of these Rules shall not affect the rights and obligations of the carrier under any statute for the time being in force relating to the limitation of the liability of owners of vessels.

Article IX Liability for Nuclear Damage

These Rules shall not affect the provisions of any international Convention or national law governing liability for nuclear damage.

Article X Application

The provisions of these Rules shall apply to every bill of lading relating to the carriage of goods between ports in two different States if:
(a) the bill of lading is issued in a Contracting State, or
(b) the carriage is from a port in a Contracting State, or
(c) the contract contained in or evidenced by the bill of lading provides that these Rules or legislation of any State giving effect to them are to govern the contract, whatever may be the nationality of the ship, the carrier, the shipper, the consignee, or any other interested person.

Appendix II Harter Act

46 U.S.C. 190-196

Sec. 190. – Stipulations relieving from liability for negligence

It shall not be lawful for the manager, agent, master, or owner of any vessel transporting merchandise or property from or between ports of the United States and foreign ports to insert in any bill of lading or shipping document any clause, covenant, or agreement whereby it, he, or they shall be relieved from liability for loss or damage arising from negligence, fault, or failure in proper loading, stowage, custody, care, or proper delivery of any and all lawful merchandise or property committed to its or their charge. Any and all words or clauses of such import inserted in bills of lading or shipping receipts shall be null and void and of no effect.

Sec. 191. – Stipulations relieving from exercise of due diligence in equipping vessels

It shall not be lawful for any vessel transporting merchandise or property from or between ports of the United States of America and foreign ports, her owner, master, agent, or manager, to insert in any bill of lading or shipping document any covenant or agreement whereby the obligations of the owner or owners of said vessel to exercise due diligence properly equip, man, provision, and outfit said vessel, and to make said vessel seaworthy and capable of performing her intended voyage, or whereby the obligations of the master, officers, agents, or servants to carefully handle and stow her cargo and to care for and properly deliver same, shall in any wise be lessened, weakened, or avoided.

Sec. 192. – Limitation of liability for errors of navigation, dangers of sea and acts of God

If the owner of any vessel transporting merchandise or property to or from any port in the United States of America shall exercise due diligence to make the said vessel in all respects seaworthy and properly manned, equipped, and supplied, neither the vessel, her owner or owners, agent, or charterers, shall become or be held responsible for damage or loss resulting from faults or errors in navigation or in the management of said vessel nor shall the vessel, her owner or owners, charterers, agent, or master be held liable for losses arising from dangers of the sea or other navigable waters, acts of God, or public enemies, or the inherent defect, quality, or vice of the thing carried, or from insufficiency of package, or seizure under legal process, or for loss resulting from any act or omission of the shipper or owner of the goods, his agent or representative, or from saving or attempting to save life or property at sea, or from any deviation in rendering such service.

Sec. 193. – Bills of lading to be issued; contents

It shall be the duty of the owner or owners, masters, or agents of any vessel transporting merchandise or property from or between ports of the United States and foreign ports to issue to shippers of any lawful merchandise a bill of lading, or shipping document, stating, among other things, the marks necessary for identification, number of packages, or quantity, stating whether it be carrier's or shipper's weight, and apparent order or condition of such merchandise or property delivered to and received by the owner, master, or agent of the vessel for transportation, and such document shall be prima facie evidence of the receipt of the merchandise therein described.

Sec. 194. – Penalties; liens; recovery

For a violation of any of the provisions of sections 190 to 196 of this Appendix the agent, owner, or master of the vessel guilty of such violation, and who refuses to issue on demand the bill of lading herein provided for, shall be liable to a fine not exceeding $2,000. The amount of the fine and costs for such violation shall be a lien upon the vessel, whose agent, owner, or master is guilty of such violation, and such vessel may be libeled therefor in any district court of the United States, within whose jurisdiction the vessel may be found. One-half of such penalty shall go to the party injured by such violation and the remainder to the Government of the United States.

Sec. 195. – Certain provisions inapplicable to transportation of live animals

Sections 190 and 193 of this Appendix shall not apply to the transportation of live animals.

Sec. 196. – Certain laws unaffected

Sections 190 to 196 of this Appendix shall not be held to modify or repeal sections 181 to 183 of this Appendix, or any other statute defining the liability of vessels, their owners, or representatives.

Appendix III Carriage of Goods by Sea Act 1936

§ 1300. Bills of lading subject to chapter

Every bill of lading or similar document of title which is evidence of a contract for the carriage of goods by sea to or from ports of the United States, in foreign trade, shall have effect subject to the provisions of this chapter.
(Apr. 16, 1936, ch. 229, § 1, 49 Stat. 1207.)

§ 1301. Definitions

When used in this chapter–
(a) The term 'carrier' includes the owner or the charterer who enters into a contract of carriage with a shipper.
(b) The term 'contract of carriage' applies only to contracts of carriage covered by a bill of lading or any similar document of title, insofar as such document relates to the carriage of goods by sea, including any bill of lading or any similar document as aforesaid issued under or pursuant to a charter party from the moment at which such bill of lading or similar document of title regulates the relations between a carrier and a holder of the same.
(c) The term 'goods' includes goods, wares, merchandise, and articles of every kind whatsoever, except live animals and cargo which by the contract of carriage is stated as being carried on deck and is so carried.
(d) The term 'ship' means any vessel used for the carriage of goods by sea.
(e) The term 'carriage of goods' covers the period from the time when the goods are loaded on to the time when they are discharged from the ship.
(Apr. 16, 1936, ch. 229, title I, § 1, 49 Stat. 1208.)

SECTION REFERRED TO IN OTHER SECTIONS

This section is referred to in section 1313 of this Appendix.

§ 1302. Duties and rights of carrier

Subject to the provisions of section 1306 of this Appendix, under every contract of carriage of goods by sea, the carrier in relation to the loading, handling, stowage, carriage, custody, care, and discharge of such goods, shall be subject to the responsibilities and liabilities and entitled to the rights and immunities set forth in sections 1303 and 1304 of this Appendix.
(Apr. 16, 1936, ch. 229, title I, § 2, 49 Stat. 1208.)

APPENDIX III CARRIAGE OF GOODS BY SEA ACT 1936

SECTION REFERRED TO IN OTHER SECTIONS

This section is referred to in section 1313 of this Appendix.

§ 1303. Responsibilities and liabilities of carrier and ship

(1) Seaworthiness
The carrier shall be bound, before and at the beginning of the voyage, to exercise due diligence to–
(a) Make the ship seaworthy;
(b) Properly man, equip, and supply the ship;
(c) Make the holds, refrigerating and cooling chambers, and all other parts of the ship in which goods are carried, fit and safe for their reception, carriage, and preservation.
(2) Cargo
The carrier shall properly and carefully load, handle, stow, carry, keep, care for, and discharge the goods carried.
(3) Contents of bill
After receiving the goods into his charge the carrier, or the master or agent of the carrier, shall, on demand of the shipper, issue to the shipper a bill of lading showing among other things–
(a) The leading marks necessary for identification of the goods as the same are furnished in writing by the shipper before the loading of such goods starts, provided such marks are stamped or otherwise shown clearly upon the goods if uncovered, or on the cases or coverings in which such goods are contained, in such a manner as should ordinarily remain legible until the end of the voyage.
(b) Either the number of packages or pieces, or the quantity or weight, as the case may be, as furnished in writing by the shipper.
(c) The apparent order and condition of the goods: *Provided*, That no carrier, master, or agent of the carrier, shall be bound to state or show in the bill of lading any marks, number, quantity, or weight which he has reasonable ground for suspecting not accurately to represent the goods actually received, or which he has had no reasonable means of checking.
(4) Bill as prima facie evidence
Such a bill of lading shall be prima facie evidence of the receipt by the carrier of the goods as therein described in accordance with paragraphs (3)(a), (b), and (c), of this section: *Provided*, That nothing in this chapter shall be construed as repealing or limiting the application of any part of chapter 801 of title 49.
(5) Guaranty of statements
The shipper shall be deemed to have guaranteed to the carrier the accuracy at the time of shipment of the marks, number, quantity, and weight, as furnished by him; and the shipper shall indemnify the carrier against all loss, damages, and expenses arising or resulting from inaccuracies in such particulars. The right of the carrier to such indemnity shall in no way limit his responsibility and liability under the contract of carriage to any person other than the shipper.
(6) Notice of loss or damage; limitation of actions
Unless notice of loss or damage and the general nature of such loss or damage be given in writing to the carrier or his agent at the port of discharge before or at the time of the removal of the goods into the custody of the person entitled to delivery thereof un-

der the contract of carriage, such removal shall be prima facie evidence of the delivery by the carrier of the goods as described in the bill of lading. If the loss or damage is not apparent, the notice must be given within three days of the delivery.

Said notice of loss or damage may be endorsed upon the receipt for the goods given by the person taking delivery thereof.

The notice in writing need not be given if the state of the goods has at the time of their receipt been the subject of joint survey or inspection.

In any event the carrier and the ship shall be discharged from all liability in respect of loss or damage unless suit is brought within one year after delivery of the goods or the date when the goods should have been delivered: *Provided*, That if a notice of loss or damage, either apparent or concealed, is not given as provided for in this section, that fact shall not affect or prejudice the right of the shipper to bring suit within one year after the delivery of the goods or the date when the goods should have been delivered.

In the case of any actual or apprehended loss or damage the carrier and the receiver shall give all reasonable facilities to each other for inspecting and tallying the goods.

(7) 'Shipped' bill of lading

After the goods are loaded the bill of lading to be issued by the carrier, master, or agent of the carrier to the shipper shall, if the shipper so demands, be a 'shipped' bill of lading: *Provided*, That if the shipper shall have previously taken up any document of title to such goods, he shall surrender the same as against the issue of the 'shipped' bill of lading, but at the option of the carrier such document of title may be noted at the port of shipment by the carrier, master, or agent with the name or names of the ship or ships upon which the goods have been shipped and the date or dates of shipment, and when so noted the same shall for the purpose of this section be deemed to constitute a 'shipped' bill of lading.

(8) Limitation of liability for negligence

Any clause, covenant, or agreement in a contract of carriage relieving the carrier or the ship from liability for loss or damage to or in connection with the goods, arising from negligence, fault, or failure in the duties and obligations provided in this section, or lessening such liability otherwise than as provided in this chapter, shall be null and void and of no effect. A benefit of insurance in favor of the carrier, or similar clause, shall be deemed to be a clause relieving the carrier from liability.

(Apr. 16, 1936, ch. 229, title I, § 3, 49 Stat. 1208.)

Codification

In par. (4), 'chapter 801 of title 49' substituted for 'the Act of August 29, 1916, commonly known as the 'Pomerene Bills of Lading Act' [49 App. U.S.C. 81 et seq.]' on authority of Pub. L. 103-272, § 6(b), July 5, 1994, 108 Stat. 1378, the first section of which enacted subtitles II, III, and V to X of Title 49, Transportation.

SECTION REFERRED TO IN OTHER SECTIONS

This section is referred to in sections 1302, 1304, 1306, 1313 of this Appendix.

§ 1304. Rights and immunities of carrier and ship

(1) Unseaworthiness
Neither the carrier nor the ship shall be liable for loss or damage arising or resulting from unseaworthiness unless caused by want of due diligence on the part of the carrier to make the ship seaworthy, and to secure that the ship is properly manned, equipped, and supplied, and to make the holds, refrigerating and cool chambers, and all other parts of the ship in which goods are carried fit and safe for their reception, carriage, and preservation in accordance with the provisions of paragraph (1) of section 1303 of this Appendix. Whenever loss or damage has resulted from unseaworthiness, the burden of proving the exercise of due diligence shall be on the carrier or other persons claiming exemption under this section.
(2) Uncontrollable causes of loss
Neither the carrier nor the ship shall be responsible for loss or damage arising or resulting from–
(a) Act, neglect, or default of the master, mariner, pilot, or the servants of the carrier in the navigation or in the management of the ship;
(b) Fire, unless caused by the actual fault or privity of the carrier;
(c) Perils, dangers, and accidents of the sea or other navigable waters;
(d) Act of God;
(e) Act of war;
(f) Act of public enemies;
(g) Arrest or restraint of princes, rulers, or people, or seizure under legal process;
(h) Quarantine restrictions;
(i) Act or omission of the shipper or owner of the goods, his agent or representative;
(j) Strikes or lockouts or stoppage or restraint of labor from whatever cause, whether partial or general: *Provided*, That nothing herein contained shall be construed to relieve a carrier from responsibility for the carrier's own acts;
(k) Riots and civil commotions;
(*l*) Saving or attempting to save life or property at sea;
(m) Wastage in bulk or weight or any other loss or damage arising from inherent defect, quality, or vice of the goods;
(n) Insufficiency of packing;
(*o*) Insufficiency or inadequacy of marks;
(p) Latent defects not discoverable by due diligence; and
(q) Any other cause arising without the actual fault and privity of the carrier and without the fault or neglect of the agents or servants of the carrier, but the burden of proof shall be on the person claiming the benefit of this exception to show that neither the actual fault or privity of the carrier nor the fault or neglect of the agents or servants of the carrier contributed to the loss or damage.
(3) Freedom from negligence
The shipper shall not be responsible for loss or damage sustained by the carrier or the ship arising or resulting from any cause without the act, fault, or neglect of the shipper, his agents, or his servants.
(4) Deviations
Any deviation in saving or attempting to save life or property at sea, or any reasonable deviation shall not be deemed to be an infringement or breach of this chapter or of the contract of carriage, and the carrier shall not be liable for any loss or damage resulting

therefrom: *Provided, however,* That if the deviation is for the purpose of loading or unloading cargo or passengers it shall, prima facie, be regarded as unreasonable.

(5) Amount of liability; valuation of cargo

Neither the carrier nor the ship shall in any event be or become liable for any loss or damage to or in connection with the transportation of goods in an amount exceeding $500 per package lawful money of the United States, or in case of goods not shipped in packages, per customary freight unit, or the equivalent of that sum in other currency, unless the nature and value of such goods have been declared by the shipper before shipment and inserted in the bill of lading. This declaration, if embodied in the bill of lading, shall be prima facie evidence, but shall not be conclusive on the carrier.

By agreement between the carrier, master, or agent of the carrier, and the shipper another maximum amount than that mentioned in this paragraph may be fixed: *Provided,* That such maximum shall not be less than the figure above named. In no event shall the carrier be liable for more than the amount of damage actually sustained.

Neither the carrier nor the ship shall be responsible in any event for loss or damage to or in connection with the transportation of the goods if the nature or value thereof has been knowingly and fraudulently misstated by the shipper in the bill of lading.

(6) Inflammable, explosive, or dangerous cargo

Goods of an inflammable, explosive, or dangerous nature to the shipment whereof the carrier, master or agent of the carrier, has not consented with knowledge of their nature and character, may at any time before discharge be landed at any place or destroyed or rendered innocuous by the carrier without compensation, and the shipper of such goods shall be liable for all damages and expenses directly or indirectly arising out of or resulting from such shipment. If any such goods shipped with such knowledge and consent shall become a danger to the ship or cargo, they may in like manner be landed at any place, or destroyed or rendered innocuous by the carrier without liability on the part of the carrier except to general average, if any.

(Apr. 16, 1936, ch. 229, title I, § 4, 49 Stat. 1210.)

SECTION REFERRED TO IN OTHER SECTIONS

This section is referred to in sections 1302, 1306, 1313 of this Appendix.

§ 1305. Surrender of rights; increase of liabilities; charter parties; general average

A carrier shall be at liberty to surrender in whole or in part all or any of his rights and immunities or to increase any of his responsibilities and liabilities under this chapter, provided such surrender or increase shall be embodied in the bill of lading issued to the shipper.

The provisions of this chapter shall not be applicable to charter parties; but if bills of lading are issued in the case of a ship under a charter party, they shall comply with the terms of this chapter. Nothing in this chapter shall be held to prevent the insertion in a bill of lading of any lawful provision regarding general average.

(Apr. 16, 1936, ch. 229, title I, § 5, 49 Stat. 1211.)

SECTION REFERRED TO IN OTHER SECTIONS

This section is referred to in sections 1306, 1309, 1313 of this Appendix.

§ 1306. Special agreement as to particular goods

Notwithstanding the provisions of sections 1303 to 1305 of this Appendix, a carrier, master or agent of the carrier, and a shipper shall, in regard to any particular goods be at liberty to enter into any agreement in any terms as to the responsibility and liability of the carrier for such goods, and as to the rights and immunities of the carrier in respect of such goods, or his obligation as to seaworthiness (so far as the stipulation regarding seaworthiness is not contrary to public policy), or the care or diligence of his servants or agents in regard to the loading, handling, stowage, carriage, custody, care, and discharge of the goods carried by sea: *Provided*, That in this case no bill of lading has been or shall be issued and that the terms agreed shall be embodied in a receipt which shall be a non-negotiable document and shall be marked as such.
Any agreement so entered into shall have full legal effect: *Provided*, That this section shall not apply to ordinary commercial shipments made in the ordinary course of trade but only to other shipments where the character or condition of the property to be carried or the circumstances, terms, and conditions under which the carriage is to be performed are such as reasonably to justify a special agreement.
(Apr. 16, 1936, ch. 229, title I, § 6, 49 Stat. 1211.)

SECTION REFERRED TO IN OTHER SECTIONS

This section is referred to in sections 1302, 1313 of this Appendix.

§ 1307. Agreement as to liability prior to loading or after discharge

Nothing contained in this chapter shall prevent a carrier or a shipper from entering into any agreement, stipulation, condition, reservation, or exemption as to the responsibility and liability of the carrier or the ship for the loss or damage to or in connection with the custody and care and handling of goods prior to the loading on and subsequent to the discharge from the ship on which the goods are carried by sea.
(Apr. 16, 1936, ch. 229, title I, § 7, 49 Stat. 1212.)

SECTION REFERRED TO IN OTHER SECTIONS

This section is referred to in section 1313 of this Appendix.

§ 1308. Rights and liabilities under other provisions

The provisions of this chapter shall not affect the rights and obligations of the carrier under the provisions of the Shipping Act, 1916 [46 App. U.S.C. 801 et seq.], or under the provisions of sections 4281 to 4289, inclusive, of the Revised Statutes of the United States [46 App. 181-188] or of any amendments thereto; or under the provisions of any

other enactment for the time being in force relating to the limitation of the liability of the owners of seagoing vessels.
(Apr. 16, 1936, ch. 229, title I, § 8, 49 Stat. 1212.)

REFERENCES IN TEXT

The Shipping Act, 1916, referred to in text, is act Sept. 7, 1916, ch. 451, 39 Stat. 728, as amended, which is classified generally to chapter 23 (§ 801 et seq.) of this Appendix. For complete classification of this Act to the Code, see section 842 of this Appendix and Tables.
Section 4288 of the Revised Statutes, referred to in text, was classified to section 175 of former Title 46, Shipping, and was repealed by act Oct. 9, 1940, ch. 777, § 7, 54 Stat. 1028.

SECTION REFERRED TO IN OTHER SECTIONS

This section is referred to in section 1313 of this Appendix.

§ 1309. Discrimination between competing shippers

Nothing contained in this chapter shall be construed as permitting a common carrier by water to discriminate between competing shippers similarly placed in time and circumstances, either (a) with respect to their right to demand and receive bills of lading subject to the provisions of this chapter; or (b) when issuing such bills of lading, either in the surrender of any of the carrier's rights and immunities or in the increase of any of the carrier's responsibilities and liabilities pursuant to section 1305 of this Appendix; or (c) in any other way prohibited by the Shipping Act, 1916, as amended [46 App. U.S.C. 801 et seq.].
(Apr. 16, 1936, ch. 229, title II, § 9, 49 Stat. 1212.)

REFERENCES IN TEXT

The Shipping Act, 1916, as amended, referred to in text, is act Sept. 7, 1916, ch. 451, 39 Stat. 728, as amended, which is classified generally to chapter 23 (§ 801 et seq.) of this Appendix. For complete classification of this Act to the Code, see section 842 of this Appendix and Tables.

§ 1310. Weight of bulk cargo

Where under the customs of any trade the weight of any bulk cargo inserted in the bill of lading is a weight ascertained or accepted by a third party other than the carrier or the shipper, and the fact that the weight is so ascertained or accepted is stated in the bill of lading, then, notwithstanding anything in this chapter, the bill of lading shall not be deemed to be prima facie evidence against the carrier of the receipt of goods of the weight so inserted in the bill of lading, and the accuracy thereof at the time of shipment shall not be deemed to have been guaranteed by the shipper.
(Apr. 16, 1936, ch. 229, title II, § 11, 49 Stat. 1212.)

§ 1311. Liabilities before loading and after discharge; effect on other laws

Nothing in this chapter shall be construed as superseding any part of sections 190 to 196 of this Appendix, or of any other law which would be applicable in the absence of this chapter, insofar as they relate to the duties, responsibilities, and liabilities of the ship or carrier prior to the time when the goods are loaded on or after the time they are discharged from the ship.
(Apr. 16, 1936, ch. 229, title II, § 12, 49 Stat. 1212.)

§ 1312. Scope of chapter; 'United States'; 'foreign trade'

This chapter shall apply to all contracts for carriage of goods by sea to or from ports of the United States in foreign trade. As used in this chapter the term 'United States' includes its districts, territories, and possessions. The term 'foreign trade' means the transportation of goods between the ports of the United States and ports of foreign countries. Nothing in this chapter shall be held to apply to contracts for carriage of goods by sea between any port of the United States or its possessions, and any other port of the United States or its possessions: *Provided, however*, That any bill of lading or similar document of title which is evidence of a contract for the carriage of goods by sea between such ports, containing an express statement that it shall be subject to the provisions of this chapter, shall be subjected hereto as fully as if subject hereto by the express provisions of this chapter: *Provided further*, That every bill of lading or similar document of title which is evidence of a contract for the carriage of goods by sea from ports of the United States, in foreign trade, shall contain a statement that it shall have effect subject to the provisions of this chapter.
(Apr. 16, 1936, ch. 229, title II, § 13, 49 Stat. 1212; Proc. No. 2695, eff. July 4, 1946, 11 F.R. 7517, 60 Stat. 1352.)

Codification

A proviso in second sentence that the Philippine Legislature might by law exclude its application to transportation to or from ports of the Philippine Islands was omitted in view of Proc. No. 2695, set out under section 1394 of Title 22, Foreign Relations and Intercourse, which proclaimed the independence of the Philippines.

§ 1313. Suspension of provisions by President

Upon the certification of the Secretary of Transportation that the foreign commerce of the United States in its competition with that of foreign nations is prejudiced by the provisions, or any of them, of sections 1301 to 1308 of this Appendix, or by the laws of any foreign country or countries relating to the carriage of goods by sea, the President of the United States may, from time to time, by proclamation, suspend any or all provisions of said sections for such periods of time or indefinitely as may be designated in the proclamation. The President may at any time rescind such suspension of said sections, and any provisions thereof which may have been suspended shall thereby be reinstated and again apply to contracts thereafter made for the carriage of goods by sea. Any proclamation of suspension or rescission of any such suspension shall take effect on a date named therein, which date shall be not less than ten days from the issue of the proclamation.

Any contract for the carriage of goods by sea, subject to the provisions of this chapter, effective during any period when sections 1301 to 1308 of this Appendix, or any part thereof, are suspended, shall be subject to all provisions of law now or hereafter applicable to that part of said sections which may have thus been suspended.

(Apr. 16, 1936, ch. 229, title II, § 14, 49 Stat. 1213; Pub. L. 97-31, § 12(146), Aug. 6, 1981, 95 Stat. 166.)

AMENDMENTS

1981–Pub. L. 97-31 substituted in first par. 'Secretary of Transportation' for 'Secretary of Commerce'.

§ 1314. Effective date; retroactive effect

This chapter shall take effect ninety days after April 16, 1936; but nothing in this chapter shall apply during a period not to exceed one year following April 16, 1936, to any contract for the carriage of goods by sea, made before April 16, 1936, nor to any bill of lading or similar document of title issued, whether before or after such date in pursuance of any such contract as aforesaid.

(Apr. 16, 1936, ch. 229, title II, § 15, 49 Stat. 1213.)

§ 1315. Short title

This chapter may be cited as the 'Carriage of Goods by Sea Act.'
(Apr. 16, 1936, ch. 229, title II, § 16, 49 Stat. 1213.)

REFERENCES IN TEXT

This chapter, referred to in text, was in the original 'This Act', meaning act Apr. 16, 1936, ch. 229, 49 Stat. 1207, as amended, which enacted this chapter and amended section 25 of former Title 49, Transportation. For complete classification of this Act to the Code, see Tables.

Appendix IV Carriage of Goods by Sea Act 1971

1971 CHAPTER 19

An Act to amend the law with respect to the carriage of goods by sea.
[8th April 1971]

1 Application of Hague Rules as amended

(1) In this Act, 'the Rules' means the International Convention for the unification of certain rules of law relating to bills of lading signed at Brussels on 25th August 1924, as amended by the Protocol signed at Brussels on 23rd February 1968 and by the Protocol signed at Brusels on 21st December 1979].
(2) The provisions of the Rules, as set out in the Schedule to this Act, shall have the force of law.
(3) Without prejudice to subsection (2) above, the said provisions shall have effect (and have the force of law) in relation to and in connection with the carriage of goods by sea in ships where the port of shipment is a port in the United Kingdom, whether or not the carriage is between ports in two different States within the meaning of Article X of the Rules.
(4) Subject to subsection (6) below, nothing in this section shall be taken as applying anything in the Rules to any contract for the carriage of goods by sea, unless the contract expressly or by implication provides for the issue of a bill of lading or any similar document of title.
(5) [repealed]
(6) Without prejudice to Article X(c) of the Rules, the Rules shall have the force of law in relation to—
(a) any bill of lading if the contract contained in or evidenced by it expressly provides that the Rules shall govern the contract, and
(b) any receipt which is a non-negotiable document marked as such if the contract contained in or evidenced by it is a contract for the carriage of goods by sea which expressly provides that the Rules are to govern the contract as if the receipt were a bill of lading, but subject, where paragraph (b) applies, to any necessary modifications and in particular with the omission in Article III of the Rules of the second sentence of paragraph 4 and of paragraph 7.
(7) If and so far as the contract contained in or evidenced by a bill of lading or receipt within paragraph (a) or (b) of subsection (6) above applies to deck cargo or live animals, the Rules as given the force of law by that subsection shall have effect as if Article I(c) did not exclude deck cargo and live animals.
In this subsection 'deck cargo' means cargo which by the contract of carriage is stated as being carried on deck and is so carried.

2 Contracting States, etc

(1) If Her Majesty by Order in Council certified to the following effect, that is to say, that for the purposes of the Rules—
(a) a State specified in the Order is a contracting State, or is a contracting State in respect of any place or territory so specified; or
(b) any place or territory specified in the Order forms part of a State so specified (whether a contracting State or not), the Order shall, except so far as it has been superseded by a subsequent Order, be conclusive evidence of the matters so certified.
(2) An Order in Council under this Section may be varied or revoked by a subsequent Order in Council.

3 Absolute warranty of seaworthiness not to be implied in contracts to which Rules apply

There shall not be implied in any contract for the carriage of goods by sea to which the Rules apply by virtue of this Act any absolute undertaking by the carrier of the goods to provide a seaworthy ship.

4 Application of Act to British possessions, etc

(1) Her Majesty may by Order in Council direct that this Act shall extend, subject to such exceptions, adaptations and modifications as may be specified in the Order, to all or any of the following territories, that is—
(a) any colony (not being a colony for whose external relations a country other than the United Kingdom is responsible),
(b) any country outside Her Majesty's dominions in which Her Majesty has jurisdiction in right of Her Majesty's Government of the United Kingdom.
(2) An Order in Council under this section may contain such transitional and other consequential and incidental provisions as appear to Her Majesty to be expedient, including provisions amending or repealing any legislation about the carriage of goods by sea forming part of the law of any of the territories mentioned in paragraphs (a) and (b) above.

5 Extension of application of Rules to carriage from ports in British possessions, etc

(1) Her Majesty may by Order in Council provide that section 1(3) of this Act shall have effect as if the reference therein to the United Kingdom included a reference to all or any of the following territories, that is—
(a) the Isle of Man;
(b) any of the Channel Islands specified in the Order;
(c) any colony specified in the Order (not being a colony for whose external relations a country other than the United Kingdom is responsible);
(d) [repealed]
(e) any country specified in the Order, being a country outside Her Majesty's dominions in which Her Majesty has jurisdiction in right of Her Majesty's Government of the United Kingdom.

(2) An Order in Council under this section may be varied or revoked by a subsequent Order in Council.

6 Supplemental

(1) This Act may be cited as the Carriage of Goods by Sea Act 1971.
(2) It is hereby declared that this Act extends to Northern Ireland.
(3) The following enactments shall be repealed, that is—
(a) the Carriage of Goods by Sea Act 1924,
(b) section 12(4)(a) of the Nuclear Installations Act 1965,
and without prejudice to section 17(2)(a) of the Interpretation Act 1978], the reference to the said Act of 1924 in section 1(1)(i)(ii) of the Hovercraft Act 1968 shall include a reference to this Act.
(4) It is hereby declared that for the purposes of Article VIII of the Rules section 186 of the Merchant Shipping Act 1995 (which entirely exempts shipowners and others in certain circumstances for loss of, or damage to, goods) is a provision relating to limitation of liability.]
(5) This Act shall come into force on such day as Her Majesty may by Order in Council appoint, and, for the purposes of the transition from the law in force immediately before the day appointed under this subsection to the provisions of this Act, the Order appointing the day may provide that those provisions shall have effect subject to such transitional provisions as may be contained in the Order.

SCHEDULE The Hague Rules as amended by the Brussels Protocol 1968

Article I
In these Rules the following words are employed, with the meanings set out below:—
(a) 'Carrier' includes the owner or the charterer who enters into a contract of carriage with a shipper.
(b) 'Contract of carriage' applies only to contracts of carriage covered by a bill of lading or any similar document of title, in so far as such document relates to the carriage of goods by sea, including any bill of lading or any similar document as aforesaid issued under or pursuant to a charter party from the moment at which such bill of lading or similar document of title regulates the relations between a carrier and a holder of the same.
(c) 'Goods' includes goods, wares, merchandise, and articles of every kind whatsoever except live animals and cargo which by the contract of carriage is stated as being carried on deck and is so carried.
(d) 'Ship' means any vessel used for the carriage of goods by sea.
(e) 'Carriage of goods' covers the period from the time when the goods are loaded on to the time they are discharged from the ship.

Article II
Subject to the provisions of Article VI, under every contract of carriage of goods by sea the carrier, in relation to the loading, handling, stowage, carriage, custody, care and discharge of such goods, shall be subject to the responsibilities and liabilities, and entitled to the rights and immunities hereinafter set forth.

Article III

1. The carrier shall be bound before and at the beginning of the voyage to exercise due diligence to—
(a) Make the ship seaworthy.
(b) Properly man, equip and supply the ship.
(c) Make the holds, refrigerating and cool chambers, and all other parts of the ship in which goods are carried, fit and safe for their reception, carriage and preservation.
2. Subject to the provisions of Article IV, the carrier shall properly and carefully load, handle, stow, carry, keep, care for, and discharge the goods carried.
3. After receiving the goods into his charge the carrier or the master or agent of the carrier shall, on demand of the shipper, issue to the shipper a bill of lading showing among other things—
(a) The leading marks necessary for identification of the goods as the same are furnished in writing by the shipper before the loading of such goods starts, provided such marks are stamped or otherwise shown clearly upon the goods if uncovered, or on the cases or coverings in which such goods are contained, in such a manner as should ordinarily remain legible until the end of the voyage.
(b) Either the number of packages or pieces, or the quantity, or weight, as the case may be, as furnished in writing by the shipper.
(c) The apparent order and condition of the goods.
Provided that no carrier, master or agent of the carrier shall be bound to state or show in the bill of lading any marks, number, quantity, or weight which he has reasonable ground for suspecting not accurately to represent the goods actually received, or which he has had no reasonable means of checking.
4. Such a bill of lading shall be prima facie evidence of the receipt by the carrier of the goods as therein described in accordance with paragraph 3 (a), (b) and (c). However, proof to the contrary shall not be admissible when the bill of lading has been transferred to a third party acting in good faith.
5. The shipper shall be deemed to have guaranteed to the carrier the accuracy at the time of shipment of the marks, number, quantity and weight, as furnished by him, and the shipper shall indemnify the carrier against all loss, damages and expenses arising or resulting from inaccuracies in such particulars. The right of the carrier to such indemnity shall in no way limit his responsibility and liability under the contract of carriage to any person other than the shipper.
6. Unless notice of loss or damage and the general nature of such loss or damage be given in writing to the carrier or his agent at the port of discharge before or at the time of the removal of the goods into the custody of the person entitled to delivery thereof under the contract of carriage, or, if the loss or damage be not apparent, within three days, such removal shall be prima facie evidence of the delivery by the carrier of the goods as described in the bill of lading.
The notice in writing need not be given if the state of the goods has, at the time of their receipt, been the subject of joint survey or inspection.
Subject to paragraph 6bisthe carrier and the ship shall in any event be discharged from all liability whatsoever in respect of the goods, unless suit is brought within one year of their delivery or of the date when they should have been delivered. This period may, however, be extended if the parties so agree after the cause of action has arisen.
In the case of any actual or apprehended loss or damage the carrier and the receiver shall give all reasonable facilities to each other for inspecting and tallying the goods.

6bis. An action for indemnity against a third person may be brought even after the expiration of the year provided for in the preceding paragraph if brought within the time allowed by the law of the Court seized of the case. However, the time allowed shall be not less than three months, commencing from the day when the person bringing such action for indemnity has settled the claim or has been served with process in the action against himself.

7. After the goods are loaded the bill of lading to be issued by the carrier, master, or agent of the carrier, to the shipper shall, if the shipper so demands, be a 'shipped' bill of lading, provided that if the shipper shall have previously taken up any document of title to such goods, he shall surrender the same as against the issue of the 'shipped' bill of lading, but at the option of the carrier such document of title may be noted at the port of shipment by the carrier, master, or agent with the name or names of the ship or ships upon which the goods have been shipped and the date or dates of shipment, and when so noted, if it shows the particulars mentioned in paragraph 3 of Article III, shall for the purpose of this article be deemed to constitute a 'shipped' bill of lading.

8. Any clause, covenant, or agreement in a contract of carriage relieving the carrier or the ship from liability for loss or damage to, or in connection with, goods arising from negligence, fault, or failure in the duties and obligations provided in this article or lessening such liability otherwise than as provided in these Rules, shall be null and void and of no effect. A benefit of insurance in favour of the carrier or similar clause shall be deemed to be a clause relieving the carrier from liability.

Article IV

1. Neither the carrier nor the ship shall be liable for loss or damage arising or resulting from unseaworthiness unless caused by want of due diligence on the part of the carrier to make the ship seaworthy, and to secure that the ship is properly manned, equipped and supplied, and to make the holds, refrigerating and cool chambers and all other parts of the ship in which goods are carried fit and safe for their reception, carriage and preservation in accordance with the provisions of paragraph 1of Article III. Whenever loss or damage has resulted from unseaworthiness the burden of proving the exercise of due diligence shall be on the carrier or other person claiming exemption under this article.

2. Neither the carrier nor the ship shall be responsible for loss or damage arising or resulting from—

(a) Act, neglect, or default of the master, mariner, pilot, or the servants of the carrier in the navigation or in the management of the ship.
(b) Fire, unless caused by the actual fault or privity of the carrier.
(c) Perils, dangers and accidents of the sea or other navigable waters.
(d) Act of God.
(e) Act of war.
(f) Act of public enemies.
(g) Arrest or restraint of princes, rulers or perople, or seizure under legal process.
(h) Quarantine restrictions.
(i) Act or omission of the shipper or owner of the goods, his agent or representative.
(j) Strikes or lockouts or stoppage or restraint of labour from whatever cause, whether partial or general.
(k) Riots and civil commotions.

(*l*) Saving or attempting to save life or property at sea.

(m) Wastage in bulk or weight or any other loss or damage arising from inherent defect, quality or vice of the goods.

(n) Insufficiency of packing.

(*o*) Insufficiency or inadequacy of marks.

(p) Latent defects not discoverable by due diligence.

(q) Any other cause arising without the actual fault or privity of the carrier, or without the fault or neglect of the agents or servants of the carrier, but the burden of proof shall be on the person claiming the benefit of this exception to show that neither the actual fault or privity of the carrier nor the fault or neglect of the agents or servants of the carrier contributed to the loss or damage.

3. The shipper shall not be responsible for loss or damage sustained by the carrier or the ship arising or resulting from any cause without the act, fault or neglect of the shipper, his agents or his servants.

4. Any deviation in saving or attempting to save life or property at sea or any reasonable deviation shall not be deemed to be an infringement or breach of these Rules or of the contract of carriage, and the carrier shall not be liable for any loss or damage resulting therefrom.

5. (a) Unless the nature and value of such goods have been declared by the shipper before shipment and inserted in the bill of lading, neither the carrier nor the ship shall in any event be or become liable for any loss or damage to or in connection with the goods in an amount exceeding 666.67 units of account] per package or unit or 2 units of account per kilogramme] of gross weight of the goods lost or damaged, whichever is the higher.

(b) The total amount recoverable shall be calculated by reference to the value of such goods at the place and time at which the goods are discharged from the ship in accordance with the contract or should have been so discharged.

The value of the goods shall be fixed according to the commodity exchange price, or, if there be no such price, according to the current market price, or, if there be no commodity exchange price or current market price, by reference to the normal value of goods of the same kind and quality.

(c) Where a container, pallet or similar article of transport is used to consolidate goods, the number of packages or units enumerated in the bill of lading as packed in such article of transport shall be deemed the number of packages or units for the purpose of this paragraph as far as these packages or units are concerned. Except as aforesaid such article of transport shall be considered the package or unit.

(d) The unit of account mentioned in this Article is the special drawing right as defined by the International Monetary Fund. The amounts mentioned in sub-paragraph (a) of this paragraph shall be converted into national currency on the basis of the value of that currency on a date to be determined by the law of the Court seized of the case].

(e) Neither the carrier nor the ship shall be entitled to the benefit of the limitation of liability provided for in this paragraph if it is proved that the damage resulted from an act or omission of the carrier done with intent to cause damage, or recklessly and with knowledge that damage would probably result.

(f) The declaration mentioned in sub-paragraph (a) of this paragraph, if embodied in the bill of lading, shall be prima facie evidence, but shall not be binding or conclusive on the carrier.

(g) By agreement between the carrier, master or agent of the carrier and the shipper other maximum amounts than those mentioned in sub-paragraph (a) of this paragraph may be fixed, provided that no maximum amount so fixed shall be less than the appropriate maximum mentioned in that sub-paragraph.

(h) Neither the carrier nor the ship shall be responsible in any event for loss or damage to, or in connection with, goods if the nature or value thereof has been knowingly misstated by the shipper in the bill of lading.

6. Goods of an inflammable, explosive or dangerous nature to the shipment whereof the carrier, master or agent of the carrier has not consented with knowledge of their nature and character, may at any time before discharge be landed at any place, or destroyed or rendered innocuous by the carrier without compensation and the shipper of such goods shall be liable for all damages and expenses directly or indirectly arising out of or resulting from such shipment. If any such goods shipped with such knowledge and consent shall become a danger to the ship or cargo, they may in like manner be landed at any place, or destroyed or rendered innocuous by the carrier without liability on the part of the carrier except to general average, if any.

Article IV *bis*

1. The defences and limits of liability provided for in these Rules shall apply in any action against the carrier in respect of loss or damage to goods covered by a contract of carriage whether the action be founded in contract or in tort.

2. If such an action is brought against a servant or agent of the carrier (such servant or agent not being an independent contractor), such servant or agent shall be entitled to avail himself of the defences and limits of liability which the carrier is entitled to invoke under these Rules.

3. The aggregate of the amounts recoverable from the carrier, and such servants and agents, shall in no case exceed the limit provided for in these Rules.

4. Nevertheless, a servant or agent of the carrier shall not be entitled to avail himself of the provisions of this article, if it is proved that the damage resulted from an act or omission of the servant or agent done with intent to cause damage or recklessly and with knowledge that damage would probably result.

Article V

A carrier shall be at liberty to surrender in whole or in part all or any of his rights and immunities or to increase any of his responsibilities and obligations under these Rules, provided such surrender or increase shall be embodied in the bill of lading issued to the shipper. The provisions of these Rules shall not be applicable to charter parties, but if bills of lading are issued in the case of a ship under a charter party they shall comply with the terms of these Rules. Nothing in these Rules shall be held to prevent the insertion in a bill of lading of any lawful provision regarding general average.

Article VI

Notwithstanding the provisions of the preceding articles, a carrier, master or agent of the carrier and a shipper shall in regard to any particular goods be at liberty to enter into any agreement in any terms as to the responsibility and liability of the carrier for such goods, and as to the rights and immunities of the carrier in respect of such goods, or his obligation as to seaworthiness, so far as this stipulation is not contrary to public policy, or the care or diligence of his servants or agents in regard to the loading, han-

dling, stowage, carriage, custody, care and discharge of the goods carried by sea, provided that in this case no bill of lading has been or shall be issued and that the terms agreed shall be embodied in a receipt which shall be a non-negotiable document and shall be marked as such.
Any agreement so entered into shall have full legal effect.
Provided that this article shall not apply to ordinary commercial shipments made in the ordinary course of trade, but only to other shipments where the character or condition of the property to be carried or the circumstances, terms and conditions under which the carriage is to be performed are such as reasonably to justify a special agreement.

Article VII
Nothing herein contained shall prevent a carrier or a shipper from entering into any agreement, stipulation, condition, reservation or exemption as to the responsbility and liability of the carrier or the ship for the loss or damage to, or in connection with, the custody and care and handling of goods prior to the loading on, and subsequent to the discharge from, the ship on which the goods are carried by sea.

Article VIII
The provisions of these Rules shall not affect the rights and obligations of the carrier under any statute for the time being in force relating to the limitation of the liability of owners of sea-going vessels.

Article IX
These Rules shall not affect the provisions of any international Convention or national law governing liability for nuclear damage.

Article X
The provisions of these Rules shall apply to every bill of lading relating to the carriage of goods between ports in two different States if:
(a) the bill of lading is issued in a contracting State, or
(b) the carriage is from a port in a contracting State, or
(c) the contract contained in or evidenced by the bill of lading provides that these Rules or legislation of any State giving effect to them are to govern the contract,
whatever may be the nationality of the ship, the carrier, the shipper, the consignee, or any other interested person.

[*The last two paragraphs of this article are not reproduced. They require contracting States to apply the Rules to bills of lading mentioned in the article and authorise them to apply the Rules to other bills of lading.*]

[*Articles 11 to 16 of the International Convention for the unification of certain rules of law relating to bills of lading signed at Brussels on 25th August 1924 are not reproduced. They deal with the coming into force of the Convention, procedure for ratification, accession and denunciation, and the right to call for a fresh conference to consider amendments to the Rules contained in the Convention.*]

Bibliography

Aikens 2006 *et al*
R. Aikens & R. Lord & M. Bools, *Bills of Lading*, London: informa 2006.

Baughen 2001
S. Baughen, *Shipping Law*, London/Sydney: Cavendish 2001.

Berlingieri 2004
F. Berlingieri, 'Uniform Interpretation of International Conventions', *Lloyd's Maritime and Commercial Law Quarterly*, p. 153-157.

Black's Law Dictionary 1968
Henry Campbell Black, *Black's Law Dictionary*, West Publishing: St. Paul, Minn. 1968.

Blackstone 1765
Blackstone, *Commentaries on the Law of England, Volume 1*, Oxford: Clarendon Press 1765.

Blussé van Oud Alblas 1929
A. Blussé van Oud Alblas, *De Hague Rules in de Brusselsche Conventie 1924*, Leiden: S.C. van Doesburgh 1929.

Boonk 1993
H. Boonk, *Zeevervoer onder cognossement*, Arnhem: Gouda Quint 1993.

Carver 1982
R. Colinvaux, *Carver's Carriage by Sea (Volume 1)*, London: Steven & Sons 1982.

Carver 2005
G. Treitel & F.M.B. Reynolds, *Carver on Bills of Lading*, London: Sweet & Maxwell 2005.

Clarke 1976
M.A. Clarke, *Aspects of the Hague Rules*, The Hague: Martinus Nijhoff 1976.

Clarke 2000
Malcolm Clarke, *The Carrier's Duty of Seaworthiness under the Hague Rules*, Lex Mercatoria: Essays on International Commercial Law in Honour of Francis Reynolds, London: LLP 2000.

Clarke 2003
M.A. Clarke, *International carriage of goods by road: CMR*, London: LLP 2003.

Cleveringa 1961
R.P. Cleveringa, *Zeerecht*, vierde druk, Zwolle: W.E.J. Tjeenk Willink 1961.

O'Connor & O'Reilly 2002
Eugene J. O'Connor & Shannon O'Reilly, *Journal of Maritime Law & Commerce, 2002*, p. 111-131.

Cooke e.a. 2007
J. Cooke e.a., *Voyage Charters*, London: Informa 2007.

Van Delden 1986
R. van Delden, *Lex Mercatoria of Ius Commune?*, Deventer: Kluwer 1986.

Donovan 1979
James J. Donovan, 'The origins and development of limitation of shipowners' liability', *Tulane Law Review* 1979, p. 999-1045.

Francis G. Jacobs 2004
Francis G. Jacobs, Varieties of approach to treaty interpretation: with special reference to the draft convention on the law of treaties before the Vienna diplomatic conference, in: Scott Davidson, *The law of Treaties*, Aldershot: Dartmouth/Ashgate Publishing Company 2004.

Gaskell 2000
Nicholas Gaskell & Regina Assariotis & Yvonne Baatz, *Bills of Lading: Law and Contracts*, London/Hong-Kong: LLP 2000.

Gilmore & Black 1975
G. Gilmore & C.L. Black, *The Law of Admiralty*, Mineola: The Foundation Press 1975.

Haak 1998
K.F. Haak, *Uitspraak & Uitleg. Rechtspraak zee- en vervoerrecht*, Deventer: Kluwer 1998.

Haak 2007
K.F. Haak, 'De internationale koers van Boek 8 BW', *NTHR* 2007, p. 155-163.

Hare 1999
J. Hare, *Shipping Law & Admiralty jurisdiction in South Africa*, Kenwijn: Juta & co 1999.

Hendrikse & Margetson 2005a
M.L. Hendrikse & N.J. Margetson, 'A comparative law study of the relationship between the obligations of the carrier and the exceptions', *ETL* 2005, p. 161-173.

Hendrikse & Margetson 2005b
M.L. Hendrikse & N.J. Margetson, 'De nautische (fout) – exceptie van de Hague Rules', *TBH* 2005, p. 480-487.

Hendrikse & Margetson 2006
M.L. Hendrikse & N.J. Margetson, 'Division of the burden of proof under the Hague (Visby) Rules', *JIML* 2006, p. 25-34.

Hodges 1999
S. Hodges, *Cases and Materials on Marine Insurace Law*, London: Cavendish 1999.

Van Huizen 1998
Ph.J.G. van Huizen, 'Samenwerkende oorzaken in het zeevervoerrecht', *TVR* 1998, p. 33-38.

Huybrechts 2007
Marc A. Huybrechts, *Language that would make a sailor blush!*, Brussel: De Boeck & Larcier 2007.

Karan 2004
Hakan Karan, *The Carrier's Liability Under International Maritime Conventions*, Lewiston/Queenston/Lapeter: The Edwin Mellen Press 2004.

Kiantou-Pompouki 1991
Aliki Kiantou-Pompouki, 'The interpretation of international maritime conventions in common law', *Revue Hellénique de Droit International* 1991, p. 7-52.

Korthals Altes & Wiarda
A. Korthals Altes & J.J. Wiarda, *Vervoerrecht*, Deventer: Kluwer 1980.

Kruisinga 2004
S.A. Kruisinga, *Non-conformity in the 1980 UN Convention on Contracts for the International Sale of Goods: a uniform concept?*, Antwerpen: Intersentia 2004.

Lamy Transport 2007
Lamy Transport, *Tome 2, Commission de transport. Mer, fer, air. Commerce extérieur*, Paris: Lamy 2007.

Loeff 1981
J.A.L.M. Loeff, *Vervoer ter zee*, Zwolle: W.E.J. Tjeenk Willink 1981.

Margetson & Margetson (2005)
N.J. Margetson & N.H. Margetson, 'House of Lords, 25 november 2004 "Jordan II": FIOST-clausule is niet in strijd met artikel 3 lid 2 Hague (Visby) Rules', *TVR* 2005, p. 58-60.

Mankabady 1974
S. Mankabady, 'Interpretation of the Hague Rules', *Lloyd's Maritime and Commercial Law Quarterly* 1974, p. 125-133.

McNair 1961
Lord McNair, *The Law of Treaties*, Oxford: At the Calarendon Press 1961.

Messent & Glass 2005
A. Messent & D.A. Glass, *CMR: Contracts for the international carriage of goods by road*, London: LLP 2000.

Nieuwenhuis 1994
J.H. Nieuwenhuis, 'Avonturen van de zee', *RMThemis* 1994, p. 203-213.

Nolst Trenité
J.G.L. Nolst Trenité, *Zeeverzekering*, Haarlem: De Erven F. Bohn 1928.

O'Conner & O'Reilly 2002
Eugene J. O'Conner & Shannon O'Reilly, 'The Fire Defenses Under U.S. Law', *JIML&C* 2002, p. 111-131.

Poor 1968
W. Poor, *Poor on charter parties and ocean bills of lading, fifth edition*, New York: M. Bender 1968.

Report from the Joint Committee 1923
Report from the Joint Committee on the Carriage of Goods by Sea Bill [H.L.] together with the proceedings of the committee minutes of evidence and appendices Ordered by the House to Commons to be printed, 16th July, 1923.

Rhidian Thomas 2006
Rhidian Thomas, 'Seaworthiness-the illusion of the Hague compromise', *JIML* 2006-12, p. 287.

Rodière 1997
René Rodière & Emmanuel du Pontavice, *Droit Maritime*, Paris: Dalloz 1997.

Royer 1959
S. Royer, *Hoofdzaken der Vervoerdersaansprakelijkheid in het Zeerecht* (diss. Leiden), Zwolle: W.E.J. Tjeenk Willink 1959.

Schadee 1954
H. Schadee, 'De inhoud van de verplichting tot vervoer over zee', *NJB* 1954, p. 725-732 en p. 763-769.

Schadee 1955
H. Schadee, 'Gevaren der Zee', *NJB* 1955, p. 689-693.

Schoenbaum 2001
Schoenbaum 2001, *Admiralty and Maritime Law*, St. Paul: West Group 2001.

Schoenbaum 2004
T.J. Schoenbaum, *Admiralty and Maritime Law*, St. Paul: Thomson/West 2004 (volume 1).

Scrutton 1984
A.A. Mocatta, M.J. Mustill & S.C. Boyd, *Scrutton on Charterparties and Bills of Lading, Nineteenth Edition*, Londen: Sweet & Maxwell 1984.

Scrutton 1996
S.C. Boyd & A.S. Burrows & D. Foxton, *Scrutton on Charterparties and Bills of Lading*, London: Sweet & Maxwell 1996.

Stevens 2001
F. Stevens, *Vervoer onder Cognossement*, Gent: Larcier 2001.

Sturley 1991
M.F. Sturley, 'The history of Cogsa and the Hague Rules', *Journal of Maritime Law and Commerce* 1991, p. 1-58.

Sturley 1997
M.F. Sturley, 'An overview of the considerations involved in handling the cargo case', *Tulane Maritime Law Journal* 1997, p. 263-358.

Swart 1971
P.J. Swart, 'Het Congnossementsverdrag en rechtstreekse werking', Appendix to *S&S* 1971-4, p. 1-16.

Tetley 1988
W. Tetley, *Marine Cargo Claims*, Montreal: International Shipping Publications Blais 1988.

Tetley 2002
W. Tetley, 'Responsibility for fire in the carriage of goods by sea', *ETL* 2002, p. 3-35.

Tetley 2003
W. Tetley, 'The UNCITRAL Draft Convention – Governing Means Choosing. Can one draft details, without first agreeing on the principles?' <http://tetley.law.mcgill.ca/publications/fairplay.htm >.

Tetley 4th ed.
W. Tetley, *Marine Cargo claims*, fourth edition
Until 2007 preliminary versions of certain chapters of this book were published on the internet. It is said that the book will be published in 2008.

Tetley 2004
W. Tetley, 'Interpretation and construction of the Hague, Hague/Visby and Hamburg Rules', *JIML* 2004-10, p. 30-70.

Travaux Préparatoires
The Travaux Préparatoires of the Hague Rules and of the Hague Visby Rules, Comité Maritime International 1997.

Trompenaars 1989
B.W.M. Trompenaars, *Pluriforme unificatie en uniforme interpretatie: in het bijzonder de bijdrage van UNCITRAL aan de internationale unificatie van het privaatrecht* (diss. UU), Deventer: Kluwer 1989.

UNCITRAL WP.21
UNCITRAL Working Group III, document A/CN.9/WG.III/WP.21.

UNCITRAL WP. 81
UNCITRAL Working Group III, document A/CN.9/WG.III/WP.81.

De Weerdt 2003
I. de Weerdt (red.), *Zeerecht,* Antwerpen: ETL 2003.

Wiel van der 2001
H. van der Wiel, 'De spanning tussen de F.I.O.S.-clausule en de Hague-Visby Rules', *TVR* 2001, p. 79-83.

Wilson 2001
J.F. Wilson, *Carriage of goods by sea, fourth edition,* Harlow, Essex: Pearson Education Limited: 2001.

Yiannopoulos 1965
A.N. Yiannopoulos, 'The unification of private maritime law by international conventions', *Law and Contemporary Problems,* 1965, p. 370-399.

Zaphiriou
G.A. Zaphiriou, 'Seaworthiness', *J.B.L.* 1963, p. 221.

Von Ziegler 2002
A. von Ziegler, *Haftungsgrundlage im internationaler Seefrachtrecht,* Baden-Baden: Nomos 2002.

Van der Ziel 2002
G.J. van der Ziel, 'Het CMI-voorontwerp voor een nieuw zeevervoersverdrag', *TVR* april 2002, p. 35-52.

Van der Ziel 2004-I
G.J. van der Ziel. UNCITRAL's attempt towards global unification of law: Survey on History and Concept, *Transportrecht* 2004, p. 275-278.

Van der Ziel 2004
G.J. van der Ziel, 'Het UNCITRAL-ontwerp voor een nieuw zeevervoersverdrag' *TVR* maart 2004, p. 43-47.

Van der Ziel 2006
G.J. van der Ziel, 'De jongste ontwikkelingen in het zeevervoer', in: *Eenvormig bedrijfsrecht: realiteit of Utopie?,* Boom Juridische Uitgevers, Den Haag: 2006.

Zwalve 2000
W.J. Zwalve, C.Æ. Uniken Venema's *Common Law & Civil Law*, Deventer: W.E.J. Tjeenk Willink 2000.

Case List

A. Meredith Jones v. Vangemar Shipping Co. (The Apostolis), [1997] 2 Lloyd's Rep. 241 / 182, 353, 373, 375
A/s J. Mowinckels Rederi v. Accinanto (The Ocean Liberty), 199 F.2d 134, 143-144 / 299
Albacora S.R.L. v. Westcott & Laurance Line, Ltd. (The Maltasian), [1966] 2 Lloyd's Rep 53 / 132, 133, 136, 173, 181, 516, 520
Amilla, Amsterdam District Court 20 December 2000, S&S 2003, 99 / 526
Amstelslot, [1963] 2 Lloyd's Rep. 223 / 93, 100
Apostolis / See A. Meredith Jones
Arktis Sky / See Associated Metals and Mineral
Asbestos Corp v. Compagnie de Navigation Fraissinet et Cyprien Fabre, (1973) A.M.C. 1683 and 480 F.2d 669 (2nd Cir.) / 304, 345
Asbestos Corp v. Compagnie de Navigation Fraissinet et Cyprien Fabre, 345 F.Supp 814 (S.D.N.Y. 1972) / 304, 358
Associated Metals and Minerals Corp v. M/V The Arktis Sky, 978 F.2d 47 / 143
Atlantic Duke, The Hague Court of Apeal 27 November 1981, S&S 1982, 24 / 148, 149
Banana Services v. M/V Tasman Star 68 F.3d 418 (11th Cir. 1995) / 315
Barentzgracht, Amsterdam Court of Appeal 18 February 1999, S&S 1999, 106 / 231
Bernd Gunda, Rotterdam District Court 15 October 1982, S&S 1983. 104 / 493
Boekanier, The Hague Court of Appeal 7 November 1991, S&S 1993, 47 / 148, 149
Boknis, Rotterdam District Court 1 July 1983, S&S 1983, 117 / 492
Boschkerk, Court of Appeal of The Hague19 June 1966, S&S 1966, 87 / 369
Bothniaborg, The Hague Court of Appeal 23 November 1999, S&S 2000, 107 / 231
Bradley Fertilizer Co. v. Lavender (The Edwin I. Morrison), (1894) 153 U.S. 199 / 416
Buckeye State, 39 F. Supp. 344, 1941 AMC 1238 / 342
Bunga Seroja / See Great China Metal Industries
Canada Shipping Co. v. British Shipowners' Mutual Protection Assn., (1889) 23 Q.B.D. 342 / 237
Canadian Highlander / See Gosse Millerd
Canadian National Steamships Ltd. v. Bayliss (1937) S.C.R. 261 / 426
Christel Vinnen, [1924] P. 208 / 205
Chyebassa / See Leesh River
City of Baroda, 25 Ll.L.L.Rep. 437 / 480
Complaint of Ta Chi Navigation (Panama) Corp S.A, 677 F.2d 225 / 314
Consolidated Mining & Smelting Co. v. Straits Towing Ltd., [1972] 2 Lloyd's Rep. 497 / 433
Consumers Import Co. v. Zosenjo, 320 U.S. 249 / 286
Coral [1992] 2 Lloyd's Rep. 158 / 399
Corrientes II, Court of Appeal of The Hague 20 April 1993, S&S 1995, 11 / 525

Damodar Bulk Carriers, Ltd. v. People's Insurance Company of China, (Damodar Tanabe), 903 F.2d 675 / 232, 316
Deidi, Amsterdam Court of Appeal 27 January 1954, S&S 1957, 70 / 99
Earle & Stoddart, Inc et al. v. Ellerman's Wilson Line, Ltd., 287 U.S. 420 / 296, 298
East and West Steamship Co. v. Hossain Brothers, (1968) 20 PLD SC 15 / 143
Edward Dawson / See Lennard's Carrying Co
Edwin I. Morrison / See Bradley Fertilizer Co.
Falconbridge Nickel Mines etc, [1973] 2 Lloyd's Rep. 469 / 427
Favoriet, SCN 19 January 1968, NJ 1968, 20 / 147, 150
Ferro, [1893] P. 38 / 264
Fiona, [1994] 2 Lloyd's Rep. 506 / 205
Flowergate, [1967] 1 Lloyd's Rep 1 / 134
Foreman and Ellams v. Federal Steam Navigation Co., [1928] 2 KB 424 / 256
Foscolo, Mango & Co., Ltd., and H. C. Vivian & Co., Ltd. v. Stag Line, 41 Ll.L.L.Rep. 165 (Stag Line) / 20, 27, 28
Friso, [1980 1 Lloyd's Rep. 469 / 402
G.H. Renton & Co., Ltd. v. Palmyra Trading Corporation of Panama, [1956] 2 Lloyd's Rep 379 / 135, 138, 141, 143, 145, 157
Gamlen, [1980] 142 C.L.R. 142 / 435, 436
Germanic / See Oceanic Steam Nav.
Giulia, 218 F. 744 / 418
Glendarroch, [1894] P. 226 / 508, 509, 517, 518, 520
Glenochil, [1896] P. 10 / 247, 265
Glymont, 66 F.2d 617 / 73
Goodfellow Lumber Sales Ltd. v. Verrault, [1971] 1 Lloyd's Rep. 185 / 431
Goodwin, Ferreira & Co. Ltd., and others v. Lamport & Holt, Ltd., 34 Ll.L.L.Rep. 192 / 462
Gooiland, Amsterdam District Court 16 June 1971, S&S 1972, 6 / 491
Gosse Millard Ltd. V. Canadian Government Merchant Marine Ltd., (1928) 32 Ll.L.Rep. 91, HL (The Canadian Highlander) / 211, 214, 215, 249, 251, 256, 258
Gosse Millerd Ltd. V. Canadian Government Merchant Marine Ltd., (1927) 28 Ll.L.L.Rep. 88, KBD (The Canadian Highlander) / 510
Gosse Millerd Ltd. V. Canadian Government Merchant Marine Ltd., (1927) 29 Ll.L.L.Rep. 190, CA (The Canadian Highlander) / 42, 269
Great A. & P. Co. v. Lloyd Brasileiro (The Pocone), 1947 A.M.C. 306 / 293
Great China Metal Industries Co. Ltd. v. Malaysian International Shipping Corporation Berhad (Bunga Seroja), [1999] 1 Lloyd's Rep. 512 / 6, 20, 32, 34, 35, 51, 117, 125, 393, 394, 407, 408, 423, 425, 429, 431, 434, 436-438, 441, 444, 445, 447, 448
Hamilton Fraser & Co. v. Pandorf & Co., (1887) 12 App. Cas. 518 / 406
Happy Ranger, [2006] 1 Lloyd's Rep. 649 / 97, 334
Hea, Amsterdam District Court 8 January 2003, S&S 2003, 76 / 231
Hector / See International Packers London
Heyn v. Ocean Steamship Co., (1927) 27 Ll.L.L.Rep. 334 / 471
Hill Harmony, [2001] 1 Lloyd's Rep. 147 / 239, 243
Hourani v. T. & J. Harrison, (1927) 28 Ll.L.L.Rep. 120 / 474, 485
Hua Fang, District Court of Rotterdam 30 December 1999, S&S 2001, 25 / 336, 368, 381, 524
Hunter Grain Pty Ltd. v. Hyundai Merchant Marine Co. Ltd., (1993) 117 ALR 507 / 143
Hyundai Explorer, 93 F.3d 641 / 322

CASE LIST

Imke, Amsterdam District Court 2 February 1966, S&S 1966, 37 / 99
International Ore & Fertilizer Corp v. East Coast Fertiliser Co. Ltd., [1987] 1 NZLR 9 / 143
International Packers London Ltd. v. Ocean Steam Ship Co., Ltd., [1955] 2 Lloyd's Rep. 218 / 137, 252
Irish Spruce, [1976] 1 Lloyd's Rep. 6 / 208
Iron Gippsland, [1994] 1 Lloyd's Rep. 335 / 262, 270, 271
Jindal Iron and Steel Co. Limited v. Islamic Solidarity Shipping Company Jordan Inc. (The Jordan II), [2005] 1 Lloyd's Rep. 57 / 36, 37, 39, 40, 41, 138-140, 145, 151, 157
Johnson v. S.S. Schickshinny, (1942) 45 F.Supp. 813 / 417
Jordan II / See Jindal Iron
Kapitan Sakharov, [2000] 2 Lloyd's Rep. 255 / 95, 96, 501
Keystone Transports v. Dominion Steel and Coal Corp., [1943] AMC 371 / 431
Kriti Rex, [1996] 2 Lloyd's Rep. 171 / 78
Kruger Inc. v. Baltic Shipping Co., [1989] C.L.D. 790 / 428, 432
Leesh River Tea Company, Ltd., and others v. British India Steam Navigation Company, Ltd. (The 'Chyebassa'), [1966] 1 Lloyd's Rep. 450 (QBD) / 224
Leesh River Tea Company, Ltd., and others v. British India Steam Navigation Company, Ltd. (The 'Chyebassa'), [1966] 2 Lloyd's Rep. 193 (CA) / 224, 226, 464, 465, 476
Lennard's Carrying Co. Ltd. v. Asiatic Petroleum Co. Ltd. (The Edward Dawson), [1915] A.C. 705, 713-714 / 332
Liberty Shipping, 509 F.2d 1249 / 305
Lilburn, (1940) 67 Ll.L.L.Rep. 253 / 197, 199
Lottowanna, 88 U.S. 558, 565-566 / 14
Makalla, 40 F.2d 418 / 419
Makedonia, [1962] 1 Lloyd's Rep. 316 / 70, 226
Maltasian / See Albacora
Maurienne / See Maxine Footwear
Maxine Footwear Co. Ltd. v. Canadian Government Merchant Marine Ltd., [1959] 2 Lloyd's Rep 105 / 76, 171, 172, 188, 190, 193, 203, 214, 215, 217, 308, 311, 372, 374
McFadden v. Blue Star Line, [1905] 1 K.B. 697 / 90, 113
Meridian Global Funds Management Asia Ltd. v. Securities Commission, [1995] 2 A.C. 500 / 329, 352
Minister of Food v. Reardon Smith Line, [1951] 2 Lloyd's Rep., 265 / 227
Mississippi Shipping Co. v. Zander & Co. (S.S. Del Sud) / 82
Morris v. KLM Royal Dutch Airlines, [2002] 2 A.C. 628 / 22
Muncaster Castle / See Riverstone Meat co.
Naples Maru (1939) 264 F.2d 32 / 413
NDS Provider, C06/082HR / 99
New India Assurance Co. Ltd. v. M/S Splosna Plovba, (1986) AIR Ker 176 / 143
Nichols v. Marland, (1876) L.R. 2 Ex.D. 1 / 405
Nikolay Malakhov Shipping Co. Ltd. v. SEAS Sapfor Ltd., (1998) 44 NS WLR 371 / 143
Nordpol, Rotterdam District Court 2 June 1959, S&S 1959, 43 / 522
Ocean Liberty / See A/s J. Mowinckels Rederi
Oceanic Steam Nav. Co. v. Aitkin (The Germanic), 196 U.S. 589 / 260, 261, 266
Paterson SS Ltd. v. Canadian Co-operative Wheat Producers Ltd. (The Sarnidoc), 49 Ll.L.L.R. 421 / 165
Pendle & Rivet Ltd. v. Ellerman Lines Ltd. 29 Ll.L.L.Rep. 133 / 480
Pericles II, Amsterdam Court of Appeal 15 April 1955, NJ 1955, 492 / 523

Pocone / See Great A. & P. Co.
Poeldijk, The Hague Court of Appeal 3 October 1980, S&S 1981, 1 / 242
Popi M, [1985] 2 Lloyd's Rep. 1 / 501, 503, 505
Portalon, SCN 8 November 1968, S&S 1969, 10 / 49
Portalon, The Hague Court of Appeal, 30 December 1966, S&S 1967, 28 / 194, 195, 351, 366
Pyrene Company, Ltd. v. Scindia Steam Navigation Company, Ltd., [1954] 1 Lloyd's Rep. 321 / 31, 138, 142, 143, 157
Quaker Oats Co. v. M/V Torvanger, 734 F.2d 238 / 482
Quo Vadis, SCN 11 June 1993, NJ 1995, 235 / 185, 191, 255, 452, 454, 455
Renton / See G.H. Renton
Rio Parana, Rotterdam District Court 4 May 1981, S&S 1981, 111 / 495
Risa Paula, The Hague Court of Appeal 18 April 1969, S&S 1970, 37 / 147
Riverstone Meat Co. Pty Ltd. v. Lancashire Shipping Co. Ltd. (The Muncaster Castle), [1961] 1 Lloyd's Rep. 57 / 20, 97, 101, 103, 105, 106, 107-110, 334
Rosalia (1920) 264 F. 285 / 412, 422
Rowson v. Atlantic Transport Co., [1903] 2 K.B. 666 / 256, 267
Sarnidoc / See Paterson SS Ltd.
Schnell & Co. v. S.S. Vallescura, 293 U.S. 296 / 207, 209, 215
Shipping Corporation of India v. Gamlen Chemical Co. A/Asia Pty Ltd., (1980) 147 CLR 142 / 143
Singapore Jaya, Rotterdam District Court 23 May 1996, S&S 1998, 105 / 231
Smith, Hogg & Co. v. Black Sea & Baltic General Insurance, 67 Ll.L.L.Rep. 253 / 91, 103, 205
Straat Soenda, Amsterdam Court of Appeal 5 February 1964, S&S 1964, 44 / 99, 100
Sunkist Growers Inv v. Adelaide Shipping Lines Ltd., 603 F.2d 1327 / 307, 312, 348, 362
Ta Chi Navigation / See Complaint of Ta Chi Navigation
Tecomar S.A, 465 F.Supp. 1150 / 359
Tempus Shipping Co., Ltd. v. Louis Dreyfus and Co., [1930] 1 K.B. 699 / 339
Thames and Mersey Marine Ins. Co. v. Hamilton, Fraser & Co., (1887) 12 A.C. 484 / 396
Tila Gorthon, [1985] 1 Lloyd's Rep. 552 / 400
Torenia, [1983] 2 Lloyd's Rep. 210 / 212-215, 402
Tubacex Inc v. M/V Risan, 45 ƒ 3rd 951 / 143
Union Oil Co. v. Point Diver, 756 F.2d 1223 / 361
Vallescura / See Schnell & Co.
Virginia Carolina Chemical Company v. Norfolk and North American Steam Shipping Company (The West Point), [1912] 1 KB 229 / 291
West Point / See Virginia Carolina Chemical Company
Westinghouse Electric Corp v. M/V Leslie Lykes,734 F.2d 199 (5th Cir. 1984) / 315, 356, 360
Xantho, (1887) L.R. 12 App. Cas. 503 / 403

Index

The numbers refer to the paragraph numbers. Numbers in bold type refer to paragraphs where the reference is discussed in more detail.

absolute warranty / 89-92
actual fault or privity / 343-349, 470
agents or servants of the carrier / 471-476
alter ego / 328, 352
applicability of the Rules / 2
bailment / 25, 50, 51, 435, 441
bill of lading / 1, 3, 12. 41, 46, 49, 50, 165, 316, 329, 427, 458
cargoworthy, cargoworthiness / 80, 114, 217
carrier / 350-363
causal connection / 161, 162, 180, 181, 183, 186, 187, 202, 214, 218, 219, 232, 233, 374
common law / 6, 32, 33, 51, 65, 70, 89, 92, 97, 100, 103, 112, 119, 125, 161, 164-167, 169, 185, 193, 197, 202, 203, 205, 223, 224, 226, 286, 289, 291, 334, 379, 380, 386, 451, 460
competing causes / 163, 164, 169, 172, 174, 198, 203
concurrent causes / 91, 192, 193, 204, 213
construction of the H(V)R / 14-67
culpable / 161, 162, 192, 193, 197, 198, 203, 215
defect / 90, 92, 97, 98, 100, 102, 103, 109, 113, 115, 212-214, 216, 223, 401
delegable / 55, 69, 101, 137, 143, 146, 147, 217, 298, 299, 305, 322, 349
departure / 82, 145, 224
design or neglect / 281, 294, 297-305, 312, 313, 324, 344-349, 354, 360
discharge / 68-70, 116, 120, 122, 125, 137, 151, 155, 165
due diligence / 93-98
duties of the carrier / 68-160
expert / 100, 102, 126, 216, 217, 232
fault or neglect / 326, 343
FIOS / 138, 139, 146, 148, 149, 156
fire / 8, 11, 47, 48, 163, 183, 188-190, 195, 196, 201, **276-391**
fire exception – burden of proof / 381-385
fire – meaning of / 335-342
fire statute / 47, 48, 279-324
foreseeable / 393-454
French / 31, 44, 64, 105, 138, 386, 458
Harter Act / 6, 89, 90, 101, 180, 187, 207, 232, 233, 236, 247, 257, 260, 261, 266, 378
historic, historical / 7, 46, 284-286, 393, 434
Implementation of the Rules / 49

loading / 70, 76, 77, 80, 86-88, 99, 122, 134, 137, 138, 140, 142, 143, 146, 147, 151, 153, 154, 155, 157, 159, 195, 217, 224, 237, 253, 260, 274, 406
management / 8, 42, 43, 58. 73, 82, 162, 210, 234-275
nautical fault / 8, 162, 210, 227, 234-275, 234-275, 389
navigation / 42, 82, 87, 114, 117, 234-260, 437, 439
neglect / 42, 163, 234, 243, 245, 249, 250, 251, 255, 258, 262, 298, 299, 305, 307, 318, 322, 326, 343, 344, 361, 362, 403, 408, 416, 417, 431, 439, 445, 454
negligence / 73, 87, 93, 104, 135, 158, 165, 168, 189, 197, 199, 200, 206, 210, 249, 255, 256, 260, 296, 299, 304, 314, 318, 320, 321-324, 327, 334, 344, 347, 358, 360, 361, 363, 370
negligent / 87, 88, 101, 102, 137, 201, 204, 207, 247, 249, 250, 252-254, 399
overriding obligation / 53, 87, 161-219, 229, 283, 297, 311, 316, 321, 324, 326, 364, 370, 375, 378-380, 389
perils of the sea / 8, 11, 35, 46, 47, 58, 125, 165, 168, 176, 197, 199, 201, 213, 223, 242, 334, **392-460**
perils of the sea – elements / 394-395
primary purpose test / 251, 260, 261, 266, 271, 272
proof / 8-11, 25, 48, 50, 55, 97, 165, 189, 212, 231-233, 381-385, 416, 431
properly and carefully – care for cargo / 122-236
Protocol of signature / 2, 49
q-clause / 461-498
q-clause – burden of proof / 477-483
seaworthiness / 112-121
seaworthiness – absolute warranty / 89-92
stages, doctrine of / 70-72, 226
stowing / 137, 138, 142-159, 176, 195, 217, 264, 334, 399, 451
third party / 41, 140, 144, 147, 150, 157
Travaux Préparatoires / 36-38, 65, 119, 217, 366, 386, 458, 460
UNCITRAL / 12, 55, 58-60, 88, 111, 145, 151, 152, 156, 162, 389
unseaworthiness / 220-233
Visby Protocol / 17, 49
voyage / 68, 69, **70-74**, 75-98
voyage – before the voyage / 76-81
voyage – the beginning of the voyage / 82-86

Curriculum vitae

Nick Margetson was born on 15 March 1968 in Colchester, England. His mother is Dutch and his father English. In 1976 Nick moved to the Netherlands with his family. He attended the nautical college of Amsterdam from 1986 to 1991. After graduating as hydrographer in 1991 Nick began work as a hydrographic surveyor. From 1991 to 1999 he worked for the Dutch dredging companies Ballast Nedam and Boskalis. Nick worked on 25 dredging and offshore projects in Europe, Asia, South and central America and the Middle East. In 1999 he decided to change his profession and started studying law at the University of Amsterdam where he graduated in 2003. From 2003 until 2005 Nick worked as a professional support lawyer for a major Dutch law firm. In 2006 he started practising law in Rotterdam.